KU-717-387

WITHDRAWN
FROM STOCK

Coláiste Oideachais Mhuire Gan Smal
Luimneach

THE EVOLVING SELF

THE
EVOLVING
SELF

Problem and Process in Human Development

R O B E R T K E G A N

Harvard University Press
Cambridge, Massachusetts, and London, England

£22·75+

233

Copyright © 1982 by the President and Fellows of Harvard College
All rights reserved
Printed in the United States of America

10 9 8 7 6 5 4 3

This book is printed on acid-free paper, and its binding materials have
been chosen for strength and durability.

Library of Congress Cataloging in Publication Data

Kegan, Robert.
  The evolving self.

    Includes bibliographical references and index.
    1. Developmental psychology. 2. Personality change. 3. Self.
4. Piaget, Jean, 1896–1980. 5. Meaning (Psychology). 6. Psychotherapy.
I. Title.
BF713.K44   155.2′5   81—6759
ISBN 0-674-27230-7   AACR2

Coláiste
Mhuire Gan Smal
Luimneach
Class No. ......755-25 KEG
Acc. No. .....71.355......

*To the living legacy
of Jean Piaget
(1896–1980)*

PREFACE

In writing this book I have taken courage from the example of Erik Erikson. Like Erikson, I came gradually and somewhat reluctantly to psychology out of a background in the humanities. And like him I was inspired by a great psychological genius in whose depth I came to find an unexpected sustenance for the very hungers that had drawn me to literature, philosophy, and theology.

Erikson's genius was Sigmund Freud. Mine has been Jean Piaget. Perhaps the reader's present associations with Piaget make his cold cognitivism seem a less likely candidate for the sustaining of great hungers. But then just how likely a candidate thirty years ago might a grimly fatalistic, body-bound id-psychology have seemed as a source of support for Erikson's essentially hopeful, psychosocial ego psychology? Erikson drew deeply on psychoanalytic theory and understanding—one has the impression—*not* to be thoroughly taken over by it, but because he sensed that at its depth he could find something he believed to be there, something he saw as intrinsic to the theory but having had hardly a chance to grow, and something that might guide or give shape to his own developing sense of what was important to remember about the human spirit. The "something," of course, was the person's "capacity to unify his experience and his action in an adaptive manner" (Erikson, 1950, p. 15), what we generally refer to as ego development, and what I call in this book the evolution of meaning. What Erikson found himself led to through Freud is what it seems to me I have been led to in a new form by Piaget—a highly elaborated surmise about the development of the ego.

Like Erikson, I have so changed the face of the theory in which I was steeped that although every one of the changes can be shown to grow out of, rather than depart from, the theory's basic premises, one is still left with the slightly uncomfortable feeling that the father of the creation might not recognize the child as his own.

Finally, I have taken courage in Erikson's choice to publish what was essentially an empirically grounded speculation, what he called "a conceptual itinerary." Like Erikson, I am holding the framework in this book to the first-order test that it be able to take account of a very wide range of complicated and carefully observed human phenomena in a consistent and substantive manner. Like Erikson, I draw these phenomena from my own and others' life experience, from my own and others' clinical experience, and from my own and others' research. Since the theoretical thinking by which I have been guided grows out of academic rather than clinical psychology, it is true that I have a larger body of rigorously gathered observations upon which to draw, especially the work of Piaget himself, his research-oriented adherents, and that of the social cognitivists, especially Lawrence Kohlberg. Although this gives me a whole additional category of phenomena which is perhaps more intersubjectively perceived than Erikson's, I am still orienting to the material of these researches as phenomena which the framework must be able to take into account rather than claiming that the researches "prove" my position. In effect the theories become themselves phenomena which the framework must engage, and I do try to suggest here the context in which a number of developmental theories might be best integrated.

I am a teacher, a therapist, a researcher-theorist. All these people have written this book. I admit that I am trying in part to engage you in the highly personal process of learning, to join you in an exploration of just how much can be understood about a person by understanding his or her meaning system, to explore with you how these meaning systems might work and how they seem to feel. As a clinician I am attending to the way this framework might help clinicians in their most fundamental activity: conveying to the client that they understand something of his or her experience *in the way he or she experiences it.* Why this activity on the part of the therapist is so crucial to the client's thriving has not been well understood, although it has long been appreciated by phenomenological and client-centered psychologists and is lately being rediscovered by psychiatry through the work of Heinz Kohut. In this book I try to demonstrate that this special kind of empathy is crucial at every phase in the lifespan because it is actually *intrinsic* to the process by which we develop. Finally, I am a researcher-theorist who finds the field of ego or personality development somewhat encumbered by a number of poorly constructed metapsychological questions: "Which is to be taken as the master in personality, affect or cognition?" or "Which should be the central focus, the individual or the social?" or "Which should be the primary theater of investigation, the intrapsychic or the interpersonal?" or even "Which is to be taken as the more powerful developmental framework, the psychoanalytic or the cognitive-structural?" In this book all these questions get reconstructed by moving from the dichotomous *choice* to the dialectical *context* which brings the poles into being in the first place. Is there some context in personality, the book asks, which is philosophically prior to, and constitutive of, these polarities—and can this context be observed and studied? The book suggests that the evolution of meaning-making is just this context, and the suggestion is supported through the consideration of a wide variety of human experience gleaned from the settings of the clinic, the research laboratory, and everyday life.

This book, in other words, is another empirically grounded speculation, another conceptual itinerary. I have written it for students and teachers of psychology; theorists and researchers of personality; psychotherapists, counselors, teachers, pastors, and all professionals who concern themselves with another's growth; and I have written it for the psychologically-minded general reader. These groups, and the individuals within these groups, trust their own personally evolved criteria for convincingness, some blend of the analytic and aesthetic by which they arrive at a sense that something does or does not seem to be true. Perhaps finally the courage I take from Erikson's example, in deciding to present this long story in the midst of my own convictions and hesitations, is the courage to trust the reader to struggle for herself or himself with the questions it raises and the tentative answers it offers.

I owe this book to ten years of conversation and company with extraordinary men and women. While we made use of the guises of student and teacher, therapist and client, researcher and subject, colleague and colleague, in order first to meet, I want to thank them here as the persons they are, before, during, and after all these roles—persons who let me learn with them and from them. Among the things they taught me is the special difficulty of acknowledging a debt such as this one. For this book's understanding of human development questions our accustomed image of each person's absolute distinctness and self-containment. An author's usual expression of gratitude—for associations he came to and came away from, ways he himself was helped or enlarged—amounts to a kind of confirmation of his independence, his individuation, the possibility of his really speaking all by himself. I should like here to acknowledge something more than my indebtedness (thereby "paying off" and being once again "free and clear"); I should like to acknowledge my embeddedness (a word which figures prominently in the chapters ahead). Not only have I taken from my connections, I am certain I speak from them as well. Where it was clear to me in the book that I was speaking from a particular connection, I tried to acknowledge the person or persons in question. But most of the time it is impossible, which is part of what it means to *be* embedded.

If I cannot always say who is speaking I can at least identify, and gratefully acknowledge, the persons and arrangements that make up the context from which I speak. For several years I have had the privilege of attentive and demanding students at the Harvard Graduate School of Education and the Massachusetts School of Professional Psychology. If this book is at all successful as a teacher it is owing to their hearing me out and their willingness to let me know when they could not hear.

I have had the benefit of participation in two genuine learning communities, one oriented to research and one to clinical practice, each inspired by a man himself inspired. Lawrence Kohlberg has been the generous, gentle, unobtrusive, and intellectually invigorating spirit behind Harvard's Center for Moral Education. He has made it possible for me to learn from him and for us all to learn from each other. Despite the wide acclaim he has received, the real nature and scope of Kohlberg's contribution to psychology and social science is only beginning to be glimpsed.

William Perry, the founder and, for thirty years, the director of Harvard's extraordinary counseling center (the Bureau of Study Counsel), saved me from an exclusively research approach to my interests. His work, too, has been way ahead of its time. On the day of his retirement his seminal book, written a good ten years earlier, was being far more widely read than it had been when it appeared. The ways I have drawn on him are numerous, but perhaps only those who have been in his presence will quite understand if I say that what has meant the most is the truth in the few words he invariably uses to introduce himself: "Bill Perry here." At the Bureau I had the chance to think and learn in an intimate community of clinicians who were, as Perry would say, "human though trained."

Over the last few years a small group of us has begun to cohere, in part for the purposes of carrying further, in research and practice, the line of thinking presented in this book. Though we have high hopes for our future, I would like here to acknowledge our past, its importance to me, and my joy in our company. I am speaking of Anne Colby, Ann Fleck Henderson, Alexandra Hewer, Gil Noam, Sharon Parks, Joe Reimer, Laura Rogers, and Zina Steinberg.

James Fowler, William Rogers, Carol Gilligan, William Torbert, and Donald Quinlan have each been important to my learning for many years. Although this book may not exactly represent the views of any of them, their own developing visions have mattered to the way I see.

I wish to acknowledge my gratitude and appreciation for the intellectual and spiritual company of Laura Rogers, who has been a part of this work from the beginning. She has been crucial to every phase of it, a research collaborator, a reader of drafts, a brilliant and buoyant partner to the endless theoretical conversation that a book like this requires.

This book is better than it might have been because of the editing of Eric Wanner and Katarina Rice. Eric kept every promise, was no later on his deadlines than I was on mine, read the book more times than I did, and was right with infuriating regularity. Katarina provided for the book exactly the experience of being heard and held which the book is about; like a client in developmental therapy the book thrived in her company. Jill Brotman prepared the manuscript and Alexandra Hewer compiled the index, each with her customary elegance. Since both cared about the material and were very familiar with it, each made suggestions that improved the book.

Finally, I am continuously grateful to the many persons who will not be identified, whose life experiences, often difficult and painful, find their way into this book. In providing us with "data" (literally, "that which is given"), they make us gifted; in revealing their courage, they encourage us.

CREDITS

Grateful acknowledgement is made for permission to reprint the following material:

Lines from "Ash Wednesday," in *Collected Poems 1909–1962* by T. S. Eliot, copyright 1936 by Harcourt Brace Jovanovich, Inc.; copyright © 1963, 1964 by T. S. Eliot. Reprinted by permission of Harcourt Brace Jovanovich, Inc.

Lines from "Burnt Norton," in *Four Quartets* by T. S. Eliot, copyright 1943 by T. S. Eliot; renewed 1971 by Esme Valerie Eliot. Reprinted by permission of Harcourt Brace Jovanovich, Inc.

Cartoon by Jules Feiffer, reprinted by permission of Jules Feiffer Dist. Publishers-Hall Syndicate.

Drawing by Charles Saxon, © 1975 The New Yorker Magazine, Inc.

Lines from *Ovid's Metamorphoses,* translated by Rolfe Humphries, reprinted by permission of Indiana University Press.

Material from "The Development, Meaning and Management of School Phobia" by S. Waldfogel, J. Coolidge, and P. Hahn, reprinted by permission of the *American Journal of Orthopsychiatry;* copyright 1957 by the American Orthopsychiatric Association, Inc.

Table 3, from *Moral Development and Behavior,* ed. Thomas Lickona, published by Holt, Rinehart and Winston; reprinted by permission of Lawrence Kohlberg.

Parts of this book have appeared previously, in considerably altered form, in the following publications: *The Andover Review* ("Rebalancing Balances: A Neo-Piagetian Perspective," Spring 1978; "The Hidden Treasure of Paid Attention," Fall 1979); *Counseling Psychologist* ("The Evolving Self: A Process Conception for Ego Psychology," vol. 8, no. 2, 1979); *Journal of Personnel and Guidance* ("Making Meaning: The Constructive-Developmental Approach to Persons and Practice," vol. 58, no. 5, 1980); *Moral and Religious Becoming,* ed. J. Fowler and A. Vergote ("There the Dance Is: Religious Dimensions of a Developmental Psychology"; Morristown, N.J., Silver Burdette, 1980).

CONTENTS

FIGURES

TABLES

In nova fert animus mutatis
dicere formas corpora . . .
My intention is to tell
of bodies changed
to different forms . . .

The heavens and all below them,
Earth and her creatures,
All change,
And we, part of creation,
Also must suffer change.

— Ovid, *Metamorphoses*
   (translated by Rolfe Humphries)

PROLOGUE

Construction and Development

Woody Allen says he was thrown out of college for cheating: it was on a metaphysics exam and he looked into the soul of his neighbor. This is something like what I understand psychology to be about. Psychology asks fundamental questions about being human; the examination is metaphysical. But we are wary of deceiving ourselves and so we "cheat" — we look into the souls of our neighbors for verification.

This is a book of psychology, then, in the literal sense: *psyche* and *logos*, a reckoning of the spirit. "The spirit," wrote Hegel in the preface to *The Phenomenology of Mind*, "is never at rest but always engaged in ever progressive motion, in giving itself a new form." This motion is the subject of this book. The book is a reckoning of the nature of these forms and the experience of this restless creativity. It is about the courage and the costs which we discover again and again in giving ourselves a new form.

Like Ovid at the beginning of the *Metamorphoses*, I have seen this book as the telling of a long story. It is the story, as he says, "of bodies changed to different forms." The story begins in Chapter 1, in which, like the seekers of old, we are given a charm by a gray-bearded elder some see as wise and others as a pleasant old fool. How powerful the charm really is and how much it will aid us in our quest, what we find, and those we meet up with along the way—all this is the story of the chapters that follow.

What are the questions that prompt the journey, and why is it important to undertake it?

In Ernest Hemingway's story "Indian Camp," a doctor's young son, Nick, joins his uncle and father when the men are called to assist an Indian woman who is having difficulty giving birth. As they arrive at the camp they hear the woman's screams, which persist for the reader through most of the story. The men of the tribe have removed themselves to a distance where, with steady conversation, they can screen out most of the sound. Nick's father solves the problem of the screams through his professionalism; Hemingway refers to him as "the doctor" in this section of the story, in contrast to more familiar appellations before and after the events at the camp. The uncle goes off in the middle of the procedure to get drunk. But the husband of the pregnant woman had earlier broken his leg, and so, unable to join his tribesmen at the camp's perimeter, he is forced to remain in the cabin, in the upper bunk, directly above his agonizing wife. The woman suffers greatly and with great courage she brings new life into the world. "Let's see how the proud father is doing," the doctor says, drawing back the blanket of the upper bunk. Nick sees his father's bloody hand and the fresh, fatal, self-inflicted wound of the husband. In the boat, riding back home, the young Nick watches his father rowing strong, regular strokes; he thinks of all he has seen at the camp, and he feels serene, grateful that he—Nick—will never die.

The story is about many things. But it reminds me that the awful and sacred human note which sounds throughout it—the agony of a woman in labor—is not a single note at all. It has as many sounds as there are people to hear it. The story's final surprise, in the mind and heart of the small boy, transcends an understanding of the woman's agony as a kind of external stimulus to which the hearers variously respond. It directs us instead to that most human of "regions" *between* an event and a reaction to it—the place where the event is privately composed, made sense of, the place where it actually *becomes* an event for that person. Strictly behaviorist theory aside, probably every personality psychology that influences counselors and therapists today directs us in some way to this zone of mediation where meaning is made.

Those of us who are professional helpers have a dual involvement with meaning-making. What we know of the way our client holds himself and his world together can help us understand what his experience means to him, including his experience of being with us in a helping relationship. We are especially helped by our awareness of the fact that the way he composes himself is at once a kind of achievement and a constraint. And yet we are unavoidably meaning-makers ourselves. And for us it is the client himself and the things he says that make up those events which come to life in our own zone of mediation. How we will understand what we hear—or, better put, what we actually do hear—will be settled there where the event is made personal sense of, there where it actually becomes an event for us. The filters and lenses we use in listening to our clients bear periodic inspection. They are themselves no less a kind of achievement and a constraint. In part, it is a professional helper's persistent recognition that her own meaning for a set of circumstances might not be the same as her client's that leads us to call her a sensitive listener; her understanding of what goes into the way her client makes meaning and what is at stake for him in defending it that leads us to call her a psychologist; and her understanding of what to *do* with her understanding that leads us to call her a therapist. It is advisable that before people become therapists they pursue the first two callings.

The zone of mediation where meaning is made is variously called by personality psychologists the "ego," the "self," the "person." From some perspectives it is one among many functions, all of which together make up the person. From other perspectives it is the very ground of personality itself—it *is* the person—and various functions are considered in its context. While any number of theorists and frameworks can be said to take an interest in the person as a meaning-maker, the psychological traditions that, in doing so, have probably had the most impact on clinical and counseling psychology are two: the neo-psychoanalytic, including both neo-psychoanalytic ego psychology (Anna Freud, 1936; Hartmann, 1939; Erikson, 1950; Kris, 1975) and neo-psychoanalytic object relations theory (Fairbairn, 1952; Jacobsen, 1964; Winnicott, 1965; Mahler, 1968; Guntrip, 1971); and the existential-phenomenological tradition (Lecky, 1945; Maslow, 1954; May, 1958; Binswanger, 1963; Angyal, 1965), whose most influential exponent for counseling and clinical psychology has surely been Carl Rogers (1951).

The contributions of each of these traditions are so crucial that any lens which does not reflect them in some way must suffer as a result. And yet each system is, by itself, in difficulty, and the integration of the two is not at all straightforward. This book does not attempt such an integration, but, in putting forward a third psychological tradition, it ends up doing honor to a surprising extent to the deepest convictions of both existential and dynamic personality psychologies. This third tradition I will call the "constructive-developmental" (it attends to the development of the activity of meaning-constructing), and it has a venerable past in the meaning-making ranks. Its origins lie in the work of James Mark Baldwin (1906), John Dewey (1938), and George Herbert Mead (1934); and its central figure has certainly been Jean Piaget (1936). It has had almost no influence on the current practice of counseling and clinical psychology (aside from psychoeducationally oriented work with children), and with very good reason. It has attended very little, if at all, to the processes of development, to the inner experience of development, or to the life of the emotions—aspects of personality central to therapeutic practice. Is this lack of attention due to intrinsic limits in the framework itself, or to the times and temperaments of its central figures? My "neo-Piagetian" approach to the person will suggest that not only is this tradition capable of addressing these issues (however different my reconstruction of that tradition may be from the reader's probable associations with Piaget), but it may be capable of doing so in a way that gives a new kind of strength to whatever lens the counselor or therapist holds most dear.

At the heart of the lens we associate with Rogers is an existential approach to the metaphors of twentieth-century evolutionary biology. In contradistinction to earlier mechanistic and homeostatic conceptions, Rogers attends to what he regards as intrinsic processes of adaptation and growth. His first principle is the "actualizing tendency":

> the inherent tendency of the organism to develop all its capacities in ways which serve to maintain or enhance the organism. It involves not only the tendency to meet what Maslow terms "deficiency needs" . . . [but] it [also] involves development toward the differentiation of organs and of functions, expansions in terms of growth, expansion of effectiveness through the use of tools, expansion and enhancement through reproduction. It is development toward autonomy and away from heteronomy or control by external forces. Angyal's statement could be used as a synonym for this term: "Life is an autonomous event which takes place between the organism and the environment. Life

processes do not merely tend to preserve life, but transcend the momentary status quo of the organism, expanding itself continually and imposing its autonomous determination upon an ever-increasing realm of events." (1959, p. 196)

This actualizing tendency Rogers regards as the sole motive of personality; there are no separate systems with motives of their own. The tensions between defense and enhancement, for example, are integrated in a single system. There is presumed to be a basic unity to personality, a unity best understood as a process rather than an entity. This process, according to Rogers' conception, gives rise to the "self," the meaning-making system with which the process gets identified. Anxiety, defense, psychological maladjustment, and the processes of psychotherapy are all understood in the context of the efforts to maintain, and the experience of transforming, the self-system. Every one of these basic convictions will be held and honed in the neo-Piagetian approach that follows.

And such refinement is needed. For there are a number of questions which even the most sympathetic Rogerian might be expected to ask of that system. First, since the emphasis is upon development ("development toward autonomy," "development toward differentiation"), is it not crucial to know something about the history of these developments, about the differences as well as the commonality between an earlier moment in this history and a later moment, between an earlier transition and a later one; about regularities among people in this history if they exist; about the different "selves" the actualizing tendency brings into being? (Rogers' descriptions of the changing self in therapy, for example, come close to suggesting it is basically one "kind of self," or one moment in the history, that requires therapy.) Second, Rogers' conception of adaptation is focused on separation ("development toward autonomy," "development toward differentiation"), when adaptation, biologists always tell us, is a matter of differentiation and integration (development toward inclusion, development toward attachment). Psychologists with a special interest in women have suggested that male bias has led to an exaggerated and wrong-headed esteem for differentiation (which becomes associated with growth) to the devaluation of integration (which becomes associated with dependency) (Gilligan, 1978; Low, 1978). Is it possible to evolve a model of personality development which takes account not only of both sides of this tension but of the tension itself? Finally, what is the real meaning, efficacy, and justification of the "client-centered response" with respect to the organismic theory of personality? Rogers' many discussions of "unconditional positive regard" and its expression by the counselor are at a level of exposition that provides more warmth than light, quickly ascending to quasi-religious piety. It is the bane of humanistic psychology in general that at precisely those moments when its powerful and transforming ideas need the protection of rigorous explication it becomes only musical and loses its voice. The meaning of client-centered therapy as a mode of practice is vulnerable to simple-minded appropriation precisely because its relation to a theory of personality has never been clearly articulated. How might this be done? These are the kinds of questions the neo-Piagetian approach addresses, and one hoped-for result is a stronger justification and operational translation of basic Rogerian convictions.

Psychoanalytically oriented ego psychology has come a great distance in elevating the meaning-making dimension of personality from the inferior position it first occupied in Freud's triumvirate. "The ego," Freud once wrote Jung, paying deference to what he felt were the greater powers of the superego and the id, "is like a clown in a circus, always trying to stick in its oar to make it look like it has something to do with what is going on" (Freud and Jung, 1974, p. 404). By the 1930s the study of the ego had become respectable and a battle was in progress, notably between Anna Freud and Heinz Hartmann, as to just what view to take of it. Anna Freud's view was a conservative one; she focused on the ego's defensive nature (1936). Hartmann claimed an adaptive potential, a "conflict-free" sphere (1939). No integration of these views was possible, given the nineteenth-century hydraulic conception of intrapsychic function that both had inherited from Freud. That very real picture of the self-protective, procrustean dimension of meaning-making could never be integrated with the equally real adaptive, self-transforming picture so long as the anxiety Anna Freud's defensive ego sought to ward off could only lead, if unchecked, to the ego's breakdown. A conception of growth tied to the ego's very activity of making meaning was needed before growth and breakthrough could be seen as a possible consequence of the ego's breakdown. This conception one can find equally in Rogers or Piaget but all psychoanalytically derived psychologies still suffer to a degree from an outdated approach to our biological reality which focuses more upon the energy system in us than the energy system in which we are.

But the fact remains that at the heart of modern ego psychology and object relations theory we find many of the same convictions expressed earlier by the existential position, and, in addition, we see the effort to engage several of the issues that elude the existentialists. For the ego psychologists and the object relations theorists, these convictions represent dramatic departures from Freudian origins. A central conviction is that personality development occurs in the context of interactions between the organism and the environment, rather than through the internal processes of maturation alone. One finds this reflected in Erikson's psychosocial approach (1950) and especially among object relations theorists, who have brought the relationship of self to other (or subject to object) to center stage. Fairbairn (1952), Winnicott (1965), Guntrip (1971), and others want to insist that "object relating" is an intrinsic interest of persons, rather than solely an extrinsic, regrettably necessary detour on behalf of a more primary goal. From the point of view of these theorists the very essence of ego activity *is* object relations, and ego activity is presumed to begin immediately at birth, rather than waiting for years to be hatched out of prior and more powerful systems, as in the classic Freudian conception. In addition, Erikson, in his famous stage theory, and object relations theorists, such as Kernberg (1966) with his stages of internalization, have attempted to chart a history of successive evolutions in self-other relating which suggest an articulation of what remains essentially undifferentiated among the existentialists. Although the neo-Piagetian framework arises out of different soil, once again it shares every one of these convictions, and, more than this, it integrates them into a consistent theoretical whole. Where possible, it has begun to translate them into a researchable program. Most of all, it joins the ego and object relations psychologists in the effort to understand the processes and stages of development in our self-other constructions.

Thus, if the Piagetian framework has traditionally seemed to have little to say to counseling and clinical psychology, its root metaphors and premises may actually make it better equipped to deal with the very issues central to those psychologies which have been most influential to the therapeutic enterprise.

The subject of this book is the person, where "person" is understood to refer as much to an activity as to a thing—an ever progressive motion engaged in giving itself a new form. The English language (in fact, all Western language) is not well suited to preserving this sense of the dialectical relation between entities and processes. Alan Watts (1936) suggests a magic trick we can perform together right now. Make a fist. Now we shall make your fist disappear. Ready? Okay—open your hand. You see?—or rather you don't see—your fist is gone! (You may wish to perform this astonishing trick a few more times before continuing.) The so-called thing (a fist) can be made to "disappear" because it is not only a thing; disguised as a noun, it is as much a process (the act of closing the hand). Western grammars separate entities and processes as if the distinction were absolute. But the Chinese, for example, do not, and their culture seems also to have less difficulty seeing that objects are also events, that the world is made up of processes as much as entities. Eastern cultures do not see night and day as static poles or distinct realms the way we do, but as subprocesses that tend toward each other (Kagan, 1972). Their thinking is less dichotomous, more dialectical. If the reader is genuinely to try on the way of seeing that constructive-developmental personality theory suggests, he or she must practice thinking a bit more like the Chinese. While it may be possible for us to accept in isolation an axiom like Hegel's, or Whitehead's (1929), that what is most fundamental about life is that it *is* motion (rather than merely some*thing in* motion), it remains that we are greatly tempted—and seduced—by our language into experiencing ourselves and the world as things that move. Even the action nouns (gerunds) which we use to refer to ourselves have lost their active dimension and get constituted as things. A writer has to strain to make the reader recover the process in the words "human being"; we talk about "a being" and "beings." This book is about human being as an activity. It is not about the doing which a human does; it is about the doing which a human is.

This notion of human being has been most powerfully represented by two separate Big Ideas which have been appearing throughout this Prologue. As big ideas should, one or both have had an influence on nearly every aspect of intellectual life in the last hundred years. These are the ideas of constructivism (that persons or systems constitute or construct reality) and developmentalism (that organic systems evolve through eras according to regular principles of stability and change). In somewhat different ways, both ideas insist on a recognition that behind the form (or thing) there exists a process which creates it, or which leads to its coming into being. What exactly do I mean by constructivism and developmentalism?

The notion that we constitute reality, rather than somehow happen upon it, is most quickly and vividly brought home in the area of perception, although perception is, of course, but one aspect of our constructivism. If you look at Figure 1, you might quickly answer the following simple questions:

1. Is the woman youngish or oldish?
2. Is she haggish or pleasant-looking?
3. Does she seem to have a large nose or a normal-sized nose?

Figure 1   A figure to figure

Originally drawn by W. E. Hill and published in *Puck,* November 6, 1905. First used for psychological purposes by E. G. Boring, "A New Ambiguous Figure," *American Journal of Psychology,* 1930.

These questions do not call for subtle distinctions. You might suppose that among your fellow readers looking at this picture you would find widespread agreement. But actually you would not. Some of you have decided the picture is of a pleasant-looking young woman with a normal-sized nose, and some of you feel you are looking at an old hag with a big nose. When a group of people discover others answering the questions quite differently I sometimes ask how it makes them feel. They generally sit up straight, compose themselves, and say it does not surprise them that much. "After all," they say, "I realize people can see the same thing different ways; that's your point, isn't it?" Well, no. I wonder whether people see the same thing different ways or whether they see *different* things different ways.

Of course the picture is a trick. It comes from the old Gestalt perception psychology of the 1930s and intentionally invites two interpretations (see Figure 2). But in this it is far less tricky than real life, which invites a myriad of interpretations. Our experience with the picture raises the question of where the picture is. We tend to act as if the picture is on the page; that is, "seeing it" seems to us to be a matter of seeing what has always been there on the page. (Why else do we tend not to look for another picture once a picture has been seen?) If twenty copies of the picture are passed out and they all look the same to us, it seems to us that everyone is getting "the same picture." (Why else does it come as a surprise to hear people giving answers different from our own?) Actually the picture is not so much on the page—the

Figure 2   Two views of Figure 1

page contains a smattering of dark and light patches, lines, and blank space—as it is composed in the metaphysical "space between" the page and a meaning-making organism—namely, you.

Before long the reader will find the expression "meaning-making organism" redundant; what an organism does, as William Perry says (1970), is organize; and what a human organism organizes is meaning. Thus it is not that a person makes meaning, as much as that the activity of being a person is the activity of meaning-making. There is thus no feeling, no experience, no thought, no perception, independent of a meaning-making context in which it *becomes* a feeling, an experience, a thought, a perception, because we *are* the meaning-making context. "Percept without concept is blind," Kant said (1969). "Experience is not what happens to you," Aldous Huxley said, "it's what you *do* with what happens to you" (1972). And the most fundamental thing we do with what happens to us is organize it. We literally make sense. Human being is the composing of meaning, including, of course, the occasional inability to compose meaning, which we often experience as the loss of our own composure.

As Herbert Fingarette writes (1963), the idea that we are constitutive of our own experience crosses philosophy, theology, literary criticism, and psychology. In psychology it is an axiom of existential, phenomenological, Gestalt, Piagetian, perception theorist, and Kelly-construct approaches. Yet, Fingarette says, it is not at all clear what it means from each approach to say the person is a meaning-maker; in fact, the word may refer to two apparently quite different activities. We may be speaking about the person's tacit "formulating of a public, logically consistent, and prediction-oriented theory," which is largely how English-speaking philosophy and psychology have used the word "meaning"; or we may be speaking of "questions and answers about life's meaning or meaninglessness . . . attempts at expressing a perception, adopting a stance, recommitting ourselves to a new life strategy," which is how Continental thought has taken the word. Thus, Fingarette concludes, the individual's presumed meaning-making may refer to a "scientific process of developing a logical, reliably interpretable and systematically predictive theory," or to an "existential process of generating a new vision which shall serve as the context of a new commitment" (pp. 62-68).

The Piagetian framework, as presently composed, powerfully embraces what Fingarette calls the scientific apprehension of meaning-making. Piaget (1936, 1937, 1948, 1962, 1969, 1970), Lawrence Kohlberg (1969, 1971, 1972, 1976), and others have taken the heretofore abstract notion of personal construction and made it almost palpable in revealing the apparently cross-culturally universal shape and sequence of "logical, reliably interpretable, and systematically predictive theories" that we grow through in the course of our development. And yet this constructive-developmental perspective has taken no interest whatever in the equally important, but quite different, side of the same activity—the way that activity is experienced by a dynamically maintained "self," the rhythms and labors of the struggle to make meaning, to have meaning, to protect meaning, to enhance meaning, to lose meaning, and to lose the "self" along the way. The Piagetian approach, viewing meaning-making from the outside, descriptively, has powerfully advanced a conception of that activity as naturally epistemological; it is about the balancing and rebalancing of subject and object, or self and other. But what remains ignored from this approach is a consideration of the same activity from the inside, what Fingarette would call the "participative." From the point of view of the "self," then, what is at stake in preserving any given balance is the ultimate question of whether the "self" shall continue to *be,* a naturally *onto*logical matter.

On the other hand, there are psychologies, notably the existential and phenomenological, which *have* raised these bigger questions about human being—questions about the *endowing* of meaning, about the process, as Fingarette put it, of "generating a new vision which shall serve as the context of a new commitment" (1963, p. 64). But these psychologies, in turn, lack the theoretical and methodological power to speak with any depth in an intersubjective way about this activity, to locate or even explore the regularities among persons in this activity, with respect to either its forms or its processes.

We are left, then, with a rigorous but reductionistic approach to meaning-making on one hand, and a vague but richer conception of psychological activity on the other. No psychology has ever successfully integrated these two conceptions of meaning-making. Were one to do so, the resulting psychology would be able to attend not only to the shape and sequence of our various consolidations of meaning, but to the universal processes themselves of constructing, defending, subordinating, surrendering, and reconstituting a meaning; to the question of what it means for us that our world designs cohere and fall apart; to crisis, anxiety, the defenses, all newly understood; to the uses of pain, to meaningfulness and meaninglessness, breakdown and breakthrough; to the very movement of meaning, as well as the systems of meaning—the stages—along the way.

The second Big Idea is that organic systems evolve through qualitatively different eras according to regular principles of stability and change. Phillip Rieff (1966) has written about the "cultural symbolic," a centering motif—a mythology, really—yielding up a rich set of images and symbols by which a whole culture might suspend its experience. He considers the Enlightenment, in the past, and Freudianism, in the present, to be examples. I would suggest that Freudianism is but a part of what is emerging as the cultural symbolic of our time, namely, developmentalism. As Norbett Mintz has said (personal communication), of those who were probably the four greatest shapers of the way modern persons experience their experience—Freud, Marx, Darwin, and Einstein—three partook of a developmental "symbolic." The three most seminal contributors to Western psychology are probably Freud, Piaget, and Skinner; two of these are developmental.

Like the idea of construction, the idea of development liberates us from a static view of phenomena. As the idea of construction directs us to the activity that underlies and generates the form or thingness of a phenomenon, so the idea of development directs us to the origins and processes by which the form came to be and by which it will pass into a new form.

This shift—from entity to process, from static to dynamic, from dichotomous to dialectical—is a shift which H. K. Wells (1972) notices in the historical development of modes of scientific thought. The first step is one of classification: botany and biology spent 2,500 years in taxonomic attention to plants and animals, astronomy classified the heavenly bodies, and so on. But the next step, after classification, is ontogeny; the attention turns to the origins, development, and direction of the phenomenon. In just the last 150 years, Wells says, nearly every social and natural science has made this transformation from a taxonomic, entity-oriented perception of the phenomena of investigation to a developmental, process-oriented perception: in astronomy with La Place (1832); in geology with Lyell (1833); in logic with Hegel (1892) and Feuerbach (1846); in history and political economy with Marx (1931); in biology with Darwin (1889).

And in psychology with Freud and Piaget. Psychoanalysis and cognitive-developmentalism have both made powerful contributions toward an understanding of psychological phenomena oriented toward origin, development, and process. Yet these understandings are essentially stranded from each other intellectually and professionally. Psychoanalytic theory now has very little life within academic psychology and yet it is the guiding source of practice in most hospitals and clinics. Cognitive-developmentalism has had a robust life in the university and almost no influence whatever in the clinic. While it can be pretended that this division of labor is an appropriate consequence of the separate tasks to which each theory is best suited, the fact remains that no whole theory of personal functioning will be possible in the absence of some higher order psychology in which to integrate the wisdom of each. Lacking such a metapsychology, both academic research and clinical practice are less than they might be.

Arriving at a metapsychology will be no small order. Although both theories are developmental, each has its own picture of what development means—where it is located, and what moves it along. These differences lead to a different sense of what is important about a phenomenon. They derive different data from a phenomenon, and the integration of the data is not at all as simple as it might first appear because in the end the data depend on differing pictures of the phenomenon. Both theories have important conceptions of equilibrium, for example. A basis for a fuller picture of human psychology seems promising with the recognition that modern psychoanalytic theory is largely concerned with the how and why of balance (available defenses, character style, ego strength) and modern cognitive-developmental theory with the what and which of balance (qualitative distinctions between universal balances, ego stages). But the ease of such an integration is quite deceptive since the conceptions of what equilibrium actually is in the first place are so different. Is the equilibrium essentially within the person, within the body, within intrapsychic representations? Or is the equilibrium in the world, in a broader field of which the person is a part, between the self and an other that actually exists beyond internal representation? A theory's conception of equilibrium springs from its particular theory of biology, which in turn is related to its underlying epistemology. Any metapsychology that does arise will have to be more than psychological, as the term implies; it will have to be explicitly attuned to the biological and the philosophical, as well as the psychological. The metapsychology that develops in this book grows out of Piaget's underlying framework, rather than his psychology, and thus meets this criterion. The underlying framework, which Piaget calls "genetic epistemology," is (as the cumbersome name implies) attuned to the biological and the philosophical.

A successful metapsychology should provide a fruitful approach to a number of tensions within personality theory upon which little progress has been made in the last thirty years. Three of these seem to me foremost: the need for a sophisticated understanding of the relationship between the psychological and the social, between the past and the present, and between emotion and thought. Psychoanalytic theory is sometimes thought of as a theory about affect, and cognitive-developmental theory as a theory about cognition; but in truth each is a theory of both, and each makes one dimension the master of personality and the other the slave. No new light on these or similar polarities will emerge until we are able to locate — philosophically, psychologically, and biologically; theoretically and empirically — a broader context in personality in which to reconstruct the questions.

This book is not shy. It eventually suggests what that broader context might be. It articulates a framework for the study of that context, a framework which brings together the big ideas of construction and development. The constructive-developmental framework studies the phenomenon in nature I call the evolution of meaning. This book is an organized way of wondering what happens if the evolution of the activity of meaning is taken as the fundamental motion in personality.

These days my daughter is learning to read. I watch her listening intently to her own announcement of each letter's sound. "SIH-AEH-NIH-DUH," she says, peering over these symbols, sitting still among these sounds which do not yet cohere for her. "SAAN-DUH." It is still an alien sound the way she says it, something strange and apart from her. She waits, strenuously. "SAND!" she says, arriving home.

It is not her experience I want to attend to here, but mine. The truth is, I find myself terribly moved by this tiny dignity. When her forehead furls and I see her there so intent, something sympathetic flexes in my heart. She grasps a word, but somehow she grasps me as well. I could even say that I love her a little harder because of this moment. I admit some small part of me feels a bit guilty in saying so. That part chides me: "What? She has to *do things* in order for you to love her? What happened to 'unconditional regard'? And is it her effort that appeals to you or her success?"

But actually most of me does not feel guilty at all. And I think this is because however much self-congratulation might be involved, however much I might appreciate her being "successful" or "smart," this just does not seem to be finally what my experience of being moved is about. There is something simpler and deeper, something else. I have felt it before, with people who aren't in any way "mine." Being in another person's presence while she so honestly labors in an astonishingly intimate activity—the activity of making sense—is somehow very touching.

This is an experience we seem to have more often with very young people than with adolescents and adults. Is this because older people less frequently display themselves in these touching and elemental ways, or because we are less able to see those ways for what they are? The personal activity of meaning actually has as much to do with an adult's struggle to recognize herself in the midst of conflicting and changing feelings as it has to do with a young girl's struggle to recognize a word; it has as much to do with a teenager's delicate balance between his loyalty to his own satisfaction and his emerging loyalty to the preservation of reciprocal relationships as it has to do with a one-year-old's effort to balance himself on two legs; it has as much to do with an adult's immobilizing depression, or a teenager's refusal to eat, as it does with a six-year-old's inability to leave the home and go off to school. The activity of meaning has as much to do with a man's difficulty acknowledging his need for closeness and inclusion, or a woman's acknowledging her need for distinctness and personal power, as it has to do with a ten-year-old's need for privacy and self-determination, or a three-year-old's need to have her adhesive relationship to significant others welcomed and supported.

If this book is apparently about a way of seeing others, its secret devotion is to the dangerous recruitability such seeing brings on. So perhaps the book should carry a warning. Though it is aimed at our vision, at helping us to see better what it is that people are doing, what the eye sees better the heart feels more deeply. We not only increase the likelihood of our being moved; we also run the risks that being moved entails. For we are moved somewhere, and that somewhere is further into life, closer to those we live with. They come to matter more. Seeing better increases our vulnerability to being recruited to

the welfare of another. It is our recruitability, as much as our knowledge of what to do once drawn, that makes us of value in our caring
for another's development, whether the caring is the professional caring of teacher, therapist, pastor, or mental health worker, or the more
spontaneous exercises of careful parenthood, friendship, and love.

And why is it so important that we be recruitable? The answer is
that a person's life depends (literally, in the first few years of life, and
in every other way in all the years that follow) on whether he or she
moves someone in this way. Our survival and development depend on
our capacity to recruit the invested attention of others to us. Nature is
nowhere more graceful than in the way she endows each newborn infant with seductive abilities. I do not know why, but the top-heavy
appearance of the infant's body (the disproportionately large head in
relation to the torso, and the disproportionately large forehead and
cranium in relation to the lower face and jaw) attracts people to it.
There is a world of mystery and hundreds of thousands of years of
genetic wisdom behind our experience that a baby is "cute." A baby's
cute body serves to draw people to the baby, but someone, usually the
mother, must not only be drawn but *stay*. There is no sadder or more
thought-provoking material in the research on infancy than the
documentation that babies fail to thrive and even die without an attachment to a consistently present caretaking person, even if the babies
are fully protected from hunger, cold, and disease. Among the ways an
infant draws another to him, none is more powerful than his eyes. It is
arguable that Nature had the assurance of these species-promoting
relationships in mind when she linked the determinants of visual attention to discrepancy. Nowhere does the body have more contours and
contrasting shapes than on the face, and nowhere is the contrast
greater than the area of the eyes. A mother can be forgiven her sense
that her infant is looking at the windows of her soul when the infant
so quickly fixes on the dark spots that are the mother's eyes. The appeal this has for the mother, who gets hooked into looking back, can
hardly be a lucky accident. A person might be a match for an infant
alone, but in these moments the baby has on his side the most powerful ally of all. Less than eight months after he is born, the infant will
actually recognize the mother's face as distinct from others, and, in a
way that must again draw the mother closer, will find other faces dis-
tressingly strange.

This capacity to hold the mother with a recognizing eye is as fundamental to our development as the prehensile capacity to hold a physical object. It has been suggested that the human being owes her capacity for higher consciousness to her thumb, that peculiar digit which can swivel itself 180 degrees and so permit the hand to hold something. The ability to grasp permits the ability to use tools and literally extends the natural functions of the body. It is arguable that tool use has some relation to the capacity to move outside one's body reflectively, the origins of self-consciousness. What is experienced physically and concretely may be later experienced metaphysically and abstractly. What is today the prehensile grasp may be tomorrow the grasp of apprehension.

But there are a number of similarly primordial experiences that begin in the infant's *social* world. What distinguishes these from the grasp of things is that they are intrinsically social; that is, the "object" which is grasped is also a self, itself a grasper. No experience is more powerful perhaps than the glance, the interplay of eyes, the looking at someone who is looking at you. The experience of being seen and not being seen, universally acted out in the game of peekaboo (in Japan the grownup says, "Nai, nai—bah!"—something like, "Nothing, nothing—here I am!") is as subject to future abstracting as the prehensile grasp. The need to be seen, to be recognized, however it changes in the complexity of its form, may never change in its intensity.

The consequence of this beguiling, the infant's relationship with her primary caretaker, like that of her relationship with physical objects, is her further development, a new kind of consciousness, a qualitative growth in her making of meaning. The infant, who before regarded the world and everyone and everything in it as a part of herself, becomes able to differentiate herself from others. Instead of being fused with the primary caretaker, she is now able to relate to him or her. In creating for the first time an "object world" or "other world" which the infant, too, sees as "other," the infant begins the history of successively joining the world rather than incorporating it, of holding the world while guaranteeing its distinct integrity—which is the history of human development.

Thus just as the object-grasping infant is doing something which, in another form, he will try to do all his life (grasp things), so the attention-recruiting infant is doing something he will try to do all his life (recognize and be recognized)—and at bottom it is the same thing: the activity of meaning. Meaning is, in its origins, a physical activity (grasping, seeing), a social activity (it requires another), a survival activity (in doing it, we live). Meaning, understood in this way, is the primary human motion, irreducible. It cannot be divorced from the body, from social experience, or from the very survival of the organism. Meaning depends on someone who recognizes you. Not meaning, by definition, is utterly lonely. Well-fed, warm, and free of disease, you may still perish if you cannot "mean."

The reasons why we are drawn to others, especially to their welfare, are surely mysterious. But so many of the eliciting situations seem to harken back to the exigencies of this basic life motion, the activity of meaning and the threat of not meaning. We are drawn to a person in heroic struggle; we are drawn to a person vulnerably alone; we are drawn to a person who seems intensely alive; we are drawn to a person whose efforts make "perfect sense" to us. I admit to wondering if our attraction is not of some force "bigger than both of us," a kind of species sympathy which we do not share so much as it shares us.

This sympathy is in great supply for newborns — and newborns share a powerful capacity to elicit it. But Nature, having done her part when it is most needed, is not so democratic after infancy. The capacity to recruit another's invested regard, so uniform at birth, becomes a various affair as people grow older: some people have a much greater ability to recruit people's attention to them than other people do. This obvious fact, so underinvestigated by psychologists and so commonly denied by teachers, is never forgotten by teenagers, who could have told researchers — before huge sums of money were spent to discover it — that the greatest inequalities in education are not between schools (of different economic strata, for example) but within them; that greater than the inequalities of social class or achievement test scores is the unequal capacity of students to interest others in them — a phenomenon not reducible to social class or intelligence, and which seems to be the more powerful determinant of future thriving.

Who comes into a person's life may be the single greatest factor of influence to what that life becomes. Who comes into a person's life is in part a matter of luck, in part a matter of one's power to recruit others, but in large part a matter of other people's ability to be recruited. People have as varying capacities to be recruited as they do to recruit others. If the capacity to be recruited is educable and depends in part on our ability to see, then perhaps the kind of exploration we undertake in a book like this one can enhance our recruitability. Accordingly, this book is concerned with practice as well as theory, with the responsibility of our response-ability, with the question of what we do once recruited.

And yet however much we learn about the effort to be of help, we can never protect ourselves from the risks of caring, which separate real help from advice, reassurance, or consolation. In running these risks we preserve the connections between us. We enhance the life we share, or perhaps better put, we enhance the life that shares us.

Let me bring these thoughts to a close with a story which comes from my experience (Kegan, 1977) among the Hasidim, modern mystics whose most fervent and scholarly discourses are always filled with stories.

This story is about Rifka, who told me right away she was no Hasid. "This you could know from the Super Duper," she said. We had been talking, as was usual with Rifka, about several things at once—Hasids, why she was so exhausted today, children. There was a story coming. How could she be a Hasid if she would buy, in a pinch, from a store that was not kosher?

"I vhass at the Super Duper food store. Les' night came home the whole family, my boys vhat are avay at collitch, and my daughter vit her husband that doesn't verk God should bless him. So, I am making for my Harold like he likes it kreplach to eat. And vit it, for my Louis that came home for the veekend vit a girl, nuch, a matza ball soup vit schmaltz. And vhat should happen—I need the aggravation—there is no schmaltz. I got a housefulla guests, a fency girl from Scarsdale vhat my Louis brings home, and—my mazel—no schmaltz."

At this I smile and Rifka frowns at me.

"So. I go to the Super Duper. I'm hurrying to get back to my dinner I valk through the aisle I see her. I saw a voman vit her child vhat vhass an idiot. You could see he vhass an idiot. I saw this voman, I saw this mother, she vhass holding two different kinds mustard. I vhass in a hurry. I had my schmaltz and I vent out of the store.

"That night when all my children and guests vere asleep I vhass not. I could not. I could not go asleep. Vhy? I din't know. I vhass thinking of all the excitement and it vhass hot but I could not go asleep.

"And then vitout—I mean I din't do it myself, I started to cry. And I cried. I cried for that mother vit her idiot vhat kept on living. I cried for that mother vhat had an idiot and vhass pricing the mustard. And I cried for the idiot vhat vhass life. He vhass life."

"It's terrible," I mumbled, not knowing what to say.

"Don't say this. Vhat is terrible?" she said. "I'm telling you you should know. I'm talking to you.

"That voman, that mother, ve did not say a vord to each other, but ve talked. Not till I came home vhass many hours later did I know ve talked. But ve talked. I heard her and she gave me. Vhat is terrible? You live, you talk. Ve talked. And you know vhat I thought vhen I vhass crying?

"I thought: 'I cry tonight now this mother vit her idiot vhat is so beautiful vhat is life, tomorrow she vill cry less.' "

PART ONE

EVOLUTIONARY TRUCES

Because I do not hope to turn again
Because I do not hope
Because I do not hope to turn
Desiring this man's gift and that man's scope
I no longer strive to strive towards such things
(Why should the agèd eagle stretch its wings?)
Why should I mourn
The vanished power of the usual reign?

Because I do not hope to know again
The infirm glory of the positive hour
Because I do not think
Because I know I shall not know
The one veritable transitory power
Because I cannot drink
There, where trees flower, and springs flow, for there is nothing again

Because I know that time is always time
And place is always and only place
And what is actual is actual only for one time
And only for one place
I rejoice that things are as they are and
I renounce the blessèd face
And renounce the voice
Because I cannot hope to turn again
Consequently I rejoice, having to construct something
Upon which to rejoice

   — T. S. Eliot, "Ash Wednesday"

ONE

The Unrecognized Genius of Jean Piaget

71.355

Some years ago I was visiting with a famous painter. He had become a renowned op artist in the heyday of that brief movement and his canvases were widely displayed. As I walked with him through his studio I admired the precision and invention that went into his pictures, which struck me largely as creative studies or explorations into the elements of painting. There seemed to me to be two kinds of paintings. One group seemed to explore the meaning and function of the line; these were all in black and white and looked like experiments into relations between kinds of line and between lines and space. The other group looked like investigations into color. These were tremendously vivid and yet almost obsessively systematic. The painter had used concentric bands of color in all of them, exploring the interesting fact that the same color looks different when the colors next to it change.

After looking at the pictures a while I mentioned my simple way of grouping them, and the artist said he thought about them similarly. I had been noticing that I was intrigued but unmoved by the paintings, and thought this had something to do with my sense that they were more like paintings about painting than expressive of something. I began thinking of paintings I loved and how alive they seemed, how they traveled beyond their canvas to something somehow true, whether natural or abstract. I was thinking about what *these* painters did with color and line. So that is probably why, when the artist agreed with my grouping idea, I heard myself ask him, "Have you ever thought of bringing these together in your painting—color *and* line?" And, since I was thinking of great masterpieces, I was astonished when he answered quite sincerely, "Actually I tried that a few times and it doesn't work." And of course if you come at it that way it cannot.

In the Prologue I discussed the themes of construction and development. The genius of Jean Piaget is not that he found a way to integrate these themes in his study of the psyche—as if this were what he set out to do—any more than Rembrandt's genius was that he found a new way to integrate color and line. Yet when we look into the unrecognized genius of Jean Piaget we will discover, I think, that this is a feature of what is distinctive about his vision and that it leads to both a new biology and a new epistemology in which to ground a new psychology of the person. Much of what equipped Piaget to see so unusually will always be ineffable, but we do know that he brought together in one man a passion for both philosophy (the constructive theme) and biology (the developmental), and thus the psychology it leads to is a natural child of this distinguished marriage. It has always been up to us to draw out and elaborate the psychology implicit in Piaget's work, for he maintained from the beginning that he was not a psychologist himself, but a "genetic epistemologist." The strange term is itself another reflection of the themes of development and construction brought together. I doubt that Piaget knew quite what he did, and I am certain that had he set out to do it when he began studying the evolution of a mollusk or a child's thinking, he would not have been able to accomplish it. He would have tried it a few times and found it didn't work.

We begin the journey toward a new understanding of the development of the person with Piaget—but not because I imagine we will find such a theory full blown in Piaget's own work, and not because I suppose that intellect or cognition is the foundation of personality. We begin here because in Piaget I believe we discover a genius who exceeded himself and found more than he was looking for.

Consider the preschool child, say a typical four-year-old. The typical four-year-old child has a host of original and (to our minds) amusingly strange views about nature. She may believe the moon follows people when they walk; and if you and she walk off in different directions it can follow both of you with no feeling on the child's part of any contradiction. Or he may believe it is possible one day to become older than his older brother, so that he can mete out the same kind of oppression his older brother is now visiting upon him. When I was four, my family would go to drive-in movies in the summer. One of my favorite things about this was that I received a whole box of popcorn all my own—probably a device to keep me occupied, since I doubt that I understood much of what was going on in the films. I do remember that at some melancholic moment the box of popcorn would begin to look closer to being empty than to being full, and I would begin to express my unhappiness at the thought that if things kept up this way I would soon have none at all. I must have been a delightful companion. In any case, my mother always performed the most extraordinary magic trick on these occasions. She took the box from me in which all the popcorn had settled, closed the lid, and with proper incantations she shook the box up. When she handed it back, I was greatly relieved that the direction in which the quantity was moving had been reversed.

Now in three or four years, all these children, even the little dummy at the drive-in, will think differently about these matters. When my daughter was four she loved the television show "Mister Rogers' Neighborhood" and was visibly moved when he told her at the end of each program, "You are special—I like you. You are my special friend." Now she is seven and she finds the show sappy and distasteful. "It's for babies," she says, stretching the point. The special intimacy, the private connection, which Mr. Rogers can make with a four-year-old, is not possible in an older child who hears these gentle testimonies and thinks, as my daughter said once with some contempt, "Y'know he's saying that to *everyone!*"

One day a mother of two was at the end of her rope with her sons' constant bickering. The current squabble was over the allocation of a dessert pastry. The mother had given two of the small squares to her ten-year-old and one to her four-year-old. She had explained to her aggrieved younger son that he had received only one because he was smaller, that when he was bigger he could have two. He was quite unappeased by this logic, as you can imagine, and he continued to bemoan his fate. The mother lost her patience, and in a fit of sarcasm she swept down on his plate with a knife, saying, "You want two pieces? Okay, I'll give you two pieces. Here!"—whereupon she neatly cut the younger boy's pastry in half. Immediately, all the tension went out of him; he thanked his mother sincerely, and contentedly set upon his dessert. The mother and the older son were both astonished. They looked at the boy the way you would look at something stirring in a wastebasket. Then they looked at each other; and in that moment they shared a mutually discovered insight into the reality of their son and brother, a reality quite different from their own.

A reality different from their own—what I am trying to convey in these tales is just that: that these quaint ways of seeing demonstrated by children are not random fancies, incomplete or dim perceptions of reality as we see it. Rather they are manifestations of a distinct, separate reality, with a logic, a consistency, an integrity all its own. Though we are here confining ourselves to a rather narrow degree of meaning-making—the physical construction of the world—we are seeing, all the same, a given meaning-system, a given moment in the evolution of meaning, the manifestations of a given evolutionary truce which "knows" the world.

Evolutionary truces establish a balance between subject and object. Can I be more precise and demonstrate exactly what balance would account for this strange way that children think? Consider Piaget's most famous study. Two identically shaped glasses or beakers are filled with equal amounts of water. The child agrees that each beaker contains the same amount. The contents of one of the beakers are poured into a taller, thinner beaker (resulting in a higher water level than in the remaining beaker), and the child is asked about the relative amounts. The child usually answers that the taller, thinner beaker has more. Now anyone's first response to such an answer is to pour the contents of the taller, thinner beaker back into the original beaker. We imagine that when the levels match once again the child will surely see that the contents of the poured beaker are equal to those of the unpoured beaker. "Yes," the typical child may say, "they are equal—*now.*" When the contents are poured once again into a shorter, wider beaker, they become less than the contents of the remaining beaker, and so on.

Now just what is going on here? Piaget's experiments are brilliant (Einstein said they were so simple they could only have been thought of by a genius) because they transform an abstract notion such as "structure" or "subject-object differentiation" into something almost palpable. The child's "error" is not something he or she is likely to catch and correct, because according to the terms of the child's present adaptive balance—or evolutionary truce—no error is being made. The deep structure of the truce, simply put, is that the perceptions are on the side of the subject; that is, the child is *subject* to his perceptions in his organization of the physical world. He cannot separate himself from them; he cannot take them as an object of his attention. He is not individuated from them; he is embedded in them. They define the very structure of his attention. For the "preoperational" child, it is never just one's perceptions that change; rather, the world itself, as a consequence, changes.

The two brothers who were bickering over the pastries could have been the same two boys who were overheard at the top of the Empire State Building. As their father reported it to me, both took one look down at the sidewalk and exclaimed simultaneously: "Look at the people. They're tiny ants" (the younger boy); "Look at the people. They look like tiny ants" (the older boy). Whether the younger boy really thought the people had become tiny we don't know (though that is just the kind of thing Piagetian psychologists might ask)—but remembering the little boy who suddenly got "two" pastries, and the one who got "more" popcorn, and the thousands throughout the world who have told researchers how the liquid "gets less" in a wider, flatter glass, we should not be too surprised if he thought exactly that. What we do know is that the older boy could take a perspective on his own perceptions; he said, "They look like tiny ants." His statement is as much about him looking at his perception as it is about the people. Of course, if we really wanted to convince ourselves of the evolutionary state of this boy's meaning-making, we would talk with him at great length and try to create a variety of opportunities for him to show us how he constructed the world, but the words sound as though they come from someone who is not embedded in his perceptions. Distinguishing between how something appears and how something *is* is just what one cannot do when one is subject to the perceptions.

So we have begun to see what a subject-object balance means (and *that* it means!). But how did our four-year-olds come to find themselves in this predicament in the first place? How did they get embedded in their perceptions? Why do they get disembedded? And what does disembedding do to the subject-object balance?

Although I have emphasized the way a four-year-old's thinking seems strange or like a kind of constraint of mind, this is actually only half the picture. It is as true to say that a four-year-old's thinking represents a kind of triumph or liberation over an even more subjective, or self-centered, way of thinking. A developmental perspective naturally equips one to see the present in the context both of its antecedents and potential future, so that every phenomenon gets looked at not only in terms of its limits but its strengths. The human being is not born with the meaning-making sophistication of a four-year-old. This is accomplished only after years of continual experience and reflection with the world, a naturally scientific method (however unaware of it we may be) which is intrinsic to personality.

A preoperational child (our typical four-year-old) is unable to distinguish between how something appears to him or her and how something is; but the newborn (Piaget's "sensorimotor" child) is unable to distinguish between itself and anything else in the world. As a newborn I live in a completely undifferentiated world, one in which nothing is on the side of the object, in which nothing is other than me, in which everything I sense is taken to be an extension of me, and where anything ceases even to *be* once it is out of my sight, touch, hearing. The newborn makes no distinction between inner and outer, between stimuli that come from her own body (for example, hunger) and those that come from outside (light), between your hand passing across her eyes and her own hand passing across her eyes. The interest of a child of four or five months can be recruited to a colorful object or crinkly piece of cellophane. But if the object is covered, the child acts as if it no longer exists. Somewhere around eight to ten months most children begin to act differently. They reach out with their little fingers and pull away whatever conceals the object. The object is somehow "there" in the world of the infant in a way it simply was not before.

Piaget's studies of the first two years of life and the gradual construction of "the permanence of the object" amount to the labors which lead to the very first truce of all—the constituting of any "objective" world itself, a world independent of my experience of it. The child is gradually moving from being subject to its reflexes, movements, and sensations, to *having* reflexes, movements, and sensations. These become the object, and the child's psychologic becomes a reflection on its reflexes and the sensorimotoric. It is not that the child was not a meaning-maker earlier or that it was unable to think. Indeed, it would even be fair to say that the child did its thinking *by* moving and sensing, that its body *was* its mind, its prehensile grasp a preabstracted forerunner to the grasp of apprehension. Like the evolution from an exoskeletal species to an endoskeletal one, the child is able to interiorize or internalize sensations and movements which before could only go on outside. The notion of development as a sequence of internalizations, a favorite conception of psychodynamic thinking, is quite consistent with the Piagetian concept of growth. And although it seems counterintuitive to describe internalization as a process by which something becomes *less* subjective, or moves from subject to object, it is just this recognition that processes of internalization are intrinsically related to the movement of adaptation which makes a Piagetian perspective so promising for a more articulated lifespan approach to basic psychodynamic categories. In fact, something cannot be internalized until we emerge from our embeddedness in it, for it is our embeddedness, our subjectivity, that leads us to project it onto the world in our constitution of reality. When the child is able to have his reflexes rather than be them, he stops thinking he causes the world to go dark when he closes his eyes.

We have begun to see not only how the subject-object balance can be spoken of as the deep structure in meaning-evolution, but also that there is something regular about the process of evolution itself. Growth always involves a process of differentiation, of emergence from embeddedness (Schachtel, 1959), thus creating out of the former subject a new object to be taken by the new subjectivity. This movement involves what Piaget calls "decentration," the loss of an old center, and what we might call "recentration," the recovery of a new center. What Piaget shows us in the first two years may be the consequence, in the narrow realm of physical meaning-making, of the first fundamental renegotiation of the evolutionary truce. It is the beginning of a history of transformations, each of which is a better guarantee to the world of its distinct integrity, a history of successive emergence from it (differentiation) in order to relate to it (integration).

The move from being my action-sensations to having them creates a new subjectivity. In "having them" they are integrated into a more articulated psychologic. That new structure—which, in being able to *reflect on* sensations and actions, is able to distinguish between a me and a not-me—I call the "perceptions." "Perceptions" refers to the organization of reflexes, sensations, and actions, their coordination, or their mediation. That which "does" the mediating constitutes a new subjectivity. Usually sometime after age two the child has completed the renegotiated truce. The sensorimotoric has "moved over" from subject to object, and the new subject, the "perceptions," has come into being. This is how our four-year-old got to be who he is—a meaning-maker embedded in his perceptions.[1]

We have already seen what it means to a child's constitution of the physical world to be subject to the "perceptions." We need only recall the two boys with their pastries, the two boys in the Empire State Building, or the child's understanding about the amounts of liquid in different-shaped glasses. But what happens in a child's evolution of meaning, typically between five and seven, that leads him or her to become like the older boys in those stories? What happens that leads a child to see the amount of liquid is the same regardless of its container?

The young child answers the way she does because she is unable to separate herself from her perceptions. Her attention is subject to her perceptions. But when this underlying structure, this psychologic, this evolutionary truce, is renegotiated, the perceptions "move over" from subject to object. Now instead of seeing the world through her perceptions, she is able to see her perceptions, like the boy who said, "The people *look like* ants." Being able to see one's perceptions leads to their being integrated or coordinated by a new psychologic. A child can coordinate her perception of the liquid at time 1 with her perception at time 2 and see that the quantity remains the same (or, she can coordinate her perception of a thinner beaker (therefore less water) with her perception of a taller beaker (therefore more) and see that the changes cancel each other out). As with every rebalancing, what had been "subject" is recast to the domain of "other." I am not my perceptions; rather, I *have* perceptions; my perceptions become the object of my attention, coordinated by what is the new subject of my attention. And what that new subject is, with respect to Piaget's focus—the precise nature of its coordinating—is a conserver of the physical world. Its capacity to move back and forth among its perceptions—what Piaget calls the reversibilities—creates a psychologic which constructs "groups" and "classes." The world which before was so labile starts to hold still; it becomes concrete. At the same time, the

---

1. Since we are confining ourselves to Piaget's part—only a portion of meaning-making—I focus on the organization of the sensorimotor as creating "the perception"; but we will see that the same overall evolution also creates "the impulse," the construction of feelings arising in *me,* which are mine as distinct from the world's. I take this up in later chapters when meaning-evolution on a fuller scale is explored.

ten-year-old child is subject to his own egocentricity, his own embeddedness. He is embedded in the concrete.

We have seen what it means to be embedded in the reflexes (the sensorimotor stage) and to be embedded in the perceptions (the preoperational stage). What might it mean to be embedded in the concrete (the
concrete operational stage)? (See Table 1.) The fully concrete operational child—a typical ten-year-old—is marvelously engaged with the
physical dimensions of the world. This is the age of collecting, of
keeping records, of memorizing baseball statistics, of the healthy
obsessive-compulsive. Now that the world has lost its fluidity and
plasticity there is an interest in pursuing its limits along the concrete
horizon in which the child is embedded, like James Joyce's Stephen
Daedalus identifying himself on his school workbook:

Stephen Daedalus
Class of Elements
Clongowes Wood College
Gallins
County Kildare
Ireland
Europe
The World
The Universe

The favorite reading of many a ten-year-old is *The Guinness Book of
World Records,* in which one can discover what is the largest cookie
ever baked (ten pounds), the most expensive stationery ever printed
(four dollars a sheet for a Spanish duke), and so on.

A few years ago I was asked to advise designers of health education
curricula for kindergarten through twelfth grade (Kegan, 1978). Of
course, I wanted to know what the children wanted to know—what
were their own questions about health and their bodies? I was greatly
aided by a study in which five thousand children of all ages were asked
just that (Byler, Lewis, and Totman, 1969). The orientations of fifth
graders, say, were strikingly different from those of their younger and
older classmates. Our preoperational friends—the kindergarteners, the
first and second graders—were expectedly "loose": the teachers found
that their interest and questions would change from one moment to
the next, often contradicting one thought with the next. Asked where
their bodies were, they said (p. 8):

TABLE 1. Piaget's eras and stages of physical-cognitive development

Era I (age 0-2): The era of sensorimotor intelligence

Stage 1.   Reflex action.
Stage 2.   Coordination of reflexes and sensorimotor repetition (primary circular reaction).
Stage 3.   Activities to make interesting events in the environment reappear (secondary circular reaction).
Stage 4.   Means/ends behavior and search for absent objects.
Stage 5.   Experimental search for new means (tertiary circular reaction).
Stage 6.   Use of imagery in insightful invention of new means and in recall of absent objects and events.

Era II (age 2-5): Symbolic, intuitive, or prelogical thought

Inference carried on through images and symbols which do not maintain logical relations or invariances with one another. "Magical thinking" in the sense of (a) confusion of apparent or imagined events with real events and objects and (b) confusion of perceptual appearances of qualitative and quantitative change with actual change.

Era III (age 6-10): Concrete operational thought

Inferences carried on through system of classes, relations, and quantities maintaining logically invariant properties and which *refer to concrete objects.* These include such logical processes as (a) inclusion of lower-order classes in higher order classes; (b) transitive seriation (recognition that if $a > b$ and $b > c$, then $a > c$); (c) logical addition and multiplication of classes and quantities; (d) conservation of number, class membership, length, and mass under apparent change.

Substage 1.   Formation of stable categorical classes.
Substage 2.   Formation of quantitative and numerical relations of invariance.

Era IV (age 11 to adulthood): Formal operational thought

Inferences through logical operations upon propositions or "operations upon operations." Reasoning about reasoning. Construction of systems of all possible relations or implications. Hypothetico-deductive isolation of variables and testing of hypotheses.

Substage 1.   Formation of the inverse of the reciprocal. Capacity to form negative classes (for example, the class of all not-crows) and to see relations as simultaneously reciprocal (for example, to understand that liquid in a U-shaped tube holds an equal level because of counterbalanced pressures).
Substage 2.   Capacity to order triads of propositions or relations (for example, to understand that if Bob is taller than Joe and Joe is shorter than Dick, then Joe is the shortest of the three).
Substage 3.   True formal thought. Construction of all possible combinations of relations, systematic isolation of variables, and deductive hypothesis-testing.

Source: Kohlberg and Gilligan, 1972.

All over me
On your head
It's with you all the time
I think it's in your feet
It's inside you
It's also outside you
It's just me!

They were filled with confusions of cause and effect (high temperatures on a thermometer cause fevers), bodily fluidity (boys could become girls, the dead could come back to life), and original notions about birth ("Muddie had a baby in her stomach and the doctor took Larry out. I wonder how he creep into her stomach"). They were completely oriented to the here and now, and to the extent that they were at all curious about their bodies, the focus was on external appearance.

The ten-year-olds were quite different. They were internally concerned with their bodies and oriented not to the surface, which they could see, but to how things looked inside. They wanted to know about physical limits.

What is the tallest you can grow?
What is the most delicate thing on your body? The strongest?
How many muscles does a person have?
How many bones are in the body?
How many cells are in a twelve-year-old male?
How many gallons of blood are in a body?
How many intestines does a person have?

They also had questions of this sort:

What happens if . . . ? (This question is often completed with stories of blood and gore, loss of or damage to limbs and organs.)
What does the doctor do if . . . ?
What if a person has too much alcohol, food, drugs, cigarettes, and so forth?

All of these questions of consequences belong to another order of concepts that do not arise without the new concrete world view. The preoperational child lives largely in the present. Later, the new-found order, regularity, and stability of the world give the child the capacity to master it in a way never before possible. This mastery is threatened by unpredictability, and questions that ask "What if . . . ?" are seeking not only information but control.

If we can see the greater objectivity of the concrete operational child's thought in comparison with the younger child's, we can also see its subjectivity in relation to the high schooler's. When the fifth graders are asked what they want to know about themselves, their answers concern the concrete activities, capacities, limits, and transformations of the physical body; but the high school students ask about the metaphysical or "psychological" self:

> What am I here for? What purpose?
> What is love—the kind that sustains marriage for forty or fifty years?
> Is it right or wrong to use drugs, have sex, drink liquor?
> Why is it wrong for me to have sex but right for my parents?
> How can I achieve happiness?
> What makes me behave as I do?

The concrete operational child explores the limits of the world, but within the terms of the evolutionary truce. From our more evolved point of view we might say it is an exploration along a plane without a recognition of the third dimension.

Once my colleagues in a research study were interviewing a nine-year-old boy and they asked, "How do you feel you make a difference in the world?" The question was a bit much for the boy, so it was rephrased: "What would the world be like if you weren't here?" The boy answered easily, "Then there'd only be four people in my family, twenty-seven in my class at school, and eleven people in my Sunday School class."

When the concrete operational child is presented with four beakers of colorless liquids and asked to figure out how to make a yellow liquid by mixing some number of some of the liquids, he proceeds haphazardly, hoping to hit upon the solution (Piaget, 1958). There is no "overall plan" in evidence. Or he may be presented with a group of metal rods that differ in all possible combinations of material, length, diameter, and shape of cross-section, and be asked what makes one rod more flexible than another (Piaget, 1958). He may experiment and declare that length is a factor, demonstrating his point with a long, small-diameter rod and a short, large-diameter rod. Asked about the difference in their diameters, since he says the difference is length but has used different diameters in his testing as well, he is likely to say that he chose them to make more emphatic the effect of differing lengths. What is happening here? The concrete operational child has no overall plan which constructs all possible ways of mixing the colorless liquids and does not isolate a single variable while holding all other factors constant, because he is subject to, or embedded in, the concrete in his construction of the physical world. An overall plan that can consider concrete events which have not yet happened requires a way of knowing the world in which the concrete moves over from the subject to the object of attention. If the reversibilities coordinate (take as "object") the perceptions for the evolutionary truce that is "concrete operations," it is the coordination of the reversibilities themselves that distinguishes the renegotiated truce that Piaget calls "formal operations."

Once again, what was the very context of meaning-making is going to be integrated into a new context. How is it that the abstract reasoning which Piaget calls formal operations and which he often found emerging around adolescence is again a consequence of this same deep structure we have been following for this whole chapter? When a concrete child is asked how he knows the amount of liquid in the taller, thinner beaker is the same as in the shorter, wider beaker, he usually says something like, "You could just pour it back into the first beaker." Sometimes he says something like, "The level in this glass is higher but the glass is also skinnier so it balances out." Both of these answers demonstrate the concrete operational ability to coordinate perceptions; they both demonstrate reversibility. But, as Piaget says, they represent different kinds of reversibility. The first is the ability to see that if you reverse a process you get back to where you started from (Piaget calls this kind of reversibility "negation" or "inversion," and represents it as: $A + (-A) = 0$; it is the kind of coordination of perceptions that creates the notion of classes or groups, one-to-one correspondence, two points coordinated in time). The second reversibility is the kind that recognizes that various adjustments can balance each other out; or that if one thing, in comparison to another, is greater in one way but lesser in another, the two things might be equivalent (Piaget calls this kind of reversibility "reciprocity," and represents it as: if $A \leq B$ and $B \leq A$, then $A = B$; it is the kind of coordination of perceptions that creates the notion of relations, of two points coordinated in space.) When the new truce is negotiated, these operations of reversibility move over from subject to object and are coordinated by the new subjectivity which constructs what Piaget calls "the inverse of the reciprocal," a way of thinking that permits the reversibilities themselves to be reflected on, or put another way, allows one to think about thought.

This new subjectivity can now construe the world propositionally, hypothetically, inferentially, abstractly. It can spin out an "overall plan" of which any given concrete event (a combination of beakers, e.g.) is but an instance. Put most simply, this new balance makes "what is" a mere instance of "what might be." This rebalancing, often the hallmark of adolescence, unhinges the concrete world. Where before the "actual" was everything, it falls away like the flats of a theater set, and a whole new world, a world the person never knew existed, is revealed. The actual becomes but one instance (and often one not very interesting instance) of the infinite array of the "possible." The underlying psychologic is transformed from the physical to the metaphysical, and a whole new *way* of making meaning comes into being, as demonstrated by the health concerns of the high schoolers in comparison to those of their younger brothers and sisters. Formal thought no longer must proceed from the actual to the theoretical. It can start right in at the theoretical; it can transcend the earth and "go through air," like Daedalus the artificer (and Stephen Daedalus, the classic adolescent) escaping the cruel dominion of his island captivity. The formal thinker can ponder about situations contrary to fact; accept assumptions for the sake of argument; make hypotheses that can be expressed in terms of propositions and tested; leave the tangible, finite, and familiar for the infinitely large or the infinitely small; invent imaginary systems; become conscious of her own thinking; and reflect on her thinking in order to provide logical justifications.

Piaget's basic research discloses four systems of thought about the physical world which people seem to grow through invariantly (although at varying speeds and with varying resting places). A favorite syllogism of Jerome Kagan's (1972) recaps the distinction between the last three of Piaget's stages: "All purple snakes have four legs. I am hiding a purple snake. How many legs does it have?" The ten-year-old is most likely to argue with the very idea of there being a purple or four-legged snake. Such snakes are not found in the concrete world, and therefore reasoning about them (which is not just "make-believe") is problematic. Here the notion of truthfulness (or veridicality) is tied to the domain of correspondence to observed phenomena. The adolescent, however, has a whole different notion of veridicality. He or she can transcend the particular givens and see that conclusions can be drawn from the propositions themselves. But our five-year-old has still another notion of veridicality, tied essentially to its own egocentric and idiosyncratic experience. The five-year-old is usually unbothered by purple or leggy snakes, but does not see that anything follows necessarily from the statements either, and is as likely to say, "My brother has a snake."

I have been trying in this rendering of Piaget's discoveries to make two points: first, that each of his stages is plausibly the consequence of a given subject-object balance, or evolutionary truce; and second, that the process of movement is plausibly the evolutionary motion of differentiation (or emergence from embeddedness) and reintegration (relation to, rather than embeddedness in, the world). That is, the rebalancing that "moves" the action-sensing of the infant from subject to object leads to the first equilibrium (the preoperational), an equilibrium that makes one's meaning-making *subject to* the perceptions which coordinate action-sensing; the rebalancing that "moves" the perceptions from subject to object leads to the next major equilibrium (the concrete), an equilibrium that makes one's meaning-making *subject to* reversibilities which coordinate the perceptions; and the rebalancing that "moves" the reversibilities (or "the concrete") from subject to object leads to the next major equilibrium (the formal), an equilibrium that makes one's meaning-making *subject to* the hypothetico-deductive (or "the possible"), which coordinates the reversibilities (or "the concrete"). Table 2—a risky procedure, because it cannot capture the qualities of *process* and *unity*, which are essential to a concept of meaning-evolution—schematizes the character of these developments in our balance-striking.

Before leaving Piaget's specific area of exploration, it might be well to suggest that, even in this narrow domain of meaning-making (the physical world), the themes of natural emergency and the experience of evolution (to which the heart of this book is devoted) can be made to emerge. Consider the situation of a given evolutionary truce com-

TABLE 2. Subject-object balancing in Piaget's stages of cognitive development

Stage	Subject ("structure")	Object ("content")
Sensorimotor	Action-sensations reflexes	None
Preoperational	Perceptions	Action-sensations reflexes
Concrete operational	"Reversibilities" (the "actual")	Perceptions
Formal operational	"Hypothetico-deduction" (the "possible")	Reversibilities (the "actual")

ing up against experience it can neither assimilate to the present balance nor ignore. A feature of preoperational embeddedness, for example, is its inability to distinguish between a group and its parts. Its inability to hold two dimensions simultaneously leaves it unable to compare one group with another which is a part of the first. For example, a child in the preoperational balance can compare nickels and pennies, but not nickels and coins. He or she cannot "class include." Jonas Langer (1969) showed children a group of same-shaped wooden beads, of which most were black, a few white. Children in the preoperational balance answer correctly when asked whether there are more black beads or white beads. But what happens when the question is, "Are there more black beads or more wooden beads?"? The preoperational child usually answers that there are more black beads, on the grounds that "there are more black beads than white beads," a demonstration of the Procrustean dimension of constructs at work. How might the preoperational child come to see the logical impossibility of his or her solution? Langer asked children to put all the black beads on one side of the table, and all the wooden beads on the other. Children who we might say were firmly in balance (either the preoperational or the concrete) handled this problem with little difficulty. The preoperationals simply divided the black and white beads — mission accomplished. They reconstructed the task in terms of their own evolutionary position and solved it. The concrete children announced that the request was ridiculous or made some unfavorable remark about the intelligence of the pestering adult.

But what of children, say of five or six or seven, who happen to be ripe for evolution? Convinced by their insufficiently differentiated notion of comparison that the groups should be separable, yet able to recognize the difficulty in doing so, these children were in an awful spot, a confusion no less profound than the inability to make the physical world cohere. Shifting the beads madly, they may move them endlessly back and forth, in a vacillation we will come to recognize as typical of transition; they may become a little upset; they may appeal to the experimenter. Clearly the nature of their "crisis" is structural; the crisis is *not* the seemingly unresolvable problem, but the way this particular problem is precisely suited to informing the preoperational balance that *something is fundamentally wrong* about the way one is being in the world. Any real resolution of the crisis must ultimately involve a new way of being in the world. Yet the resistance to doing so is great, and will not occur in the absence of repeated and varied encounters in natural experience. Assimilation is defense, but defense is also integrity (even in the literal, biological, sense), that which makes a system a system. Children may be ingenious in their efforts to settle the problem without suffering the loss of their evolutionary position. Some children have, for instance, lined up all the beads in a row, with the whites on one side and the woodens "on the other." (This picture of defense as the effort to resolve without reorganizing is one which will reappear in fuller color and refinement later in this book.)

Eventually, preoperational children do evolve, constructing, as a result, a new organization of the physical world. And when they do, it is not because they have listened more carefully to tutoring grownups, or had it unfold within them like their developing physiologies, so much as it is because of their own activity in the world, evolutionary activity—an activity biologists speak of as the move toward the greater coherence of one's organization. Robert White (1959) referred to it as "competence" and I call it the evolution of meaning.

For over fifty years, in volume after volume, Jean Piaget published the results of his studies. I often wonder which is the greater impediment to our understanding him: the opaque, involuted, Latinate quality of his writing; or the absolute clarity of the fact that he was fascinated by and respectful of the minds of children. In any case, Piaget is taken to be about intellectual development, stages, and children, none of which, in my view, was central to his concern.

Twenty years ago Piaget was seen as a charming fellow who sat on the shores of Swiss lakes talking with children about the wind. Today his program of work is taken as the very guide to universally regular features in intellectual development from birth to adolescence. Yet twenty years from now — long after the current passion for descriptive stages in the life course has spent itself — Piaget may "be about" stages or cognitive development only in the way that Newton "is about" gravity, or Columbus the West Indies, or Jefferson reconciling the claims of the individual with claims of the state, or Joyce a literary approach to consciousness. These were the "problems" that consumed these men and they resolved them brilliantly — but so brilliantly that the resolutions become Trojan horses lying in wait to reveal what they were really about (Perry, 1970). Coaxed out of the fortress of our established habits of mind by the interesting figure on home territory, we look into the matter, only to have the contents explode upon us, an army spreading all around and capturing the fortress as figure upon it. What was but a dazzling construction on familiar ground becomes now the new ground itself as a new scientific, geographic, civil, or aesthetic grammar is articulated. Columbus' voyage changed the shape of the world. He may have discovered America, but in doing so, he caused every other part of the world to be rediscovered as well. His discovery, initially of just another "part," was of that extraordinary sort that "re-cognizes" the relationships of the parts to the whole.

In this chapter we have been exploring Piaget's "part" ("cognition," "stages") in the context of the bigger discovery it leads to — *the process of evolution as a meaning-constitutive activity*. My own research, clinical work, and theorizing amounts to an organized way of wondering whether Piaget's part does not compose a Trojan horse with an army inside as daring as psychoanalysis. Might that army, were it to be released, claim as broad a field for its attentions (the whole person in development — dynamically, cognitively, behaviorally)? Might it be possessed of its own transdisciplinary complexity; its own potential for understanding and helping persons in pain; its own promise of generating a rich fund of those most basic metaphors and images by which we come to experience our experience?

No framework can hope to supply a theory of the developing person without some profound acknowledgment of our biological reality. Psychoanalysis provided one, and no framework since has offered an alternative vision with anything like comparable scope or plausibility.

A profound acknowledgment of our biological reality addresses how we are animated, but it is much more than a theory of motivation. At bottom it is a conception of the life force itself and how we figure in it. Whether from psychoanalysis, genetic biology, or the more recent "sociobiology," the prevailing image of our biological reality is, and has been, essentially deterministic and body-based. The theater of activity is located within each separate, biologically autonomous system (the individual), which carries within itself an inherited code that unfolds (and causes the individual to develop) along a largely predetermined path or sequence. This locating of the individual or the separate body as the fundamental source of life's movement contrasts with the behaviorist notion that tends to place the source of the "action" in the environment to which the person responds. If Piaget is better known than he is understood, it is partly because his vision is neither a nativist, maturational one nor an environmental one, though these two options have come to seem exhaustive of the possibilities. Indeed, Piaget often said that it is difficult to have a third alternative even seen, since the tendency is for those who think maturationally to take his vision as maturationalist, and those who think environmentally to take his vision as environmentalist.

In fact, Piaget's vision derives from a model of open-systems evolutionary biology. Rather than locating the life force in the closed individual or the environmental press, it locates a prior context which continually elaborates the distinction between the individual and the environment in the first place. This is a conception whose meaning and implications we will grow into gradually; it is admittedly complicated and unlike the way we are accustomed to thinking. But perhaps we can begin by saying that it does not place an energy system within us so much as it places us in a single energy system of all living things. Its primary attention, then, is not to shifts and changes in an internal equilibrium, but to an equilibrium in the world, between the progressively individuated self and the bigger life field, an interaction sculpted by both and constitutive of reality itself. •

Central to Piaget's framework—and often ignored even by those who count themselves as Piagetian—is this activity, equilibration. Whether in the study of the mollusk or the human child, Piaget's principal loyalty was to the ongoing conversation between the individuating organism and the world, a process of adaptation shaped by the tension between the assimilation of new experience to the old "grammar" and the accommodation of the old grammar to new experience. This eternal conversation is panorganic; it is central to the nature of all living things. Piaget's work has demonstrated—and the work of many modern biologists in other areas confirms—that this conversation is not one of continuous augmentation, but is marked by periods of dynamic stability or balance followed by periods of instability and qualitatively new balance. These periods of dynamic balance amount to a kind of evolutionary truce: further assimilation and accommodation will go on in the context of the established relationship struck between the organism and the world. The guiding principle of such a truce—the point that is always at issue and is renegotiated in the transition to each new balance—is what, from the point of view of the organism, is composed as "object" and what as "subject." The question always is: To what extent does the organism differentiate itself from (and so relate itself to) the world?

Seen only "biologically," this process may seem to be pretty cold stuff— differentiation and reintegration, assimilation and accommodation. It is the business of protozoa, coleus plants, and elephants as well as of human beings. And yet, as this book proceeds, I think we will be drawn to a radical consideration: that this evolutionary motion is the prior (or grounding) phenomenon in personality; that this process or activity, this adaptive conversation, is the very source of, and the unifying context for, thought and feeling; that this motion is observable, researchable, intersubjectively ascertainable; that its understanding is crucial to our being of help to people in pain; and that unlike other candidates for a grounding phenomenon, this one cannot be considered arbitrary or bound over to the partialities of sex, class, culture, or historical period. It is an activity we have always shared and always will share. Seen "psychologically," this process is about the development of "knowing" (each evolutionary truce, striking a subject-object balance, becomes a way of knowing the world); but at the same time, we *experience* this activity. The experience, as we will see, may well be the source of our emotions themselves. Loss and recovery, separation and attachment, anxiety and play, depression and transformation, disintegration and coherence—all may owe their origins to the felt experience of this activity, this motion to which the word "emotion" refers. I use the word "meaning" to refer to this simultaneously epistemological and ontological activity; it is about knowing *and* being, about theory-making *and* investments and commitments of the self (Fingarette's seminal ambiguity resolved).

While this evolutionary process may be described in purely biological terms, it is as true that the same ongoing tension between self-preservation and self-transformation is descriptive of the very activity of hope itself, which Holmes (1974) calls "a dialectic of limit and possibility." Were we "all limit" (all "assimilation"), there would be no hope; "all possibility" (all "accommodation"), no need of it. That "energy field" which to the evolutionary biologist may be about "adaptation," is as much as anything about the very exercises of hope. Might we better understand others in their predicament if we could somehow know how their way of living reflects the state of their hoping at this depth? — not the hopes they have or the hoping they do, but the hopes and hoping they are?

T W O

The Evolution of Moral Meaning-Making

When I first graduated from college I taught literature to a group of seventh-grade boys. Much of the year I had a terrible time. This was the 1960s and I had arrived with some basic convictions along the lines of "universal brotherhood," "good will toward men," and "don't go fighting a land war in Southeast Asia." I discouraged competition in my class. I was forever assigning group projects, cooperative tasks, teamwork situations; but nothing really took. They would do these things if I provided all the structure, but the class did not, of its own, become a going concern. It always seemed to me that I was the one who had to put its spirit into motion each time, and guide that spirit to a conclusion.

As Bill Perry says, if you hit a donkey over the head with a two-by-four you can usually get its attention. One day the students finally got me to attend to who they were, and it led me to thinking about why the class was the way it was. I had assigned them a story much anthologized at the time, "The New Kid" by Murray Heyert. The city block and the nearby playing field form the universe of the story, which opens with the choosing of sides for baseball. This ritual is a humiliating one for Marty; he is always chosen last and relegated to the outfield. Here he prays fervently that no ball will leave the infield, much less come his way. But, as it happens, at the crucial moment the ball soars toward Marty who, sprouting extra arms, fails the chance and costs his side the game. As he trudges in from the field his teammates heap abuse upon him. We get the impression that this is not only an awful experience for Marty, but a rather common one. He isn't Willy Mays. Then one day a new kid appears on the block. He's little. His clothes are too nice. His socks match. There are buckles on his shoes. All bad signs. In other words, he may be more of a wimp than Marty. He is invited to the ballfield and sides are chosen. For the first time Marty is not the least favored. The new kid is put in the outfield. He belongs to the same religion as Marty and prays that nothing will be hit to him, but as luck (or artistic license) would have it, the new kid must handle the crucial, last-inning blow. He fails spectacularly—not merely at catching it, but at running after it, grasping it, and throwing it. He returns from the field with his chin on his knees, and who should begin—who should lead, who should sustain—the round of humiliating invective, but Marty himself!

Now I asked my twelve-year-old students the moral of this story (though I doubt I used this word), and their answers ran something like this:

> The story is saying that people may be mean to you and push you down and make you feel crummy and stuff, but it's saying things aren't really all that bad because eventually you'll get your chance to push someone else down and then you'll be on top.

I found myself quite amazed with my students' understanding of "The New Kid." I think Murray Heyert might have been surprised by it, too. It was not only that they all seemed to agree that that was what the story was about, but that it seemed no one could even *invent*—even if they didn't believe it—what I took to be the obvious moral of the story. At first I thought they were teasing me, boasting perhaps, acting "hard." "Do you really think it was okay the way Marty acted?"

> It was more than okay; it was the right thing to do.
> It was the only thing to do.
> Look, we were sixth graders last year, right?—the oldest in the school. We pushed the little kids around. Now we're the little kids and we're getting pushed around. Wait till we're seniors! Fair is fair!

It seems clear that what we are looking at here is not so much what kids know but how they know. It began to occur to me that if how they were making sense of this story was so different from how I was making sense of it, perhaps we were not all living in exactly the same classroom.

From the point of view of the matters at hand, it is also worth noting that however harsh their interpretation might sound (or, for that matter, actually *be*), theirs was a staunchly and explicitly moral formulation. It was not an amoral position they adopted, or an immoral one. They spoke their point of view with a righteous sense that indeed we were touching here on solemn matters of right and wrong, and, as any moralist might, they were championing the right as they saw it. In fact, much as in my consideration of the boy whose dessert could be doubled by cutting it in half, I will resist the temptation to talk first about the limits of this way of making meaning. For once again, it is as true to say that my students' words signal an accomplishment when they are heard in the context of a history of meaning-making already long under way.

The students' analyses of the story have an undeniable ring of reciprocity to them, even if they strike us as an odd, or logically circular, sort of reciprocity. It is a kind of reciprocity that seems to let slip away just the different pieces that need to be held together—for example, that Marty, better than anyone, should know how the new kid felt. This refusal to let yourself be the context in which the two sides are joined is reminiscent of a famous Groucho Marx exchange: "What if everyone felt the way you did?" "Well then," says Groucho, "I'd be a fool to feel otherwise!" What is funny or exasperating in Groucho's ability to purposely slip out of a kind of meaning he is capable of making is actually quite close to a structure of meaning an elementary school child has no choices about. He or she is embedded in it, as Jules Feiffer captures in one of his cartoons (Figure 3).

As I say, there is an undeniable reciprocity here, an ability to put two things together—what he did and what I should do as a consequence—even though it does seem a rather imprisoning circle. I point out this reciprocity because, odd as it is, it gives me one way into speaking of the triumph of this way of thinking (as well, obviously, as of its limits). Another way of thinking about both its sophistication and its immaturity is to consider the ability of the student to think about how another person feels. The students revealed an understanding of how Marty felt (he felt awful when picked on; he was happy and relieved to have someone else to pick on) and of how the new kid felt (he felt awful when picked on, too; but he'd have his chance). Of

Figure 3 By permission of Jules Feiffer, Dist. Publisher-Hall Syndicate

course, they could not consider simultaneously the way each felt, orienting each to the other. But even the ability for simple reciprocity, or the ability to "take the role" of a single other person (Mead, 1934; Selman, 1980) is the result of long years of meaning.

Lawrence Kohlberg's study of the development of moral reasoning has represented the single most significant extension of the Piagetian framework. His twenty years of careful research and conceptual work have demonstrated the power of the framework to address the development of the personal construction of the *social* world, and to take account of development in meaning-making beyond adolescence into adulthood. I want to offer a reading of Kohlberg's stages (see Table 3) that is analogous to the one I have just offered of Piaget. That is, in part I am interested in looking at the theory as an account of universally regular evolutions of meaning with respect to a given domain of personality (one's sense of right and wrong, the moral, fairness). But I also want to show how these part-meanings are plausibly the consequence of the same basic motion which I have suggested underlies Piaget's stages, and which, in future chapters, I will suggest is the fundamental motion in personality itself.

It should not be hard to see that the young child's perception-bound psychologic will account for more of his meaning-making than merely the construction of the physical world. *Social* objects (that is, people) will be known in the same egocentric way. The child who thinks there can be more popcorn in a box just by shaking it also happens to have one brother. If we asked him if he has a brother he would say yes. If we asked him if his brother has a brother he would say no. He is unable to get outside of himself, to look at things from his brother's point of view and see that, indeed, his brother does have a brother, and it is he. The meaning-constructive activity which we colloquially refer to as "getting outside of oneself" is analogous to what I have meant by "moving from subject to object," or "disembedding" or "differentiating."

Kohlberg's first stage, I am suggesting, is a consequence of that first evolutionary truce in which the perceptions (social *or* physical) are "on the side of" the subject. Piaget's preoperational children give strange answers to conservation tasks because they cannot take the role of their perceptions while still being themselves, someone other than their perceptions. The first Kohlberg stage is the social correlate, the inability to distinguish between the other and my perception of the other, the inability to get behind my perceptions and see the other as himself having to do with his properties.

Piaget told preoperational and concrete operational children a story (1948): One little boy was told by his mother not to touch some fragile cups, but he purposely picked one up and smashed it to bits on the floor. Another little boy was not told anything about not touching the cups: to help his mother, he tried to carry a tray of twelve cups to where she needed them. He accidentally dropped all of them onto the floor, and they were smashed to bits. "Are these children equally at fault (la même chose vilain)?" Piaget asked. If not, "Which of the two children is the naughtier, and why?" Some children think the first child is naughtier, and some think the second, but not at all randomly. The children who do not see that there is the same amount of liquid in the beakers, or who in other ways appear preoperational, tend to feel that the child who broke the twelve cups is the naughtier; the concrete kids think the first boy is naughtier. The perception-bound children (stage 1) are orienting to the results because they are embedded in the social surface; the children who have renegotiated this truce, I am suggesting, can pierce this surface, can move beyond result to intention. Just as their disembeddedness permits them to see that the liquid has properties of its own and that they are not determiners of its properties, so they can see that they are not the determiners of another's properties. The other is allowed a measure of self-creation which in the earlier balance is not permitted. It is not until a child moves to the new balance that she stops seeing her parents as "mean" whenever their behaviors deprive her, whether or not the parents intend to be depriving.

It is this evolutionary renegotiation (in which we differentiate ourselves from the "perception" as the psychologic which defines us) that brings into being the kind of simple reciprocity we saw in my students' interpretation of the story about the new kid. Simple *reciprocity* is analogous to the concrete operational *reversability*. The ability to take the role of another person, to see that their behaviors are the consequence of something which generates their behaviors, a "something" distinct from my perception, is analogous to the concrete operational ability to transcend the shadows of Plato's cave to see that there is a something which projects those shadows, to get behind the perceptual surface. We could even compare the kinds of reciprocity evident in the social interpretations we've seen with the kinds of reversability Piaget speaks of (see Table 4). Piaget talked of the ability to

TABLE 3. Kohlberg's moral stages

Level and stage	What is right	Reasons for doing right	Social perspective of stage
		LEVEL I–PRECONVENTIONAL	
Stage 1–Heteronomous Morality	To avoid breaking rules backed by punishment, obedience for its own sake, and avoiding physical damage to persons and property.	Avoidance of punishment, and the superior power of authorities.	*Egocentric point of view.* Doesn't consider the interests of others or recognize that they differ from the actor's; doesn't relate two points of view. Actions are considered physically rather than in terms of psychological interests of others. Confusion of authority's perspective with one's own.
Stage 2–Individualism, Instrumental Purpose, and Exchange	Following rules only when it is to someone's immediate interest; acting to meet one's own interests and needs and letting others do the same. Right is also what's fair, what's an equal exchange, a deal, an agreement.	To serve one's own needs or interests in a world where you have to recognize that other people have their interests, too.	*Concrete individualistic perspective.* Aware that everybody has his own interest to pursue and these conflict, so that right is relative (in the concrete individualistic sense).
		LEVEL II–CONVENTIONAL	
Stage 3–Mutual Interpersonal Expectations, Relationships, and Interpersonal Conformity	Living up to what is expected by people close to you or what people generally expect of people in your role as son, brother, friend, etc. "Being good" is important and means having good motives, showing concern about others. It also means keeping mutual relationships, such as trust, loyalty, respect and gratitude.	The need to be a good person in your own eyes and those of others. Your caring for others. Belief in the Golden Rule. Desire to maintain rules and authority which support stereotypical good behavior.	*Perspective of the individual in relationships with other individuals.* Aware of shared feelings, agreements, and expectations which take primacy over individual interests. Relates points of view through the concrete Golden Rule, putting yourself in the other guy's shoes. Does not yet consider generalized system perspective.

Stage	What Is Right	Reasons for Doing Right	Social Perspective of Stage
Stage 4—Social System and Conscience	Fulfilling the actual duties to which you have agreed. Laws are to be upheld except in extreme cases where they conflict with other fixed social duties. Right is also contributing to society, the group, or institution.	To keep the institution going as a whole, to avoid the breakdown in the system "if everyone did it," or the imperative of conscience to meet one's defined obligations.	*Differentiates societal point of view from interpersonal agreement or motives.* Takes the point of view of the system that defines roles and rules. Considers individual relations in terms of place in the system.

LEVEL III—POSTCONVENTIONAL, or PRINCIPLED

Stage	What Is Right	Reasons for Doing Right	Social Perspective of Stage
Stage 5—Social Contract or Utility and Individual Rights	Being aware that people hold a variety of values and opinions, that most values and rules are relative to your group. These relative rules should usually be upheld, however, in the interest of impartiality and because they are the social contract. Some nonrelative values and rights like *life* and *liberty*, however, must be upheld in any society and regardless of majority opinion.	A sense of obligation to law because of one's social contract to make and abide by laws for the welfare of all and for the protection of all people's rights. A feeling of contractual commitment, freely entered upon, to family, friendship, trust, and work obligations. Concern that laws and duties be based on rational calculation of overall utility, "the greatest good for the greatest number."	*Prior-to-society perspective.* Perspective of a rational individual aware of values and rights prior to social attachments and contracts. Integrates perspectives by formal mechanisms of agreement, contract, objective impartiality, and due process. Considers moral and legal points of view; recognizes that they sometimes conflict and finds it difficult to integrate them.
Stage 6—Universal Ethical Principles	Following self-chosen ethical principles. Particular laws or social agreements are usually valid because they rest on such principles. When laws violate these principles, one acts in accordance with the principle. Principles are universal principles of justice: the equality of human rights and respect for the dignity of human beings as individual persons.	The belief as a rational person in the validity of universal moral principles, and a sense of personal commitment to them.	*Perspective of a moral point of view* from which social arrangements derive. Perspective is that of any rational individual recognizing the nature of morality or the fact that persons are ends in themselves and must be treated as such.

Source: Lickona, 1976.

TABLE 4. Common meaning-evolution in the physical and sociomoral domains

Physical meaning-making (Piaget)		Sociomoral meaning-making (Kohlberg, Selman)	
The reversibilities		The social reversibilities	
	Two points in time (classes)		
CONCRETE OPERATIONS	Inverse	Role-taking	INSTRU-MENTALISM (STAGE 2)
	Two points in space (relations)		
	Reciprocal	Simple reciprocity ("tit-for-tat")	
The integration of the reversibilities		The integration of the social reversibilities	
EARLY FORMAL OPERATIONS	Inverse of the reciprocal	Reciprocal role-taking	INTERPERSONAL CONCORDANCE (STAGE 3)

hold two points in time (inverse) and two points in space (reciprocal). We can consider the capacity to coordinate two social perceptions in social time and social space. For example, the capacity to take the role of another is related to the ability to create the notion of a continuing social other which retains its properties from one social perception to the next. This is like Piaget's inverse and brings into being the social equivalent of the class or group, which in simpler terms is the social "self," a social object conserved through time. Similarly, the kind of tit-for-tat reciprocity is analogous to the compensating form of reversibility Piaget called the reciprocal; a kind of social "space" is conserved by the way retribution evens out the initial assault.

We can also see that the limits of concrete operations and Kohlberg's stage 2 are equally parallel, by virtue of their embeddedness in the reversibilities. The consequence of this underlying evolutionary truce in Piaget's domain is that there is no way to integrate the reversibility of inversion with that of negation. Its consequences in Kohlberg's domain are that there is no way to integrate the reciprocity of social space with that of social time. And similarly, just as the renegotiation of this truce makes the Piagetian reversibilities the object of a new psychologic integrative of the reversibilities ("the inverse of the reciprocal"), so this same underlying renegotiation brings into being the integration of role-taking and simple reciprocity ("reciprocal role-taking"). This new psychologic allows one to take the point of view of Marty and the new kid simultaneously and in relation to each other, and it is just this extraordinary renegotiation of the terms of our evolutionary contract which makes the meaning we call mutuality or interpersonalism.

My seventh-grade English class was not so monolithic in its response as I have portrayed. There were a very few kids who had a different idea about what the story might mean. One of these, Richie, was a particularly fortunate young fellow; he was bright and a good athlete and not afraid to stand alone. He listened to the answers of his classmates and finally managed a dissenting view. It was hard for him to put into words exactly, but he felt that somehow Marty should be able to think about how he felt when he was picked on and therefore not pick on the new kid. This intrigued and irritated the other students in the class; and, of course, it is just this sort of recruited at-tention—often eliciting intrigue and curiosity—which facilitates the evolution of meaning. Young Richie, his heart the same distance from the earth as his classmates', was a far more effective "moral educator" than I, because his meaning-making was so much closer to, had so recently been identical to, that of the other kids in the room.

What was happening to Richie's meaning-evolution? Was he simply less sadistic than the others? Do some children interpret the story one way because they are more hostile or more conflicted about aggression than others? Or is it more a matter of having a whole different meaning, a different psychologic, which makes the story really two quite different stories? Maybe this forced choice is unfair, but what can be argued forcefully, I think, is that until one can "reciprocally role-take," until one can orient one perspective to an-other, there is no possibility that one is going to be able to make sense of the story as we imagine the author intended.

Reciprocal role-taking is what is required to understand something like the Golden Rule. Selman's outstanding program of work on social reasoning and role-taking (1976a, 1976b, 1980) includes asking chil-dren about the Golden Rule—what it is, how it works, whether it's a good rule, and why. He found that concrete operational kids could recite the Golden Rule perfectly, but when he asked them what it says you should do if someone comes up and hits you, they tended to answer, "Hit 'em back. Do unto others like they do unto you." (This is identical, at its own developmental level, and in its own domain, to preoperational children knowing their left from their right, but giving a strange answer when you stand in front of them and ask which is *your* left.)

One of Selman's subjects captures nicely the enormous effort that goes into understanding the complexity of the Golden Rule when one is only freshly differentiated from the boundedness to the concrete and is still struggling with the new integration this makes possible:

> Well, the Golden Rule is the best rule because like if you were rich you might dream like that you were poor and how it felt, and then the dream would go back in your own head and you would remember and you would help make the laws that way.

Another boy about the same age, from Fowler's research on faith development (1976), gives us a view of this evolutionary renegotiation just a little further along:

> [after saying that what is bad is what causes people pain] (Why is causing them pain bad?) Well, that's what I've been taught. Um—some other people have been taught a bit different—that what's bad is to do anything unfair. You know, it's fair to draw all over their things because, they'd drawn all over yours. That's good, that's good to do. But I think no matter what they've done to you, it really doesn't matter. The point is that it gets done, so what?

As a child making the same discovery said to Piaget (1948), forgiveness is preferable to revenge, not because of some Sunday School sermonizing, but because "there's no end to revenge." Perhaps, as the boy says, it is a matter of his having been taught one way and the other another, but the research offers a compelling degree of evidence to suggest that this is not a matter of cultural teaching, but rather of individual meaning-making. If children develop and change their notion of what is fair, it is always in the direction from this instrumentality (stage 2) to interpersonal concordance (stage 3), never the reverse; children who reason at stage 2 will prefer a stage 3 solution to a given conflict if they can be made to understand it, but children at stage 3 already understand the stage 2 solution and never prefer it (Rest, 1973). That is, it is a matter, literally, of their "knowing better" and not of their having been taught a "bit different." This knowing better Sullivanians will recognize as the essence of Sullivan's described shift from "cooperation" (involvement with the other to enhance the self) to "collaboration" (involvement with the other which considers the other's enhancement), which permits the possibility of chumship and the capacity for what Sullivan calls intimacy (1953).

If "reciprocal role-taking" is an evolutionary triumph over the subjectivity of the earlier truce, it is as true to say that it is in its own way overly subjective, a function of its overembeddedness in the interpersonal. It is a way of making meaning lodged in the structures and benefits of the interpersonal context, unable to appeal the demands of that context to any higher, or mediating authority—for this *is* the highest authority. There is no one who runs the interpersonal; rather than "having" the interpersonal, one *is* the interpersonal. A person's social meaning-making at this point in the evolutionary history is highly vulnerable to the influence of the social environment. A white teenager living in a liberal northern suburb may espouse values of racial egalitarianism if that is the prevailing peer ethic, only to become a holder of racist views among racist friends if her family relocates to a school and neighborhood in the South or closer to the action in the North. The prevailing wisdom here will be that the teenager has changed as a result of new friends and new influences; it would be as true to say, however, that the teenager's way of making meaning has remained the same.

Central to the limits of interpersonal embeddedness in the domain of sociomoral meaning-making is the inability to construct a social order regulative of the interpersonal. The social order at this point gets conceived, as Kohlberg says, as "primarily composed of dyadic relations of mutual role-taking, mutual affection, gratitude and concern for one another's approval" (1971, p. 198).

In an experiment on the relationship of moral judgment to moral action (Krebs and Rosenwald, 1977), subjects were paid in advance for "two psychological tests lasting two hours." The first hour was a standard Kohlberg moral judgment interview, after which a confederate entered the room to announce that, due to scheduling errors, the room would have to be vacated for other parties. The experimenter, having paid the subject and never having recorded a name or address, informed him or her that the second test was a paper-and-pencil type of test and that he could go home, fill it out on his own, and return it. This second test was, of course, of no interest to the experimenters other than as a task which the subjects, whose moral meaning-making had been assessed in the interview, either would or would not accomplish. What the experimenters found was that people who from the interview appeared to be at stages 2 or 3 did not return the tests, while those at 4 or 5 did.

Why, if stages 3 and 4 are both "conventional," should persons at this level act differently? Well, we don't know; but I have one plausible interpretation. The subjects at Kohlberg's stage 2 fail to return the tests because they can do so and get away with it. For persons who construct the world at Kohlberg's stage 3 (orienting to dyadic interpersonal relationships), commitments flow out of relationships. Although concern for friends or loyalty to parents has some temporal dimension — that is, the concern and loyalty may persist in the absence of the friend or the parent — the commitment has its origin in the physical presence of the other, is bound to shared space. Only when one transcends an embeddedness in the interpersonal and takes it as object, can one's psychologic integrate dyadic relations into a construction of the social group and its rules. The place-bound stage 3 subject, who genuinely commits himself to fulfilling his obligation to the experimenter, is likely to be waylaid by more deeply obligated (interpersonal) commitments when he moves into other spaces and places. The time-bound stage 4 subject, whose commitment is less to the experimenter than it is to a place-independent norm of keeping one's word, is more likely to return the test.

We can get a picture of the kind of situation which is likely to spur the evolution of meaning in the sociomoral domain, and at the same time consider the limits of the interpersonalist truce, through the story of a superbly illustrative, although uncommonly public, event. The subject is a former five-term New York state assemblyman. Year after year legislation for abortion reform came before the assembly, and year after year he voted against it. When his children came of age they developed pro-abortion positions, confronted him on this, and discovered, with what must have been the most mixed of emotions, that he was personally in favor of the reform legislation. But he continued to vote the other way. Why? Because of a sense of obligation to represent the majority opinion of his constituency?

And I tried to explain to them [his children] the practicalities of my—my dilemma. That I was representing a district. Not a district so much, I think the district wanted the bill. It was my county committee that was very upset about this thing.

But what is one to do when members of other important interpersonal relationships—one's own children—make a competing claim?

Mr. Speaker, one of my sons has called me a whore for the vote that I cast against this. Just before I left for Albany this week, my son, who, as you recall, Mr. Speaker, gave the invocation to this Assembly on February fourth, said, "Dad, for God's sake, don't let your vote be the vote that defeats this bill."

How powerfully the son, a rabbi, invoked the Assembly history does not record, but his invocation to his father was certainly efficacious. The image of the whore runs throughout the subject's interview until it reaches its terrible conclusion—that a man can be as easily a whore for the coin of his children's approval as for that of his political cronies'. No resolution could come of merely choosing between the two kinds of whoredom. Again, the crisis *is* a crisis because it directs the man precisely to the limits of his way of knowing the world; if personal expectation is the source of right-making, this ethical construction will fail him where important expectations are conflicting.

In the ingenious ways we devise to resolve such crises without surrendering the construct, the subject became responsive to the other party's offers to buy his legislative seat with a cushy appointment.

I was selling out, and yet, by the same token, so was everybody else doing the same thing there, and I felt that if this was an opportunity I should seize it. And the men whom I had the closest relationships with said I'd be foolish not to take it.

When the time came for the actual vote the bill's leaders felt it was going to come down to a dead tie. Earlier they had thought they had a majority of three, but when they took their last tally they thought there would be three defections. Thus, they approached the subject of our story, knowing his true feelings on the matter. They told him they were aware of the "secret" about his new appointment, and urged him, now that he no longer needed the support of his county committee, to vote as he actually believed. Now this reasoning could not attract him, for his "bond" to the committee seemed not to be based on an exchange of favors (stage 2), but on mutual expectation and obligation ("What would they think of me?"). On the other hand, the adequacy of such right-making was itself under assault by the inability to resolve the competing claim of his children ("What will *they* think of me?"). Still, he was able to hold off the discrepancy a while longer, and temporarily resolved this in a stage-maintaining contortion that we will see again in more private arenas: Certain in his own mind, he said, that it could not come down to a tie, he gave the bill's supporters his word that he would switch his vote if it did come to a tie. But as the roll call began and one of the suspected defectors switched his vote, our subject was summoned to the Speaker's chamber. The Speaker told him to vote as he pleased, but to decide then and not to switch his vote in the event of a tie. That would draw all the attention to him, the Speaker explained, and when it was announced later he was being appointed to a commission seat it would not look good. Thus he left the Speaker's chamber aware of the consequences of switching his vote: he could destroy himself utterly, as he would be cut off both from the commission seat and from his county committee. Accordingly, when his name was called the subject cast his vote on the abortion issue as his committee wished, confident that it would not be his vote that defeated the bill.

After the second suspected defector did indeed cast his vote against the reform, our subject began behaving in a way he can report only because so many people told him he did in fact act that way; he himself has no recollection of it. He began literally bobbing up and down in his seat. Eventually he went to the third suspected defector and strenuously and continuously implored—begged—this man not to switch his vote. With this behavior he seems to have been saying: Please don't create a situation which brings me finally and unavoidably to the limits of my capacity to *know*; don't drive me out of my mind.

But when the third vote did collapse, when life imitated art and the assembly was exactly divided, no escape from the contradiction of his world design was possible.

I think at that point I just about cracked. I didn't know what to do. I—didn't—know—what—to—do. And my options were fading fast because there wasn't too much time left, and I—the chamber was just jammed with people, and everything else; photographers, and some assemblymen who are now judges, who had come up from New York to watch this. Men that I know. And I didn't know what to do. As I finally—it—it was almost by impulse. And the next thing I remember there I was. It was like a wild dream. There I was, saying things that, uh, just off the top of my head. Things that I was sorry that I said afterwards. I remember saying, "Mr. Speaker, I once read a book called *Profiles in Courage*." I don't know why I said that. I think what I was intending to say was that up until this point I was showing far more profile than courage.

What he actually did say, or most of it, was recorded by a reporter who realized from the quiver and intensity of the man's voice that something unusual was about to happen.

Mr. Speaker, less than a week ago, I learned that I was being seriously considered by you, sir, for a very important post in state government. Mr. Speaker, so that there will be no misunderstanding I release you from any commitment which you have made to me, sir. I am also fully aware of the fact that many people in my district may not only condemn me for what I am about to do, but, in many respects, perhaps, my law firm will suffer as a result of this. But Mr. Speaker, I say to you in all candor, and I say this very feelingly to all of you: "What's the use of getting elected or reelected if you don't stand for something?" Mr. Speaker, one of my sons has called me a whore for the vote that I cast against this. Just before I left for Albany this week, my son, who, as you recall, Mr. Speaker, gave the invocation to this Assembly on February fourth, said, "Dad, for God's sake, don't let your vote be the vote that defeats this bill." I had hoped that this would never come to pass. But if I am going to have any peace in my family, ladies and gentlemen, I cannot go back to my family on the first Passover seder and tell them that I defeated this bill. I fully appreciate that this is the termination of my political career, but I cannot in good conscience, stand here and thwart the obvious majority of this house, the members of whom I dearly love and for whom I have a great deal of affection. I'll probably never come back here again to share these things with you, but, Mr. Speaker, I must have some peace in my family. I, therefore, request you, Mr. Speaker, to change my negative vote to an affirmative vote.

There was more changing here than a vote, more being passed than a bill. After this speech the man slumped in his chair, put his head in his hands, wept, and said, over and over again, "What have I done?

What have I done?" The last words of his speech indicate that he really was not sure what he had done. We heard at one moment a justification from the perspective of his family's expectations; at the next moment, from that of the rights of the group. Transition often sounds like this (Turiel, 1969, 1972). When he was interviewed a year after the episode, he was found to be in Kohlberg's stage 4. The stage 4 perspective subordinates the claims of my interpersonal affiliations to the needs of the group, a group which is known to me *as a group,* replete with its norms and rules and roles which, cutting through time, across all particular interpersonal relationships, can resolve the kind of conflict our subject encountered. Moments before his experience he had been begging a man to prevent it; now it seems to him, despite the fact that it did cut him off completely from political life, to be "the summit of my life." The Chinese depict the word for crisis with two characters: one means danger; the other, opportunity. From thinking, like T. S. Eliot in "Ash Wednesday," that he would "not turn again," from "knowing I shall not know," from finding the air so "thoroughly small and dry" that his wings were "no longer wings to fly / But merely vans to beat the air," he looks back on the moment from the "opportunity" side of crisis, the summit of his life.

With the evolution that accounts for Kohlberg's stage 4, persons begin unselfconsciously to engage a problem which has recruited the interest of political philosophers for hundreds of years: How are the claims of the individual and the claims of the state to be reconciled? The three evolutionary movements which Kohlberg has best demonstrated empirically in address to this question are his stage 4, stage 4½ (a transitional period), and stage 5. The first of these decides for the group at the expense of the individual (as we will see, this may be due to the lack of any meaning construction of "an individual" apart from the group); the second decides for the individual at the expense of the group (this may be due to a differentiation from the societal, without yet integrating it or recognizing it as "other"); the third represents an integration of the individual and the group.

While the emergence from embeddedness in the interpersonal frees one from the subjectivity of constructing one's morality on the basis of arbitrary affections and empathies, the new stage is subject to its own arbitrariness. In constructing that which subtends or coordinates the interpersonal it is likewise embedded in that construction, the social order or social group. Each new evolutionary truce guarantees the world a more distinct identity, and at Kohlberg's stage 4 social objects of the world (people) are not guaranteed their distinctness apart from their identification with the social order. Kohlberg's stage 4 is essentially the psychological birth of ideology, which is a meaning system that is above all factional (Mannheim, 1936) — that is, it is a truth for *a* group, caste, class, clan, nation, church, race, generation, gender, trade, or interest group. This ideology can be implicit and tacit, or explicit and public. It is identified, in any case, by the extent to which it makes the maintenance and protection of its own group the ultimate basis of valuing, so that "right" is defined on behalf of the group, rather than the group being defined on behalf of the right. It is identified by the way it tends to draw the lines of membership in the human community according to the particular faction it makes ultimate, creating what Erikson (1972) called the "pseudo-species." The classic picture of the limits of this construction is the law-and-order philosophy in which the right is defined *by* the law rather than seeing the law as an imperfect, organic, in-process attempt to serve the right.

Such a construction of the sociomoral has no way to separate manners from morals, custom and tradition from ethics. In its more benign or amusing forms this can translate into a moral investment in manners of dress and address. In its more lethal forms it amounts to nothing less than the inability to protect a person against arbitrary abuses and exclusions simply because he or she seems to be against the interests of the group. This is seen in the periodic opinion polls in which a majority of citizens would deny all of us the rights which, unknown to them, are actually guaranteed us in the Bill of Rights (Yankelovich, 1969). It is seen in the Kentucky police case (*Glasson* v. *Louisville,* 1975) in which "peace officers," in an effort to preserve the peace, confiscated anti-administration signs from demonstrators at a presidential rally (the demonstrators sued and the Supreme Court upheld them), raising the question of whether "peace officer" is a sufficiently guiding identity. (Perhaps "rights officers" would be more to the point.) It is seen in a former United States president telling a television interviewer that "legal is whatever the Chief Executive says is legal. If he does it, it cannot be against the law" (Frost, 1978). It is seen in the Rochester, New York, flag case, in which the citywide administrators of the school system fought passionately and successfully for several years to keep a young — and, by their own concession, excellent — teacher out of their high schools because she silently refused to say the Pledge of Allegiance each morning when she had been teaching (Lang, 1973). "He assigned an almost hallowed quality to the Pledge, comparing it to a chapel reading," Lang writes of one of the society-sacralizing administrators (p. 45). The teacher, Mrs. Russo, is most confused by the way she and others can both use a word like "community"—in reference to the same group of people—so fervently, and so contradictorily. In her most sensitive and hard-working deliberations upon her tormenters, Mrs. Russo recognizes that devotion or sincerity or commitment themselves are not what distinguish her from them. Lang writes: "Mrs. Russo fell silent a moment. When she spoke again, a look of anger crossed her face. Fairly wresting the words out, she said, 'I believe Don Loughlin loves this country as much as I do' " (p. 40). She does not need a "meaning-evolutionist" to tell her that it is the shape of their love, not the force of it, which divides them. She might be interested to know, though, as the study of meaning-evolution might instruct her, just how different those constructions are; or how difficult it is for her counterplayers to understand her; or how deeply her confrontation places her in the meaning of her own personal history. And, in her confusion at being made to feel an outlaw, she may be interested to know that she articulates the question posed at the boundary between the two world views: When is someone who recognizes society, respects it, but stands outside of it in her construction of community, not an alien? When is an outlaw not an outlaw?

We should not imagine, however, that in constructing the stage 4 balance we become cowardly conformists. We do not so much submit to a system as *create* it. That a parent in this world view might vilify his own civilly disobedient child is not a matter of failed courage, nor mere capitulation to what others will think. The parent can understand his child's action only in the parent's own terms, or in more primitive terms that the parent himself has rejected; in either case, the parent sees the action not as courageous or conscienced but as actually cowardly or destructively sentimental. The parent has his own kind of courage. He is not controlled by what others will think so much as he is the others who are thinking, a difficult job when it leads to rejecting one's own child, and a way into our understanding of the nature of that courage which is his. Societally embedded parents *are* the society, and bring the full force of it to bear on their children, a benefit to the development of their children when young, perhaps, but when applied to those who need a more articulated tension for their development, a societal parent in a stage 4 culture may resemble nothing quite so much as a species which eats its young. Anyone who has seen the film of the Milgram experiment (Milgram, 1974), in which obedient subjects administer what they believe to be near-fatal voltages of electric shock to fellow subjects, must conclude that good Germans gunning down defenseless Jews were in their own way courageous. This, after all, is the real source of contempt in the use of the word "good." The Milgram shockers are not sadists; they abhor what they "have to" do; they sweat; they sob at the controls. But life is like this. Sometimes you have to do what is most difficult to do. And that is why they are *good.* They can conceive of quitting the experiment in no way other than cowardice. They continue courageously. Passion is thus ever driven back to reason, and reason to passion.

It is this kind of absolutism, practically excluding from the human community those who fall outside the ideological or social group, which can come to an end when the evolution of meaning transcends its embeddedness in the societal. One begins to differentiate from the societal; it begins to "move" from subject to object; it is no longer ultimate. As the societal is relativized those judgments which have owed their justification to the societal come in for a critique. They are found to be arbitrary as one comes to see that, from another system, the same situation could be (and is) valued in quite a different way with equal consistency. The differentiation from the societal invents a kind of tolerance which could not have been present before. It is no longer palatable to generalize one's own values to another culture, or, for that matter, to another person. A common expression of this new construction of morality might be a statement such as this one: "People have a right to their own views, their own ideas, to live the way they think best. If it's sincere, if it's what they really think, then it's right *for them.* Who am I to say what's right for them? Who are *you?* The idea that you can say it's wrong is just a sign that you are trapped in your own cultural context. You think it's *the* truth, but it's just *a* truth. And there are a lot of other ones; ones we haven't even heard of. Anybody's telling anybody else they're right or wrong is just another version of old English anthropologists calling other cultures 'primitive' and looking at them completely out of their own framework without any awareness of the defining nature of their own framework. If there *is* a truth it's in the *person*, in each person. You can't come down on one person with some other person's truth."

Such a position, as I have suggested, has much to admire in it. Getting behind the self-constructed nature of a system of valuing, it generates a protective tolerance for difference and the beginning of a sense of individual rights. As it stands, however, it is a position in serious jeopardy because it is fraught with an internal self-contradiction. Note, for example, that laced through this plea for non-judgmentalism is a judgment against those who would make judgments. Is the speaker himself not "coming down" on other persons with his own truth? When the speaker sees the Kentucky policemen denying other people the right to peacefully express themselves, or the school board punishing the teacher for refusing to express herself the way it would like toward the American flag, he is likely to say, "The police and the school board are laying their notions of right and true on other people and they should not do that." "They should not do that"? Is *he* not then making a judgment? Certainly he does not mean, "My own arbitrary sense is that they should not do this, but if, from their point of view, it is right to control people's expressions, then I guess there is no saying it is wrong."

Indeed the tolerance won out of the differentiation from the societal is not a balanced position from which to construct the moral world (how can you be tolerant of the intolerant?) precisely because it does not represent a new evolutionary balance. It is differentiation without reintegration. It has separated from the societal, but has as yet found no way to integrate its claims into a new system. Kohlberg's stage 4 resolved the historic conflict between the individual and the group by deciding entirely for the group (failing actually to construct the individual); the position we are looking at here, Kohlberg's 4½, a transitional place, decides entirely for the individual (probably because it is unable to hold onto the construction of an individual apart from the group if it has to also *consider* the group). This position, cultural or ethical relativism, the conviction that there is no nonarbitrary basis for judging anything, amounts to confusing two ideas. It confuses the idea that all persons are entitled to hold whatever beliefs they wish with a second idea, that there is no nonarbitrary basis upon which to compare these beliefs. The second idea does not necessarily follow from the first, but, developmentally, the two are fused at this point. Another way to state the confusion might be to say that the recognition that value systems are self-constructed (that there is an unavoidable "subjectivity" to valuing) does not *have to* lead to the conclusion that there is no way to compare value systems.

The sense of the self-contradictory nature of ethical relativism can lead a person to consider whether there *is* any basis upon which to make judgments that have a validity beyond oneself and are not, at the same time, a form of the old absolutism. Development is not a matter of differentiation alone, but of differentiation *and* reintegration. Certainly Kohlberg's most exciting claim—and if he is right, his most significant contribution—is that by carefully studying the development of persons' moral meaning-making, one can be led to a solution in the two-thousand-year-old quandary of the relation between the individual and the group.

This solution, which Kohlberg calls the construction of universalizable principles, may be the consequence of an evolution which not only differentiates from the societal, but reintegrates it into a wider system of meaning which reflects on and regulates it. The result is that one comes to distinguish moral values apart from the authority of groups holding those values. These values do not make the law or the maintenance of the group ultimate, but rather orient to a process by which the laws are generated, to which they can be appealed for modification on behalf of equally protecting the dignities and opportunities of *all* parties.

Certainly a central feature of this new evolution is the creation of two hitherto nonexistent realities—rights, and what I will call interindividuality. Rights amount to protections or guarantees that obtain to a person not by virtue of idiosyncratic affection or fealty to a common group or belief but because the person is a member of the human community and is accorded the status of an individual. Although the notion of individuality as a highly evolved creation may evoke the typically Western image of over-esteem for the isolated, decontextualized, autonomous, and unattached figure, it is important to understand that what is meant here by individuality amounts as much to a recognition of, and concern for, the most fundamental connections that do exist between persons. However distinctly given persons may be known, the construction of individuality suggests a way of knowing them which is common among them. This way of knowing essentially creates a category ("individuality") in which all persons are seen as eligible to participate. It endows to this category all those powers which persons might want for themselves but would at the same time be willing for others to have; all those responsibilities which persons would want others to meet, but at the same time would be willing to meet themselves. The construction of "individuality" is thus really "interindividuality"; neither any one person nor the group as an unindividuated whole, it is a category of interpenetration.

Although Kohlberg's most evolved position is seen by some as an ode to the highly abstracted, disaffiliated "lone contemplator" who ignores human particulars on behalf of some disembodied generalizable principle (Gilligan and Murphy, 1979), I think it would be more accurate to say that what Kohlberg has found in his principled subjects is a capacity to transcend an ultimate orientation to exclusive connections on behalf of more inclusive ones. This shift, I am suggesting, is the consequence of meaning-evolution, which is not a matter of increasing differentiation alone, but of increasing relationship to the world. These "increases" are qualitative and they involve, first of all, a better recognition of what is separate from me so that I can be related to it, rather than fused with it.

I would like to give three brief examples of what seem to me to illustrate the evolution to principles or postconventionality, and I would ask about each of them whether it demonstrates increasing isolation and disaffiliation or a qualitatively more expanded form of connection.

The first example comes from an ancient text, the Hagaddah, a collection of Hebrew stories and prayers that commemorate the Jews' exodus from Egyptian captivity. Much of the Hagaddah is flagrantly ideological. The borders of humanity often get drawn where the Chosen People stop and their oppressors begin. God is urged to punish those who are not on the side of the Jews and He is often seen as the private possession of one group. But there are at least two moments of a different nature in this story. When it comes time to recount the ten plagues which were visited upon the Pharoah's people for refusing to "let my people go," it is traditional to spill a few drops of wine from one's cup at the mention of each terrible plague. And why? The gesture expresses a different sentiment. Jews are instructed, in response to a recitation of the plagues, to diminish their own lot, to reduce their own pleasure, in recognition that the suffering of *any* person, even one's enemy, is most of all a suffering shared by all; that however divided the Jews and the Egyptians might be, it is a preliminary division in the face of their truer commonality in the human community. A similar moment comes after the Egyptian soldiers are drowned by the closing of the Red Sea. The Jews are joyous, but the angels in Heaven weep. "Are not these who have drowned also God's children?"

For a more local and current example of the contrast between the conventional and postconventional positions, we can turn to the controversies around forced busing for school desegregation in Northern cities. I would not suggest that one could conclude anything about a person's moral meaning-making on the basis of whether he or she was for or against busing; as always, the issue is *how* one constructs the situation. One of the confrontations in the Boston crisis that I found most interesting was between the white, Irish judge who ordered the busing and a white, Irish school committeewoman who opposed it. The committeewoman seemed to speak at the time for a large portion of a heavily Irish neighborhood which was against the disruption forced busing would cause in its community. The judge had carefully studied the school situation and concluded both that black children in largely black schools were not being afforded an equal opportunity to quality education, and also that the school committee was unable or unwilling to rectify the situation on its own. In her testimony in one of many suits arising out of the controversy, the committeewoman made a fascinating statement—she said, "Integration is being forced upon us by a man who is Irish and doesn't want to be." The statement fails to understand the possibility of taking action against one's special interest group on behalf not of some other group, but of the bigger community of persons to which *all* special interest groups are relativized.

The last example returns us to the Mideast, where the tensions between groups continues three thousand years after the Exodus. Roberta Steinberg and I did a study some years ago on Israeli soldiers' attitudes toward their Arab enemies (Steinberg and Kegan, 1978). Steinberg gave Israeli soldiers Kohlberg moral judgment interviews and open-ended interviews about their attitudes. Most of the soldiers were conventional, and most drew the lines of the human community as firmly as their predecessors in the Hagaddah; the Arabs were simply not considered as human as the Israelis. A few of the soldiers interviewed were principled in the moral judgment interview and also took a remarkably different view toward their real-life situation. While they were fighting with no less a sense of having their backs to the sea, they maintained a sense of being only part of a bigger collective to which even the Arabs had also to be admitted, however begrudgingly. This was a matter not merely of speculation and concept, but also of actual behavior. Soldier-medics were asked about their treatment of enemy wounded. Most would take little or no measures to care for them and one even suggested it was preferable to murder them to eliminate the chance of their killing more Israelis. One man, Asher, dealt quite differently with the situation:

> In the last war and also in this war I took care of the enemy's wounded. Now if you understand from that that I took care of them in the exact same manner as I took care of Israelis—well, if you're talking about the medical part it's correct. If you're referring to the spiritual part it's incorrect. If he has to receive some kind of treatment he'll receive it, just as every Israeli and every other soldier, without any problem. But with an Israeli I always have a desire, some kind of empathy with him, some kind of will to work and do everything, in order that he'll be saved. Regarding the Arab I'll do the same actions, but I'll do it not out of love—well, out of—I don't know, not out of love for the man, but out of some kind of a duty I feel I have toward him.

I find this a moving and authentic statement. It seems to me he is speaking the very language of a differentiation *and* an integration greater than the group-bound, stage 4 morality. Of course it does not feel exactly the same, he says, treating one's enemy and treating one's own; there is a special affection for a member of one's own group, nation, or ideology. But he is also saying that, in a way which may even seem a bit strange to him, this group affection is not finally ultimate; it is never forgotten, but it is not controlling either. Somehow there is a supervening affection toward something else, toward something that looks more like the human community, the community of all persons, to which this man feels even more strongly compelled.

This may be an example, I suggest, of Kohlberg's postconventional stage at work, a consequence of a long history of evolutionary negotiations (see Table 5). It can be argued that before this man could relate himself to the world in this way, he lived, as a young child, embedded in his social perceptions (where he might have felt the boy with better intentions—but more broken cups—was the naughtier); that he

TABLE 5. Subject-object balancing in Kohlberg's stages of moral development

Stage	Subject ("structure")	Object ("content")
(1) Punishment and obedience orientation	Social perceptions	Reflexes, sensations, movements
(2) Instrumental orientation	Simple role-taking, marketplace reciprocity	Social perceptions
(3) Interpersonal concordance orientation	Mutuality, reciprocal role-taking	Simple role-taking, marketplace reciprocity
(4) Societal orientation	Societal group, institutional society	Mutuality, reciprocal role-taking
(5/6) Universal principles orientation	Community of the whole, rights, inter-individuality	Societal group, institutional society

emerged from this truce to take his perceptions as the object of simple role-taking and marketplace reciprocity (where he might have felt it was only right for Marty to give as good as he got to the new kid); that this balance became figure upon the ground of mutuality or reciprocal role-taking (where he might have felt it was right to hate Arabs since all his friends hated Arabs); that he emerged from this embeddedness, and moved from "being" the interpersonal to "having" the interpersonal, which brought into being the social group as an institution regulated by rules and laws rather than a collection of affiliations regulated by particular affections (where he might have felt the population to whom he owed his "duty" was defined by a national border); and that finally he transcended the embeddedness in the societal to take it as figure upon the ground of the universal community of persons. With each move he made a better guarantee to the world of its distinct integrity, qualitatively reducing each time a fusion of himself with the world, thereby creating a wider and wider community in which to participate, to which to be connected, for which to direct his concern. Each of these moves, each of Kohlberg's stages, like each of Piaget's, may be the consequence of a single underlying process of evolution, an evolution that is imagined to go on not within the body alone but within the life-surround, an evolution which continually reconstructs the relationship of the organism to this bigger environment, an evolution more of the mind than of the brain. Having considered the consequences of this evolution in the physical-cognitive and social-cognitive domains, we turn now to the larger domain of the self, to its constructions and its emergencies.

THREE

The Constitutions of the Self

Diane is twenty years old, attractive, and extremely depressed. She took forty-two pills, "not to die," she says, "but to show him how much he hurt me." She had lived with a man for nearly a year and now he was seeing another woman. Her hopes for "an exclusive relationship" were destroyed. She was furious with him but she was afraid that if she expressed this she would lose him completely. She had no one else with whom to share her unhappiness, because after she moved in with him she gradually stopped seeing other friends. As her anxiety and depression increased she had terrifying nightmares with recurring images of death. Minor irritations with her boyfriend brought on in her several episodes of rage, during which she pictured herself sitting on the mouth of a large plastic head resembling her own, staring at the back of the inside of the structure. She had several experiences of waking up abruptly and relating to her boyfriend "as if he were my father and I was about four years old"; then she would fall back to sleep and wake with no memory of these events. As she began to make plans to separate from her boyfriend she became extremely upset and took an overdose of drugs. This had happened to her before, she says. She finds a man, finds herself becoming increasingly dependent upon him; he eventually finds the relationship too burdening and moves to end it or reduce its intensity; she then feels, "I can't live with him and I can't live without him." On two other occasions when things got to this state she tried to kill herself. Now she has tried again. This time she has admitted herself to the psychiatric unit of a local hospital. What is happening? This is what she and I both want to know.

In the last two chapters we looked at the consequences of meaning-evolution in the circumscribed domains of physical and sociomoral construction. We were embarked not on an exhaustive study of Piaget and Kohlberg so much as on a search for the common origin of the stages they discovered. I suggested that the underlying motion of evolution, setting terms on what the organism constitutes as self and other, may both give rise to the stage-like regularities in the domains they explore and describe the process of movement from one stage to the next. I tried to indicate the great variety of phenomena such a proposal seems to take into account and for which it seems to offer a more integrative explanation. In this chapter I seek to widen even further the phenomenal domain of which the sequence and process of "psychologics" might be able to take account. I consider the meaning of each evolutionary truce for the basic organization of the psychological self—a lifespan developmental approach to object relations which describes a sequence of emotional, motivational, and psychodynamic organizations, as well as the now familiar cognitive and sociomoral ones.

The same week Diane entered the hospital, Terry arrived on the ward. Though the ward is a "voluntary" one, Terry, at fifteen, was not herself the volunteer. She was admitted by her mother after her parents decided they could no longer deal with her. The final blow had come that week when the mother called the school and had discovered that her daughter had skipped. When Terry returned home at the appropriate afterschool hour, her mother confronted her with the information; Terry then flew into a rage at what she regarded as her mother's intrusiveness and demanded that her mother give her her bankbook so she could run away. Her mother refused, so Terry took twenty dollars from her mother's purse and barricaded herself in her room. When the mother forced entry, Terry escaped through a window and led the mother, assorted allies, and eventually the police on a seven-hour chase which Terry reports in the hospital with glee. On the checklist at admission Terry's mother describes Terry as bright, egocentric, narcissistic, and manipulative. Terry characterizes her mother as stern, strong, stubborn, nagging, unwilling to compromise, and headstrong.

In the hospital, where group therapy and participation in the life of a ward community are the primary media of treatment, Terry is having a terrible time. She can be seen in group meetings struggling unsuccessfully to talk about herself in a way the staff will approve. When she says, in many different ways, "My problems are not mental; they have to do with getting along with my family," the staff, however gently and indirectly, is not satisfied with the formulation and takes it as resistance to dealing with herself, her own feelings and responsibilities. The staff can see that when she does speak the language of internal reflexivity she is doing it by triangulation or imitation, that she is not really speaking her own voice; this, too, they take as a kind of slipperiness or dishonesty. Their exasperation with her grows, and when it is discovered both that she spoke to people outside the ward about people inside the ward (a cardinal violation of patient-patient bonds) and that she used "unprescribed drugs" during a weekend pass (a violation of patient-staff bonds), the staff throws her out of the community. They understand her behavior as hostility and acting out, and they justify their own on the grounds that she "would not do the work of the ward," "was argumentative," "was disruptive," "was inciting to other patients," and "was a staff-splitter." In short, this outstanding professional staff is no more successful in being helpful (or even staying with) Terry than were her parents. But *why* are the staff and the milieu treatment so unsuccessful? This is what they and I both want to know.

Whatever else might be said about Terry and Diane, they seem to share a concern about personal boundaries. Their sense of what is "self" and what is "others" seems either to be shaky or to have become shaky. Difficulties of this sort — especially the inability to maintain the differentiation between self and other — are now widely understood to reflect on the vicissitudes of earliest life, the infant's separation and individuation from its undifferentiated state at birth (Mahler, 1975). From this point of view the phenomena of infancy become the context to which all further considerations of object relations throughout the life span are referred. Recurring issues of differentiation and integration throughout life come to be understood as the consequences, reflections, or offspring of this earliest period. The recognition of this crucial era prior even to the oedipal years has led in effect to a restatement of Freud's dictum: now it is the *infant* who is father to the man.

The constructive-developmental approach, which develops not out of the psychoanalytic tradition but out of the Piagetian one, takes a somewhat different view—both of the phenomena of infancy and of their representations in the later living of a Terry or a Diane. Its argument, in effect, is a shift of figure and ground. It suggests that rather than understanding issues of differentiation and integration in the context of infancy, the phenomena of infancy are better understood in the context of the psychological meaning of evolution, a lifetime activity of differentiating and integrating what is taken as self and what is taken as other. The consequences of doing so are not only a somewhat different conception of infancy, but the possibility of understanding—in some way which would not otherwise be available—that Terry and Diane are not eighteen months old any longer.

Everyone has heard the story of the man who was searching for something under a streetlight. "You lost it around here?" he is asked. "No, over there," he says, pointing to a dark corner some distance away. "Well why are you looking for it here?" he is asked. "Because," he says, "this is where the light is good." I admit to hoping that a constructive-developmental approach to object relations might light up some of these dark corners so that we are not forced to understand all evolutionary phenomena by default in terms of the one transformation we understand well.

What is an object? People frequently find the term "object relations" strange or distasteful. What we are most of all speaking about, they say, is other human beings, and the notion of persons as things seems unfortunate. And yet there is a meaning to the word "object" that must not be lost and that no other word conveys. We can start by looking for this in its very etymology. The root (*ject*) speaks first of all to a motion, an activity rather than a thing—more particularly, to throwing. Taken with the prefix, the word suggests the motion or consequence of "thrown from" or "thrown away from." "Object" speaks to that which some motion has made separate or distinct from, or to the motion itself. "Object relations," by this line of reasoning, might be expected to have to do with our relations to that which some motion has made separate or distinct from us, our relations to that which has been thrown from us, or the experience of this throwing itself. Now I know this preliminary definition sounds peculiar, but it has more in its favor than a Latin pedigree: it is the underlying conception of object relations to be found in neo-Piagetian theory.

Central to that theory is an understanding of motion as the prior context of personality. Simply put, this is the motion of evolution; less simply, it is evolution as a meaning-constitutive activity. As the prior context of personality (I mean, of course, philosophically prior; not temporally), it is argued to be not only the unifying, but also the generating, context for both (1) thought and feeling (about which more later), and (2) subject and object, or self and other (about which more now). Evolutionary activity involves the very creating of the object (a process of differentiation) as well as our relating to it (a process of integration). By such a conception, object relations (really, subject-object relations) are not something that go on in the "space" between a worldless person and a personless world; rather they bring into being the very distinction in the first place. Subject-object relations emerge out of a lifelong process of development: a succession of qualitative differentiations of the self from the world, with a qualitatively more extensive object with which to be in relation created each time; a natural history of qualitatively better guarantees to the world of its distinctness; successive triumphs of "relationship to" rather than "embeddedness in." By such a conception the term "object relations" is an acceptable, even welcome term (more welcome than something more human sounding), because, properly understood, the term does not relate persons to things, but creates a more general category. In the term is a recognition that any given person may differ from us not only by her distinctness from other persons, but by the differing ways in which we ourselves make sense of her, of which differences none may be so important as the extent to which we distinguish her from ourselves.

Psychoanalytic object relations theory looks to the events of the first years of life for its basic themes and categories. While early infancy has great importance from a neo-Piagetian view, it is not, in its most fundamental respect, qualitatively different from any other moment in the lifespan. What is taken as fundamental is the activity of meaning-constitutive evolution. It is true that infancy marks the beginning in the history of this activity. As such, infancy initiates themes that can be traced through the lifespan and inaugurates a disposition on the part of the person toward the activity of evolution. The first years of life do indeed have great salience. But it is not a salience *sui generis;* the distinctive features of infancy, it is suggested, are to be understood in the context of that same activity which is the person's fate throughout his or her life. The recurrence of these distinctive features in new forms later on in development are not understood as later manifestations of infancy issues, but contemporary manifestations of meaning-making, just as the issues of infancy are, in their own time, contemporary manifestations of meaning-making. What does it mean to look at the psychological phenomena of infancy in the context of meaning-making, rather than to look at meaning-making in the context of infancy?

Piagetian and psychoanalytic psychologies share a conception of the newborn's state. Both consider the newborn to live in an objectless world, a world in which everything sensed is taken to be an extension of the infant, where out of sight (or touch or taste or hearing or smell) can mean out of existence. Freud considered "mental functioning" eventually to be under the sway of "the pleasure principle" and "the reality principle," but in the newborn only under the first (1911). Piaget considers mental functioning eventually to be under the sway of "assimilation" (fitting one's experience to one's present means of organizing reality) and "accommodation" (reorganizing one's way of making meaning to take account of experience), but in the newborn only under the first (1936). Taken at a general level, the notion of "orality" is consistent with the Piagetian conception of the all-assimilative, incorporative newborn. Both perspectives see the central psychological achievement of the first eighteen months in terms of an end to this objectless world and the dawn of object relations.

From a psychoanalytic point of view the baby's binding energy is directed away from himself toward another, or some part of another. The infant's natural narcissism, or self-absorption, gradually comes to an end as he withdraws an attachment to himself in favor of a new "object choice" outside himself. The notion of object relations as an energy redirection or an object choice can be contrasted with the neo-Piagetian notion of object creation. By this understanding the dawn of an object world is the consequence of the organism's gradual "emergence from embeddedness" (Schachtel, 1959). By differentiating itself from the world and the world from it, the organism brings into being that which is independent of its own sensing and moving. As Piaget himself writes, such an understanding makes early life narcissistic only in a very special sense of the word: "One could not describe it as a focus of emotion on the activity itself, as a self contemplation of self, precisely because the self has not yet developed. Narcissism is nothing other than emotion associated with the non-differentiation between the self and the non-self (the adulatory stage of Baldwin, emotional symbiosis of Wallon). The primary narcissism of nursing is really a narcissism without Narcissus" (1964, p. 35).

From a neo-Piagetian view, the transformation in the first eighteen months of life—giving birth to object relations—is only the first instance of that basic evolutionary activity taken as the fundamental ground of personality development. The infant's "moving and sensing," as the basic structure of its personal organization (the reflexes), get "thrown from"; they become an object of attention, the "content" of a newly evolved structure. Rather than being my reflexes, I now have them, and "I" am something other. "I" am that which coordinates or mediates the reflexes, what we mean by "impulses" and "perceptions." This is the new subjectivity. For the very first time, this creates a world separate from me, the first qualitative transformation in the history of guaranteeing the world its distinct integrity, of having it to relate to, rather than to be embedded in. But this transformation does not take place over a weekend, and it does not take place without cost to the organism, which must suffer what amounts to the loss of itself in the process. The laborious gradualness and personal cost of this transformation can be considered in the context of the two best researched phenomena of this period—the construction of the permanence of the object, and the infant's protest upon separation from the primary caretaker. From a neo-Piagetian view, both phenomena are easily misunderstood.

In a film describing their scales for measuring object permanence, Uzguris and Hunt (1968) show us the same infants from the first months of their lives until after their second birthdays. The experimenter interests a child in some small object, and then, right under the child's eyes, conceals it in some way—a bead necklace is covered by a small blanket, or a ball is rolled under a chair. Before the object is covered the child of four or five months is able to involve himself with the toy, pursuing it with eyes and hands, holding it, bringing it to his mouth; but when the object is covered all involvement with it ceases. This cannot be attributed to a loss of interest in the toy, for the experimenter has only to lift the cover and the child lights up, vocalizes, reaches again for the object. It seems not that the child loses interest in the covered object, but that the covered object loses its existence for the child. Beginning somewhere around eight to ten months, children make some tentative efforts to retrieve the covered object, though if it is covered by more than one screen or displaced from one screen to another, their exploration often comes to an early halt. By the time they are two years old they usually have no problem retrieving the hidden object, despite the experimenter's multiple displacements.

These widely known experiments are not so widely understood. When I show graduate students the Uzguris and Hunt film for the first time, they usually become bored and restless halfway through. It is clear that the children are behaving "as they should," that as they get older they get "better at finding the object." The theme is set early on and the predictability of the infants' behavior makes the film tiresome. And yet I have seen students watch the film again and again once they understood what they were seeing, and I find that I do not tire of seeing it repeatedly. For the film amounts to time-lapse photography of the most difficult sort—the evolution of a relationship. The process in the film is not as simple as the unfolding of a rose or the physical growth of a single organism (a child). Rather, the film is time-lapse photography of the relationship between an organism and its environment. If one turns an eye to it, one can see the child being "hatched out" (to use Mahler's term, 1975) of a world in which he was embedded.

It is difficult, for anyone, unless forewarned, to resist the perception that the little necklace or the rubber ball is remaining the same throughout the film while only the infant is changing; that the two-year drama contains two characters—an infant and an object—whose entitivity remains the same. The film takes on a whole new life if one sees that a single dynamic organism, "baby-and-ball," is gradually undergoing a process of transformation. Over the period roughly from nine to twenty-one months, the baby-and-ball begins to be something other than a single entity, but does not quite constitute, as yet, two distinct entities. Although the hidden object is not immediately given up, its pursuit is easily defeated. One has the sense of a differentiation so fragile, so tentative, that it can very easily merge back into oneness. Even the experimenter taking the object out of the infant's hands becomes a fascinating picture of a scientist probing the integrity of a specimen in a critical period in its evolution. Having given the object to the infant to enhance his interest in it, the experimenter then routinely pulls it gently away in order to cover it. In the early months the child gives it up without protest of any kind. He does not, it seems clear, *have* it, in the sense of its being something apart from, something to be bound up with. As he gets older it seems that it is not only his physical grasp that intensifies and articulates (from gross to fine motor coordination, for example), but a psychological one as well. All in all, the film, then, is capturing a motion, the motion of "throwing from," of differentiation, which creates the object, and the motion of integration, which creates the object relation.

But what can be found can also be lost. The process of differentiation, creating the possibility of integration, brings into being the lifelong theme of finding and losing, which before now could not have existed. The universal infant reaction of protest upon separation from the primary caretaker, a great number of researchers tend to agree, first appears around ten months, peaks at twelve months, and ceases at about twenty-one months (Kagan, 1971).

From the neo-Piagetian perspective these simultaneous phenomena—the gradually developing capacity to orient to the object even when it is absent, and the definable course of protest upon separation—are the cognitive and affective dimensions of a single, more basic phenomenon, the evolutionary transition from an undifferentiated state to the first equilibrium. In arguing for evolutionary activity as the fundamental ground in personality, constructive-developmental theory is not choosing between "affect" or "cognition" as the master of development—a choice which has limited both classical Freudian and Piagetian theory—but is putting forth a candidate for a ground of consideration prior to, and generative of, cognition *and* affect. When we view this evolutionary activity with respect to any particular subject-object differentiation which is being maintained, we are considering its implications for knowing. The events of the first eighteen months culminate with the creation of the object and make evolutionary activity henceforth an activity of equilibration, of preserving or renegotiating the balance between what is taken as subject or self and what is taken as object or other. I suggest that human development involves a succession of renegotiated balances, or "biologics," which come to organize the experience of the individual in qualitatively different ways. In this sense, evolutionary activity is intrinsically cognitive, but it is no less affective; we *are* this activity and we experience it. Affect is essentially phenomenological, the felt experience of a motion (hence, "e-motion"). In identifying evolutionary activity as the fundamental ground of personality I am suggesting that the source of our emotions is the phenomenological experience of evolving—of defending, surrendering, and reconstructing a center. The universally recognized anxiety between nine and twenty-one months I understand as that distress which attends every qualitative decentration—which from the point of view of the developing organism amounts to the loss of its very organization.

"Separation anxiety," by this account, is not well understood as an anxiety about the loss of an object or another, of the caretaker or the comforts the caretaker provides. It seems more correct to imagine that, from the perspective of the infant (the only perspective that counts when we attempt to understand an infant's anxiety), the distress is not about the loss of an object—for an object does not yet wholly exist, and the time when it does wholly exist (around twenty-one months) is exactly when the anxious behavior comes to an end. Central to the experiences of qualitative change or decentration (phenomenologically, the loss of my center) are the affects of loss—anxiety and depression. Infant distress understood as the felt experience of an evolutionary transformation—an emergence from embeddedness—seems to be not so much a matter of separation from the object as separation from myself, from what is gradually becoming the old me, from which I am not yet sufficiently differentiated to integrate as other. The extraordinary vulnerability of the infant to an actual prolonged separation from the primary caretaker, which according to Spitz and others does not seem to exist before six months or much after two years (Spitz, 1946, 1950; Bowlby, 1973), seems to be due to the misfortunate combination of an actual disappearance of what was part of me at the very time I am psychobiologically beginning to separate myself from it.

Anxiety and depression may be the affective experience of the wrenching activity of differentiation in its first phases, but sooner or later the balance as to which self is "me" begins to shift, and the old equilibrium can be reflected upon from the new, emerged position. This experience, which begins the process of integration, of taking the old equilibrium as "object" in the new balance, is often affectively a matter of anger and repudiation. From a neo-Piagetian perspective the familiar sequence from depression to anger is not so much a matter of redirecting an emotion from self to other—from one target to another—as it is moving the target of the anger itself from self to other. Emergence from embeddedness involves a kind of repudiation, an evolutionary re-cognition that what before was me is not-me. This we see, too, on a universal basis in the first years of life. Could the "terrible twos" with their rampant negativism and declarations of "No!" be a communication to the old self, now gradually becoming object, more than to those exasperated parents who feel they are being defied as distinct and separate people? When the new balance becomes more secure, the infant will have less of a need to "protest too much" and the parents will become "others" rather than "not-me's."

I started by discussing how "object creating" must mean "subject losing"; I have come round to showing how "subject losing" can lead to "object finding." This is a rhythm central to the underlying motion of personality. Its discovery during difficult periods in the lives of Terry or Diane may not be so much a matter of revisiting an infancy rhythm, as experiencing the contemporary manifestation of a lifelong activity which begins in infancy.

Let me summarize some of the implications of this section. It should be clear that my conception neither subsumes affectivity to the cognitive realm, as traditional Piagetians tend to do (Schaefer and Emerson, 1964), nor makes intellectual life the offspring servant of affect, as psychoanalysis tends to do. "Thinking," from such a perspective, does not have to wait upon the discovered insufficiencies of "primary process," as classic psychoanalysis would suggest. It begins in its own form at birth with the moving hand and the sensing eye, the newborn's body being its mind. As Piaget himself has said (despite the inability of his own work to realize it fully): "There are not two developments, one cognitive and the other affective, two separate psychic functions, nor are there two kinds of objects: all objects are simultaneously cognitive and affective" (1964, p. 39). This is because all objects are themselves the elaboration of an activity which is simultaneously cognitive and affective.

It should also be clear how such a model speaks directly to the ambition of modern psychoanalytic theorists to recognize — rather than just posit — an intrinsic motivation for object relations (Fairbairn, 1952; Winnicott, 1965; Guntrip, 1968; Sandler and Sandler, 1978). Though the person is seen now to "think" from birth, it is not "thinking" which motivates her growth. Though she "feels" from birth, it is not "feeling" or drive states or energetics which motivate her growth. Psychoanalytic theory views the individual as primarily motivated by the desire to reduce or eliminate unpleasurable affect. By this reasoning the individual turns away from herself to the object (whether it is the object's representation, as in primary process, or the world of real objects, as in secondary "cognition") because her own system of warding off noxious experience has broken down. Object relations are thus formed extrinsically, a kind of necessary inconvenience. Freud depicted ego formation and reality orientation as an unavoidable "detour" the psychic system must make to secure for itself the peace which it has desired since inception and which was much more efficiently obtained in utero. While I share the perception that it is the newborn's inability to satisfy herself that brings on the birth of object relations, this perception is couched in a conception of human motivation which is not tied to affect alone. It is the greater coherence of its organization which is the presumed motive (White, 1959), a transorganic motive shared by all living things. A more cognitive-sounding translation of the motive is to say that the organism is moved to make meaning or to resolve discrepancy; but this would not be different than to say it is moved to preserve and enhance its integrity.

In any case, the neo-Piagetian view concurs that it is the infant's inability to satisfy himself that prompts his development, but gives a rather different reason why. The in utero state represents a kind of nirvana. One of its most impressive features is that the needs of the fetus are perfectly met; the host organism nourishes it, breathes for it (through the host's blood), and so on. It is most appealing, in light of the neo-Piagetian understanding of growth as a process of emergence from embeddedness, to consider the experience of birth itself as the beginning of the transition out of the first evolutionary position. What must be most dramatic about this new world for the infant is an end to this harmony. Innate reflexes may cause the eyes to close automatically before bright light, but the stomach contractions brought on by hunger do not cause food to enter the system. These discrepant experiences the organism is prompted to resolve—not, the neo-Piagetian perspective would understand, in order to return to the homeostatic state of the fetus, but to bring its organization into a coherence that can take account of the greater complexity with which it is faced; not to return to an old reality, but to establish a meaning for, or make sense out of—yes, even at one year of age—its present reality. The further elaboration this occasions, which always brings about a qualitatively new object relation, is hence neither an effort to recreate the fetal state nor an extrinsic detour. Object relations, from a neo-Piagetian view, are oriented to the present reality, and are brought into being for their own intrinsic value. While growth is no merry ride, neither is each qualitative change regarded as a greater defeat, or further indebtedness, an ever more complex and less elegant way of keeping the system free of stimulation. Rather, each qualitative change, hard won, is a response to the complexity of the world, a response in further recognition of how the world and I are yet again distinct—and thereby more related.

Table 6 indicates six different levels of subject-object relations throughout the lifespan and their expression in a number of developmental theories. The table differs from any number of similar comparisons of theories in its suggestion of the underlying structure in which the various theories might be rooted.

THE IMPULSIVE BALANCE (STAGE 1)

What we traced in the preceding section on infancy was the transition from the incorporative stage to the impulsive stage. This transformation was accomplished through a process which we will see repeated. It has been called a process of decentration (Piaget, 1937), emergence from embeddedness (Schachtel, 1959), the recurring triumph over egocentrism (Elkind, 1974); it has been referred to as a process in which the whole becomes a part to a new whole (Perry, 1970); in which what was structure becomes content on behalf of a new structure (Piaget, 1968); in which what was ultimate becomes preliminary on behalf of a new ultimacy (Kegan, 1980); in which what was immediate gets mediated by a new immediacy (Kegan, 1981). All these descriptions speak to the same process, which is essentially that of adaptation, a differentiation from that which was the very subject of my personal organization and which becomes thereby the object of a new organization on behalf of a new subjectivity that coordinates it. In Mahler's terms, we are "hatched out"—but over and over again. And, as we shall see in succeeding chapters, we are vulnerable each time to a qualitatively new kind of separation anxiety.

In disembedding herself from her reflexes the two-year-old comes to have reflexes rather than be them, and the new self is embedded in that which coordinates the reflexes, namely, the "perceptions" and the "impulses." The tremendous lability, cognitive and emotional, of the

TABLE 6. Balances of subject and object as the common ground of several developmental theories

	Stage 0 *Incorporative*	Stage 1 *Impulsive*	Stage 2 *Imperial*	Stage 3 *Interpersonal*	Stage 4 *Institutional*	Stage 5 *Interindividual*
Underlying structure (subject vs. object)	S— *Reflexes, (sensing, moving)* O— *None*	S— *Impulses, perceptions* O— *Reflexes (sensing, moving)*	S— *Needs, interests, wishes* O— *Impulses, perceptions*	S— *The interpersonal, mutuality* O— *Needs, interests, wishes*	S— *Authorship, identity, psychic administration, ideology* O— *The interpersonal, mutuality*	S— *Interindividuality, interpenetrability of self systems* O— *Authorship, identity, psychic administration, ideology*
Piaget	Sensorimotor	Preoperational	Concrete operational	Early formal operational	Full formal operational	Post-formal[b] Dialectical?
Kohlberg	—	Punishment and obedience orientation	Instrumental orientation	Interpersonal concordance orientation	Societal orientation	Principled orientation
Loevinger	Pre-social	Impulsive	Opportunistic	Conformist	Conscientious	Autonomous
Maslow	Physiological survival orientation	Physiological satisfaction orientation	Safety orientation	Love, affection, belongingness orientation	Esteem and self-esteem orientation	Self-actualization

	Power orientation	Affiliation orientation	Achievement orientation	Intimacy orientation?[b]
McClelland/Murray	—	—	—	—
Erikson	Initiative vs. guilt	Industry vs. inferiority	Affiliation vs. abandonment?[a]	Identity vs. identity diffusion	—

a. I believe Erikson's theory misses a stage between "industry" and "identity." His identity stage—with its orientation to *the self alone*, "who am I?", time, achievement, ideology, self-certainty, and so on—captures something of late adolescence or early adulthood, but it does not really address the period of connection, inclusion, and highly invested mutuality which comes between the more independence-oriented periods of latency and (early adult) identity-formation.

b. Piaget does not posit a post-formal stage, nor does the McClelland/Murray typology posit an intimacy orientation. These are my own hunches about where their models point. For an excellent conceptual and empirical exposition of "dialectical operations," see Basseches, 1980. For a developmental approach to intimacy as an orientation following achievement, see Richardson, 1981. The relationship between "intimacy" and "dialectics" is explored in Chapter 8.

preschool child is suggested to be a function of this new embeddedness. The child is able to recognize objects separate from herself,
but those objects are *subject to* the child's perception of them (this is, I
suggest, the underlying structure of Piaget's preoperational stage). If
the child's perception of an object changes, the object itself has
changed, in the child's experience; she is unable to hold her perception
of the liquid in one container with her perception of the liquid in the
taller, thinner container, precisely because she cannot separate herself
from her perceptions. The same is true of the structurally equivalent
psychological category, the "impulse." The preschooler has poor impulse control, it is suggested, not because she lacks some quantitative
countering force, but because her "biologic" (the living logic which
she *is*) is composed in a qualitatively different way. Impulse control requires mediation, but the impulses are *im*mediate to this subject-object
balance. When I am subject to my impulses, their nonexpression raises
an ultimate threat; they risk who I am. Similarly, the preschooler's inability to hold two perceptions together (which is what gives the object world its concreteness, à la Piaget) is paralleled in the preschooler's
inability to hold two feelings about a single thing together—either the
same feelings about a thing over time which creates the "enduring
disposition" (the psychological structure I call "needs, interests,
wishes" in Table 6), or competing feelings at the same time. This latter suggests why the preschooler lacks the capacity for ambivalence,
and it understands the tantrum—the classic expression of distress in
this era—as an example of a system overwhelmed by internal conflict
because there is no self yet which can serve as a context upon which
the competing impulses can play themselves out; the impulses *are* the
self, are themselves the context.

   The extremely varied phenomena suggesting a fundamental shift between the ages of five and seven (White, 1970; Gardiner, 1978) find a
unifying context when we see that the underlying shift is exactly that
of the *next* transformation in object relations, from the impulsive
balance to the imperial one. Consider findings as apparently disparate
as these: (1) Children on the early side of the five to seven shift seem to
need rewards which are fairly immediate, sensual, and communicating
of praise; children on the older side seem to feel more rewarded by the
information that they have been correct. (2) Children who lose a limb
or become blind before they are through the shift tend not to have
phantom limb responses or memories of sight; children on the other

side of the shift do. A child's capacity to take her impulses and perceptions as an object of her meaning-making not only brings an end to the lability of the earlier subject-object relation, but brings into being a new subject-object relation which creates a more endurable self—a self which does its own praising, so to speak, but needs the information that it is correct as a confirmation; a self which can store memories, feelings, and perceptions (rather than being them), so that a feeling arm or a seeing eye lives on in some way. The examples make clear, I think, that the context which is evolving is more than cognition *or* affect.

THE IMPERIAL BALANCE (STAGE 2)

One way of characterizing the new subject-object relation (stage 2: the imperial balance) is in terms of the construction of the role. This is true whether we are speaking of the social-cognitive capacity to take the role of another person, or the affective differentiation within the impulse life of the family, which permits me to take my appropriate role as a "child" in relation to a "parent" rather than *being* my impulse life bound up with another. A distinguishing feature of this new subject-object relation is that the child seems to "seal up" in a sense; there is a self-containment that was not there before; the adult no longer finds himself engaged in the middle of conversations the child has begun all by himself; the child no longer lives with the sense that the parent can read his private feelings. He *has* a private world, which he did not have before.

It is not just the physical world which is being conserved but internal experience, too. With the constitution of the enduring disposition (what I call, for shorthand purposes, the "needs"—but it should be clear I am not talking about need as a content), there comes as well the emergence of a self-concept, a more or less consistent notion of a me, *what* I am (as opposed to the earlier sense of self, *that* I am, and the later sense of self, *who* I am).

With the capacity to take command of one's impulses (to have them, rather than be them) can come a new sense of freedom, power, independence—agency, above all. Things no longer just happen in the world; with the capacity to see behind the shadows, to come in with the data of experience, I now have something to do with what happens. The end of Kohlberg's first moral stage, where authority is all-powerful and right by virtue of its *being* authority, is probably brought on by this construction of one's own authority. Recall Terry, the sixteen-year-old runaway. She was asked during an interview on the ward, "What's the most important thing involved in a mother-daughter relationship?"

> A lot of love and understanding but a lot of times that understanding has been misplaced and over-protectiveness takes its place. I guess if the mother doesn't know when to break the bond. When a kid is born, till five they are really dependent on the mother. Then they want to break away a little bit and the mother doesn't know. She has been so used to "Mommy, Mommy, Mommy, should I do this? Mommy, help me with that." The child has total dependency and the mother doesn't want to break that because she has been subjected to it for five years and it is hard to break. It is hard to break out of the habit. The kid doesn't see it because the kid, of course, is getting maturer and maturer while the mother has dependency and it is hard.

As is the case with every new development, the new liberation carries new risks and vulnerabilities. If I now have something to do with what happens in the world, then whether things go badly or well for me is a question of what I can do. Looming over a system whose hallmark is newly won stability, control, and freedom, is the threat of the old lability, loss of control, and what now appears as the old subjugation from without. How much of the control and manipulation we experience when we are the object of this meaning-making balance is a matter of a person's efforts to save herself from an old world's threat of ungovernable and overwhelming impulse life?

Every new balance is a triumph over the constraints of the past evolutionary truce, but a limit with respect to the truce which might follow. What are the limits of stage 2, the imperial self? If I betray a confidence because it suits my needs to do so, I do not experience whatever it is one experiences when one simultaneously considers one's own impulse coordinating with another's (often called "guilt"). What I may experience is concern about whether the person I have betrayed will find out, and what the consequences of their finding out will be. I am certainly prepared for their dissatisfaction with my deed, as I am able to see that they, like me, have needs and interests. I am able to understand how they might feel about being betrayed, but how *they* will feel is not a part of the very source of my own feeling or meaning-making. For it to be so would require me to be able to integrate one needs-perspective with another, which would be not just an additive but a qualitative construction of the balance in which I hang. Such a reconstruction entails not just a new level of social perspective, but a new organization and experience of interior life as well. When my own needs and another's are not integrated, I am unable to hold the other imaginatively and so must seek to hold him in some other way. This is because, being unable to hold him imaginatively, I am left having to await or anticipate the actual movements or happenings of others in order to keep my world coherent.

The creation of guilt, or the development of conscience, may seem to some a terrible burden and a terrible loss. And, of course, in some way it is; but it is also quite liberating, as it frees one of having to exercise so much control over an otherwise unfathomable world. It frees me of the distrust of a world from which I am radically separate. Without the internalization of the other's voice in one's very construction of self, how one feels is much more a matter of how external others will react, and the universal effort to preserve one's integrity will be felt by others as an effort to control or manipulate. When you are the object of my stage 2 balance you are subject to my projecting onto you my own embeddedness in my needs. I constitute you as that by which I either do, or do not, meet my needs, fulfill my wishes, pursue my interests. Instead of seeing my needs I see through my needs. You may experience this as manipulation, or being imperialized, because in order for me to "keep my balance" I have to actually control, or at least predict, the behavior "out there" of people who, in carrying around their own agendas separate from me, make it impossible, unless I can exercise such control, for me to gauge reality, the essence of which, at this point, is knowing the consequences of my actions. What makes the balance imperial is our sense of the absence of a shared reality. The absence of that shared reality names the structural limits of the second stage.

Terry discussed her understanding of Kohlberg's dilemmas while she was in the hospital. She was told about a teenager whose mother had promised her she could go to a special rock concert if she earned the money herself. She saved up the cost of the ticket—five dollars—plus another three, by babysitting, but then her mother changed her mind and told Judy she had to spend the money on new clothes for school. Judy was disappointed and decided to go to the concert and tell her mother she had only saved three dollars. That Saturday she went to the performance and told her mother that she was spending the day with a friend. A week passed without her mother finding out. Judy then told her older sister that she had gone to the concert and lied to their mother about it. The older sister wonders whether to tell their mother what Judy did. Should she?

Should the older sister tell their mother that Judy lied about the money or should she keep quiet?

If she did, she would be a rat. Because it was important to the kid, the kid wanted to go and she had saved up for it, and she still had three dollars left over. The sister should not have said anything, because she knew she would get her sister in trouble. That's a kid's point of view.

What is the other point of view?

She shouldn't have lied. Her mother said it was for clothes. It did take a long time for her to save the money up?

Pretty long.

She still had three dollars left over, I don't know. I don't know.

What is the problem here, what do you see as the conflict?

Between adult and kid, the girl wanted it, she saved up for a long time. Of course it was a disappointment to her. But it wasn't exactly fair in her mother's rights. She wasn't exactly understanding to say no after the girl had saved up for a long time. I think that the mother should have made some kind of compromise.

You are taking both points of view, the mother's and the kid's.

Yes. This is too close to home, that is why I am having problems with it, it really is.

What would be the best reason for the older sister to keep her mouth shut?

Because the younger sister will probably rat-fink on her sometime. She would experience something worse. If she had told her mom, it would not have been right from a sister, sibling position; you don't tell on me. You tell on me, I tell on you. That's the way it is between kids. Plus I think there would be a lot of problems in that family and they would be better left alone; no one was hurt. She got away with it. Besides, there would be just as many problems if she didn't go because she and her mother would be bitching at each other for who knows how long. If she was saving up for a long time. It was a goal and her mother shot it for her. Still it wasn't like five dollars was all she had, she had eight dollars, and she had three dollars left over; I am sure if she did as much babysitting as she did before, she could get more money. I am sure she could suffice without clothes—of course, she has clothes, but not new clothes—a little while. You could kill two birds with one stone; if you could get away with it, go ahead.

Would it be right to?

No, I don't think so. It would be wrong for her to tell.

How come?

There would be too many hassles, there would be a lot of fighting. There really would.

* * *

How about the older sister; she has a relationship with her younger sister and you said she wants to keep a trust going, but she also has a relationship with her mother and if she tells on her sister, she breaks the sister bond. If she doesn't tell on her sister she is in a dishonest relation with her mother.

In a way, if she does suffer guilt feelings. I wouldn't suffer guilt feelings. I couldn't.

You don't think it would be violating your trust with your mother?

Sure, because it is just your concern that the mother does know about it, the mother probably wouldn't find out. If she did—she wouldn't come to it—it wouldn't be as fresh, it would be an old issue and time would have kind of erased it from my mind, the circumstances.

* * *

Was it right for Judy to do it?

Yah, in the sense that she has worked for it. No, in the sense that she is going to always worry, what if her mommy finds out. She would have to worry about that, won't enjoy it as much.

What makes the thing wrong?

It is hard, because there are reasons for both. You can make something right if you want to make it right. If you want it to be wrong, you can make something wrong.

What is the wrong reason, how is it wrong?

Because she didn't have her mother's permission to go. She misused the money in her mother's eyes, but not in her eyes.

How about in your eyes?

I would have gone because it is something I worked for. It was important to me.

From the very start of the interview we see that Terry herself frames the dilemma in terms of what the kid wants versus what the adult wants. This is a construction mindful that different parties have different needs or wants, but it is not a construction integrative of these different wants. She does not orient to a *relationship*—to the nature of a promise, for example, or to the cost of sustaining a shared relationship when one partner acts like the mother is acting, or to the impact of the mother's or the daughter's violation on the bond between the two people. Might this truncated orientation arise because the shared context does not yet quite exist for Terry; because the intercourse between people is not so much a context in itself as an avenue for expedient exchange? The older sister should not tell on Judy "because the younger sister will probably rat-fink on her sometime."

Terry demonstrates no spontaneous sense that the older sister may be in a conflict of her own between her interpersonal obligations to her sister and those to her mother, the sort of conflict that is bound to raise grave problems for the interpersonalist balance. When a question is put on just this subject, Terry answers that the older sister would only be in such a bind "if she suffers guilt feelings." In this fascinating section of the interview we begin to see what "guilt" is like when viewed from the outside. Guilt is apparently something that some people—it is clear to her perceptive observation—do suffer from, but she has no personal experience of it. She would not suffer guilt feelings, she says; "I couldn't." What she would have instead is a "worry" as to whether her mother would find out, and so long as she didn't find out things would either be okay, or continuously worrisome. Was it right for Judy to go to the concert? "Yah, in the sense that she has worked for it. No, in the sense that she is going to always worry, what if her mommy finds out." Notice here how both notions of its being right and wrong stem from the same context—what would or would not be of benefit to one party (herself). Guilt has to do with having a problem simply because the lie exists and one is implicated thereby; the mother in such a case is a part of the interior life. Worry has to do with potential consequences of the lie's being discovered; here the mother is outside. Though persons at stage 2 will sometimes use the word "guilt" to refer to their own experience, when we look into what they mean it turns out they are talking about an anxious anticipation of what the other will do. Similarly, their favorite guilt-free expression, "What they don't know won't hurt them," really means, "What they don't know won't hurt *me*." In the recent movie *Peppermint Soda*, the lives of two sisters, seventeen and fourteen, are explored. One day the two are walking with their mother, and the younger sister steals an apple off a cart. The mother is embarrassed. That night the sisters are talking in their bedroom and the older sister asks, "How could you do that to Mama?" The younger one replies, "I didn't think I'd get caught." This is a conversation at cross-purposes precisely because it crosses two different evolutionary balances. The older girl orients to the idea of stealing, and to its violation of an "internalized" bond between herself and her mother. The younger girl orients to the consequences of the behavior, and whether mother will find out. This is because the mother is "out" in a way she is not for the older sister.

With the emergence from an embeddedness in one's needs, gradually a new evolutionary truce is struck. "I" no longer *am* my needs (no longer the imperial I); rather, I *have* them. In having them I can now coordinate, or integrate, one need system with another, and in so doing, I bring into being that need-mediating reality which we refer to when we speak of mutuality. The theory presented in this book is at once a theory of interpersonal and intrapsychic reconstruction. The context of meaning-evolution is taken as prior to the interpersonal *and* the intrapsychic; it gives rise to each. The interpersonal consequence of moving the structure of needs from subject to object is that the person, in being able to coordinate needs, can become mutual, empathic, and oriented to reciprocal obligation. But during the transition the old balance can experience this change as an unwelcome intrusion upon the more independent world of personal control and agency. The intrapsychic consequence of moving the structure of needs from subject to object is that the person is able to coordinate points of view within herself, leading to the experience of subjectivity, the sense of inner states, and the ability to talk about feelings experienced now *as* feelings rather than social negotiations. But once again, *during* the transition, this change can be felt as a perplexing complexification of one's inner experience, the most common expression of which is adolescent moodiness.

THE INTERPERSONAL BALANCE (STAGE 3)

In the interpersonal balance the feelings the self gives rise to are, a priori, shared; somebody else is in there from the beginning. The self becomes conversational. To say that the self is located in the interpersonal matrix is to say that it embodies a plurality of voices. Its strength lies in its capacity to be conversational, freeing itself of the prior balance's frenzy-making constant charge to find out what the voice will say on the other end. But its limit lies in its inability to consult itself about that shared reality. It cannot because it *is* that shared reality.

My stage 3 ambivalences or personal conflicts are not really conflicts between what I want and what someone else wants. When looked into they regularly turn out to be conflicts between what I want to do as a part of this shared reality and what I want to do as part of that shared reality. To ask someone in this evolutionary balance to resolve such a conflict by bringing both shared realities before herself is to name precisely the limits of this way of making meaning. "Bringing before oneself" *means* not being subject to it, being able to take it as an object, just what this balance cannot do.

When I live in this balance as an adult I am the prime candidate for the assertiveness trainer, who may tell me that I need to learn how to stand up for myself, be more "selfish," less pliable, and so on, as if these were mere skills to be added on to whoever else I am. The popular literature will talk about me as lacking self-esteem, or as a pushover because I want other people to like me. But this does not quite address me in my predicament, or in my "hoping." It is more that there *is* no self independent of the context of "other people liking." It is not as if this self, which is supposedly not highly esteemed, is the same self as one that can stand up for itself independent of the interpersonal context; it is rather a wholly different self, differently constructed. The difference is not just an affective matter—how much I like myself, how much self-confidence I have. The difference goes to that fundamental ground which is itself the source of affect and thought, the evolution of meaning. With no coordinating of its shared psychological space, "pieced out" in a variety of mutualities, this balance lacks the self-coherence from space to space that is taken as the hallmark of "identity." From such perspectives this more public coherence is what is meant by ego itself, but in my view it would be wrong to say that an ego is lacking at stage 3, just as it would be wrong to say that at stage 3 there is a weaker ego. What there is is a qualitatively—not a quantitatively—different ego, a different way of making the self cohere.

This balance is "interpersonal" but it is not "intimate," because what might appear to be intimacy here is the self's *source* rather than its aim. There is no self to share with another; instead the other is required to bring the self into being. Fusion is not intimacy. If one can feel manipulated by the imperial balance, one can feel devoured by the interpersonal one.

A person in stage 3 is not good with anger, and may, in fact, not even *be* angry in any number of situations which might be expected to make a person angry. Anger owned and expressed is a risk to the interpersonal fabric, which for this balance is the holy cloth. My getting angry amounts to a declaration of a sense of self separate from the relational context—that I still exist, that I am a person too, that I have my own feelings—which I would continue to own apart from this relationship. It is, as well, a declaration that you are a separate person, that you can survive my being angry, that it is not an ultimate matter for you. If my meaning-making will not permit me to know myself this way, it will surely not permit me to guarantee this kind of distinctness to you either. There are a myriad of reasons why people might find it hard to express anger when they feel it, but it appears that persons in this balance undergo experiences, such as being taken advantage of or victimized, which do not make them angry at all, because they cannot know themselves separate from the interpersonal context; instead they are more likely to feel sad, wounded, or incomplete.

Thus, if the interpersonal balance is able to bring inside to itself the other half of a conversation the imperial balance had always to be listening for in the external world, the interpersonal balance suffers the vicissitudes of its own externalities. It cannot bring onto itself the obligations, expectations, satisfactions, purposes, or influences of interpersonalism; they cannot be reviewed, reflected upon, mediated—and so they rule.

Diane, too, discussed Kohlberg's famous dilemmas. She was told the story of Heinz, who needed a drug to save his dying wife, but faced a druggist who had invented the drug and wanted a huge sum of money for it which Heinz had no way of paying.

> He had created this thing to try to help people and then shut it off for his own monetary gains. I think that's wrong. His aim couldn't have been to help people, but to glorify and enrich himself. And that sets up the whole subject of selfishness, which selfishness to that degree I think is wrong.

Get back to Heinz—what if he doesn't feel close or affectionate to his wife, does he have the obligation—first of all, do you think he has any obligation in any case to steal the drug? You said it was the right thing to do.

No, I don't think it is an obligation, I think it comes under does he care enough about his wife, for his wife, to put himself in jeopardy.

But if he doesn't, would he be right not to, if he decided that he doesn't care enough about his wife to put himself in jeopardy, do you think what he is doing is the right thing to do?

I think he should go to his wife and let her know how he feels and help her; they have spent a number of years together, parts of themselves and their lives together, and he should help her to see if there is any way that she can get the drug, but if he feels that he can't—if he puts getting himself in trouble over his wife—

I am trying to get oriented. I understand when you say you think it was more important to try to save the woman's life than observe the druggist's rights.

Yah, I don't think he or any person on the street is under any obligation to steal.

So when you say the value of life would make it right to do it, you are saying the husband has an obligation to do it?

No.

Would it be just as right to do it if he no longer loved her, or he was no longer intimately concerned about her welfare?

I think it would be right, I think doing something like that would show that he did care, I don't think he would do it if he didn't care. But I still think it would be right if he didn't, if he felt that he wanted to do this, he would probably feel in that sense, that he owed her something, but I think if he felt he wanted to do this for her, as another human being, it would be all right.

Why do you think it wouldn't be an obligation? Or a duty? Do you think the wife would have a right to expect him to do it for her?

No. Not at all.

Why not?

Because I don't know that you can expect to put other people in that jeopardizing situation for your own good if they don't care to. Anyone doing this for this woman obviously cares a great deal for the woman and I don't think that she could expect that from someone who didn't care about her.

Because someone who didn't wouldn't do it? Or it would be wrong to expect it?

If she has invested nothing in this other person, I don't see how she can expect a return.

So suppose it was not for a person, but it was Heinz's pet dog? Would it be right for him to steal to save the dog's life?

Save the dog's life—I think I would look at that as being somewhat an extreme and an irrational measure for a dog. Then that is putting human life over animal life, and separating the two. But I could go back to the same argument of he has invested in the dog, and I guess I do have some tendency of feeling that animals aren't independent in their own right and I don't think that the dog really has invested himself in a person. I can see how he could, just somehow, I don't see what it is, but something in me is not letting me justify that.

You think it would be wrong if he did it, would you say that was wrong? Or wouldn't you want to talk about it as being right or wrong?

I think you could talk about it being right or wrong, but I just feel at this point I am not able to make that decision.

Whatever it is about a human's life that you are willing to base a justification on it, the person's investment in that life, wouldn't hold for a dog.

Yah, there is something of a sense in here, that dogs hold a shorter life than humans and you can get over those things. There is an interaction between humans that I think becomes much stronger than that of an animal and a person, and that difference, taking that, I guess I would say it was wrong.

Diane spontaneously frames the dilemma either in terms of the relative affective "investments" persons might have in profit-making "things" versus other human beings, or in terms of "selfishness" (what stage 2 looks like from the perspective of stage 3) versus caring for others. The rightness of Heinz's theft is lodged entirely within the expectations, requirements, satisfactions, and influences of mutual, interpersonal relationships. Life is valuable by virtue of people's investment in it, or its investments in others (rather than by virtue of its benefits to me, as was the case in the earlier balance). But stealing is sanctioned with no spontaneous construction of a social or legal system generalized beyond the interpersonal, to some extent regulative of the interpersonal, and requiring some kind of "answer" in the face of a sanctioned theft. The subordination of the druggist's rights are justified finally in terms of the inferior claims of selfishness in comparison to altruism. ("He has created this thing to help people and then shut it off for his own monetary gains. I think that's wrong. His aim couldn't have been to help people, but to glorify himself and enrich himself. And that sets up the whole subject of selfishness, which selfishness to that degree I think is wrong.") Thus this much of the interview suggests the kind of self-and-other balance in which the universe is subject to the interpersonal, the self is constructive of the interpersonal, and the important question for the "other" is framed in terms of its recognition of, and availability for, the rigors of mutuality. Does this give us some sense of how great were the proportions of Diane's loss when her relationship ended? Does it suggest something of what must be further lost if she is to be able to live more successfully outside the hospital?

Each new balance sees you (the object) more fully as you; guarantees, in a qualitatively new way, your distinct integrity. Put another way, each new balance corrects a too-subjective view of you; in this sense each new balance represents a qualitative reduction of what another psychology might call "projected ambivalence." In the imperial balance (stage 2), you are an instrument by which I satisfy my needs and work my will. You are the other half of what, from the next balance, I recognize as my own projected ambivalence. In the move to the new evolutionary grammar of stage 3, I claim both sides of this ambivalence and become internally "interpersonal." But stage 3 brings on a new "projected ambivalence." You are the other by whom I complete myself, the other whom I need to create the context out of which I define and know myself and the world. At stage 4, I recognize this as well, and again claim both sides as my own, bringing them onto the self. What does this mean for my inner life?

THE INSTITUTIONAL BALANCE (STAGE 4)

In separating itself from the context of interpersonalism, meaning-evolution authors a self which maintains a coherence across a shared psychological space and so achieves an identity. This authority—sense of self, self-dependence, self-ownership—is its hallmark. In moving from "I am my relationships" to "I have relationships," there is now somebody who is doing this having, the new I, who, in coordinating or reflecting upon mutuality, brings into being a kind of psychic institution (*in* + *statuere*: to set up; *statutum*: law, regulation; as in "statute" and "state").

As stage 3, in appropriating a wider other, was able to bring onto itself the other half of a conversation stage 2 had always to be listening for in the external world, stage 4's wider appropriation brings inside those conflicts between shared spaces which were formerly external-ized. This makes stage 4's emotional life a matter of holding both sides of a feeling simultaneously, where stage 3 tends to experience its am-bivalences one side at a time. But what is more central, perhaps, to the interior change between the interpersonal and the institutional, is the way the latter is regulative of its feelings. Having moved the shared context over from subject to object, the feelings which arise out of in-terpersonalism do not reflect the structure of my equilibrative know-ing and being, but are, in fact, reflected upon by that structure. The feelings which depend on mutuality for their origin and their renewal remain important but are relativized by that context which is ultimate, the psychic institution and the time-bound constructions of role, norm, self-concept, auto-regulation, which maintain that institu-tion. The sociomoral implications of this ego balance are the construc-tion of the legal, societal, normative system. But what I am sug-gesting is that these social constructions are reflective of that deeper structure which constructs the self itself as a system, and makes ultimate (as does every balance) the maintenance of its integrity.

Talk of "transcending the interpersonal" often makes people uneasy who want to point out—and rightly, I think—that other people should remain what is important to us throughout our lives. But others are not lost by an emergence from embeddedness in the in-terpersonal. (On the contrary, in a sense they are found.) The question always is *how* "other people" are known. The institutional balance does not leave one bereft of interpersonal relationships, but it does ap-propriate them to the new context of their place in the maintenance of a personal self-system.

A strength of this is the person's new capacity for independence, to own herself, rather than having all the pieces of herself owned by various shared contexts; the sympathies which arise out of one's shared space are no longer determinative of the "self," but taken as preliminary, mediated by the self-system. But in this very strength lies a limit. The "self" is identified with the organization it is trying to run smoothly; it *is* this organization. The "self" at ego stage 4 is an administrator in the narrow sense of the word, a person whose mean-ings are derived out of the organization, rather than deriving the or-ganization out of her meaning/principles/purposes/reality. Stage 4 has no "self," no "source," no "truth" before which it can bring the operational constraints of the organization, because its "self," its "source," its "truth" is invested within these operational constraints. In this sense, ego stage 4 is inevitably ideological (as Erikson, 1968, recognized must be the case for identity formation), a truth for a faction, a class, a group. And it probably requires the recognition of a group (or persons as representatives of groups) to come into being; either the tacit ideological support of American institutional life, which is most supportive to the institutional evolution of white males, or the more explicit ideologies in support of a disenfranchised social class, gender, or race.

Emotional life in the institutional balance seems to be more internally controlled. The immediacy of interpersonalist feeling is replaced by the mediacy of regulating the interpersonal. Regulation, rather than mutuality itself, is now ultimate. For stage 3 it is those events risking the integrity of the shared context that mobilize the "self's" defensive operations; for stage 4 it is those events that threaten chaos for the interior polity. The question is not, as it was earlier, "Do you still like me?" but, "Does my government still stand?" A variety of feelings, particularly erotic or affiliative feelings and doubts around performance and duty discharge, come to be viewed as potential dissidents which must be subjected to the psychic civil polity. Stage 4's delicate balance is that in self-government it has rescued the "self" from its captivity by the shared realities, but in having no "self" before which it can bring the demands of that government, it risks the excesses of control that may obtain to any government not subject to a wider context in which to root and justify its laws.

Rebecca is in her mid-thirties. The very self-sufficiency Diane desperately needed when she entered the hospital has long been familiar to Rebecca. It has become now too familiar; it has worn out its welcome. But because "it" is how Rebecca is herself composed, she is herself worn out. We will return to her in more detail later, but in her words, presented here, I think one can hear: (1) a fleeting glance back to the interpersonalist balance, long ago transcended; (2) the personal authority and integrity of the institutional self; and (3) the courage and fatigue of experiencing its limits:

> I know I have very defined boundaries and I protect them very carefully. I won't give up the slightest control. In any relationship I decide who gets in, how far, and when.

What am I afraid of? I used to think I was afraid people would find out who I really was and then not like me. But I don't think that's it anymore. What I feel now is—"That's me. That's mine. It's what makes me." And I'm powerful. It's my negative side, maybe, but it's also my positive stuff—and there's a lot of that. What it is is me, it's my self—and if I let people in maybe they'll take, maybe they'll use it—and I'll be gone.

Respect above all is the most important thing to me. You don't have to like me. You don't have to care about me, even, but you do have to respect me.

This "self," if I had to represent it I think of two things: either a steel rod that runs through everything, a kind of solid fiber, or sort of like a ball at the center that is all together. What you just really can't be is weak.

I wasn't always this way. I used to have two sets of clothes—one for my husband and one for my mother who visited often. Two sets of clothes, but none for me. Now *I* dress in *my* clothes. Some of them are like what my mother would like me to wear but that's a totally different thing.

How exhausting it's becoming holding all this together. And until recently I didn't even realize I was doing it.

THE INTERINDIVIDUAL BALANCE (STAGE 5)

The rebalancing that characterizes ego stage 5 separates the self from the institution and creates, thus, the "individual," that self who can reflect upon, or take as object, the regulations and purposes of a psychic administration which formerly was the subject of one's attentions. "Moving over" the institutional from subject to object frees the self from that displacement of value whereby the maintenance of the institution has become the end in itself; there is now a self who runs the organization, where before there was a self who *was* the organization; there is now a source before which the institutional can be brought, by which it is directed, where before the institution was the source.

Every ego equilibrium amounts to a kind of "theory" of the prior stage; this is another way of speaking about subject moving to object, or structure becoming content. Stage 2 is a "theory" of impulse; the impulses are organized or ordered by the needs, wishes, or interests. Stage 3 is a "theory" of needs; they are ordered by that which is taken as prior to them, the interpersonal relationships. Stage 4 is a kind of theory of interpersonal relationships; they are rooted in and reckoned by institutions. Stage 5 is a theory of the institutional; the institutional is ordered by that new self which is taken as prior to the institutional. Kohlberg's moral stage 5 requires a "prior-to-society perspective," by which he refers to that dislodging by which the self is no longer subject to the societal; this is accomplished at the transitional disequilibration between his stages 4 and 5. To be at stage 5 in Kohlberg's framework, a person must have, in addition to this prior-to-society perspective, a kind of theory that roots the legal institution in principles which give rise to it, to which conflicts in the law might be appealed, and by which the rights that the legal institution protects might be hierarchized. What this amounts to, more than disequilibrial transition out of the stage 4 balance, is the re-equilibration by which the legal institution has been recovered or recollected as object in a new balance. No longer is "the just" derived from the legal, but the legal from a broader conception of the just. And no longer is the past balance disowned (as in, " 'Should' is no longer in my vocabulary"). The hallmark of every rebalancing is that the past, which may during transition be repudiated, is not finally rejected but reappropriated.

But that which is a kind of theory of the legal institution may be an expression, in the moral domain, of the deep structure which is a theory of the self as institutional. And that which constructs this theory—the new subjectivity—is the next ego balance.

What happens to one's construction of community at ego stage 5? The capacity to coordinate the institutional permits one now to join others not as fellow-instrumentalists (ego stage 2) nor as partners in fusion (ego stage 3), nor as loyalists (ego stage 4), but as individuals—people who are known ultimately in relation to their actual or potential recognition of themselves and others as value-originating, system-generating, history-making individuals. The community is for the first time a "universal" one in that all persons, by virtue of their being persons, are eligible for membership. The group which this self knows as "its own" is not a pseudo-species, but the species. One's self is no longer limited to the mediation and control of the interpersonal (the self as an institution) but expands to mediate one's own and others' "institutions." If the construction of the self as an institution brought the interpersonal "into" the self, the new construction brings the self back into the interpersonal. The great difference between this and stage 3 is that there now is a "self" to be brought to, rather than derived from, others; where ego stage 3 is interpersonal (a fused commingling), ego stage 5 is interindividual (a commingling which guarantees distinct identities).

This new locating of the self, not in the structure of my psychic institution but in the *coordinating* of the institutional, brings about a revolution in Freud's favorite domains, "love" and "work." If one no longer *is* one's institution, neither is one any longer the duties, performances, work roles, career which institutionality gives rise to. One *has* a career; one no longer *is* a career. The self is no longer so vulnerable to the kind of ultimate humiliation which the threat of performance-failure holds out, for the performance is no longer ultimate. The functioning of the organization is no longer an end in itself, and one is interested in the way it serves the aims of the new self whose community stretches beyond that particular organization. The self seems available to "hear" negative reports about its activities; before, it *was* those activities and therefore literally "irritable" in the face of those reports. (Every balance's irritability is simultaneously testimony to its capacity to grow and its propensity to preserve itself.) Every new balance represents a capacity to listen to what before one could only hear irritably, and the capacity to hear irritably what before one could hear not at all.

But the increased capacity of the stage 5 balance to hear, and to seek out, information which might cause the self to alter its behavior, or share in a negative judgment of that behavior, is but a part of that wider transformation which makes stage 5 capable, as was no previous balance, of intimacy. At ego stage 4, one's feelings seem often to be regarded as a kind of recurring administrative problem which the successful ego-administrator resolves without damage to the smooth functioning of the organization. When the self is located not in the institutional but in the coordinating of the institutional, one's own and others, the interior life gets "freed up" (or "broken open") within oneself, and with others; this new dynamism, flow, or play results from the capacity of the new self to move back and forth between psychic systems within itself. Emotional conflict seems to become both recognizable and tolerable to the "self." At ego stage 3, emotional conflict cannot yet be recognized by the self; one can feel torn between the demands from one interpersonal space and those from another, but the conflict is taken as "out there"; it is the ground and I am the figure upon it. At ego stage 4, this conflict comes inside. The dawn of the "self-as-a-self" (the institutional self) creates the self as the ground for conflict and the competing poles are figures upon it. Emotional conflict is recognized but not tolerable; that is, it is ultimately costly to the self. The self at ego stage 4 was brought into being for the very purpose of resolving such conflict, and its inability to do so jeopardizes its balance. Ego stage 5 which recognizes a plurality of institutional selves within the (interindividual) self is thereby open to emotional conflict as an interior conversation.

Ego stage 5's capacity for intimacy, then, springs from its capacity to be intimate with itself, to break open the institutionality of the former balance. Locating itself now in the coordination of psychic institutions, the self surrenders its counter-dependent independence for an interdependence. Having a self, which is the hallmark of stage 5's advance over stage 4, it now has a self to share. This sharing of the self at the level of intimacy permits the emotions and impulses to live in the intersection of systems, to be "re-solved" between one self-system and another. Rather than the attempt to be both close and auto-regulative, "individuality" permits one to "give oneself up" to another; to find oneself in what Erikson has called "a counter-pointing of identities," which at once shares experiencing and guarantees each partner's distinctness, which permits persons—again Erikson's words— "to regulate with one another the cycles of work, procreation, and recreation" (Erikson, 1968). Every re-equilibration is a qualitative victory over isolation.

The stories of Terry, Diane, and Rebecca are not complete. Each story will continue when we meet each woman again in the chapters to follow. But perhaps a last picture of them now will help me to suggest an overarching image for this history of evolutionary truces.

Although I said that Terry, Diane, and Rebecca all seem to be involved with boundary issues, it should be clear that some distinctions within this generalization can be made. Chief among these is that Terry and Rebecca (the youngest and oldest of the three) seem to express their concerns in terms of preserving a boundary which feels like it is giving way. Diane, on the other hand, expresses her concerns in terms of a fearful inability to preserve the lack of a boundary. Terry and Rebecca seem to be guarding a precious sense of differentiation or separateness, whereas Diane seems to be guarding an equally precious sense of inclusion or connection.

These two orientations I take to be expressive of what I consider the two greatest yearnings in human experience. We see the expression of these longings everywhere, in ourselves and in those we know, in small children and in mature adults, in cultures East and West, modern and traditional. Of the multitude of hopes and yearnings we experience, these two seem to subsume the others. One of these might be called the yearning to be included, to be a part of, close to, joined with, to be held, admitted, accompanied. The other might be called the yearning to be independent or autonomous, to experience one's distinctness, the self-chosenness of one's directions, one's individual integrity. David Bakan called this "the duality of human experience," the yearnings for "communion" and "agency" (1966). Certainly in my experience as a therapist—a context in which old-fashioned words such as "yearn" and "plea" and "long for" and "mourn" have great meaning—it seems to me that I am often listening to one or the other of these yearnings; or to the fear of losing a most precious sense of being included or feeling independent; or to their fearful flip sides—the fear of being completely unseparate, of being swallowed up and taken over; and the fear of being totally separate, of being utterly alone, abandoned, and remote beyond recall. Those who are religiously oriented will note that the same old-fashioned language finds its way into prayer, and that much liturgy and scripture is an expression of one or the other of these two longings. I think of Schliermacher's "ultimate dependence," on the one hand (1958), and Luther's "Here I Stand," on the other; of the fervent communalism of Hasidism, on the one hand (1960), and the lonely Job, talking to (even cursing) the Lord, on the other.

But what is most striking about these two great human yearnings is that they seem to be in conflict, and it is, in fact, their *relation*—this tension—that is of more interest to me at the moment than either yearning by itself. I believe it is a lifelong tension. Our experience of this fundamental ambivalence may be our experience of the unitary, restless, creative motion of life itself.

Biologists talk about evolution and its periods of adaptation—of life organization—as involving a balance between differentiation and integration. These are cold and abstract words. I suggest they are a biological way of speaking of the phenomena we experience as the yearnings for autonomy and inclusion.

Every developmental stage, I said, is an evolutionary truce. It sets terms on the fundamental issue as to how differentiated the organism is from its life-surround and how embedded. It would be as true to say that every evolutionary truce—each stage or balance I have sketched out in this chapter—is a temporary solution to the lifelong tension between the yearnings for inclusion and distinctness. Each balance resolves the tension in a different way. The life history I have traced involves a continual moving back and forth between resolving the tension slightly in the favor of autonomy, at one stage, in the favor of inclusion, at the next. We move from the overincluded, fantasy-embedded impulsive balance to the sealed-up self-sufficiency of the imperial balance; from the overdifferentiated imperial balance to overincluded interpersonalism; from interpersonalism to the autonomous, self-regulating institutional balance; from the institutional to a new form of openness in the interindividual. Development is thus better depicted by a spiral or a helix, as in Figure 4, than by a line.[1]

While any "picture" of development has its limitations, the helix has a number of advantages. It makes clear that we move back and forth in our struggle with this lifelong tension; that our balances are slightly *im*balanced. In fact, it is because each of these temporary balances is slightly imbalanced that each *is* temporary; each self is vulnerable to being tipped over. The model suggests a way of better understanding the nature of our vulnerability to growth at each level.

The model also recognizes the equal dignity of each yearning, and in this respect offers a corrective to *all* present developmental frameworks which univocally define growth in terms of differentiation, separation, increasing autonomy, and lose sight of the fact that adaptation is equally about integration, attachment, inclusion. The net effect of this myopia, as feminist psychologists are now pointing out (Gilligan, 1978; Low, 1978), has been that differentiation (the stereotypically male overemphasis in this most human ambivalence) is favored with

1. The general notion of depicting development as a helix I owe to conversation with William Perry. George Vaillant, I have since discovered, has a similar conception which grows out of his reconstruction of Erikson's model.

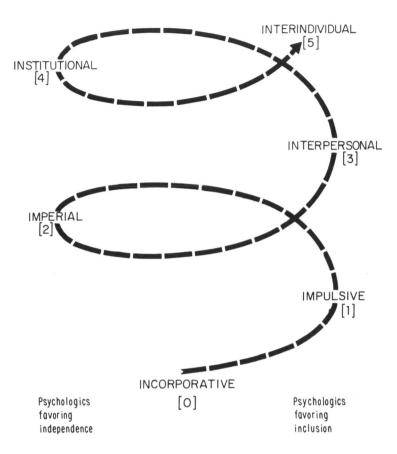

Figure 4   A helix of evolutionary truces

the language of growth and development, while integration (the stereotypically female overemphasis) gets spoken of in terms of dependency and immaturity. A model in pursuit of the psychological meaning and experience of *evolution*—intrinsically about differentiation *and* integration—is less easily bent to this prejudice.

Finally, the model makes graphically clear the way we revisit old issues but at a whole new level of complexity. Diane's overinclusiveness, as we will see in Chapter 7, recalls the overinclusiveness of the oedipal years, and while the model recognizes the cousinhood of the impulsive balance to the interpersonal one, it also suggests a distinction between them. Rebecca's overdifferentiated defense recalls Terry's, and the model suggests why that might be so; it also has a way of recognizing the difference between, for example, the control of the other's behavior and the control of one's own psychological definition.

The image of the helix may serve as a guide over the next several chapters, for we turn now to an exploration of its experience. Especially we consider those periods in a life when the terms of our evolutionary truce must be renegotiated. These terms *are* the self. Their renegotiation is a natural emergency.

PART TWO

THE NATURAL EMERGENCIES
OF THE SELF

At the still point of the turning world. Neither flesh nor fleshless;
Neither from nor towards; at the still point, there the dance is,
But neither arrest nor movement. And do not call it fixity,
Where past and future are gathered. Neither movement from nor towards,
Neither ascent nor decline. Except for the point, the still point,
There would be no dance, and there is only the dance.
I can only say, *there* we have been: but I cannot say where.
And I cannot say, how long, for that is to place it in time.
The inner freedom from the practical desire,
The release from action and suffering, release from the inner
And the outer compulsion, yet surrounded
By a grace of sense, a white light still and moving,
Erhebung without motion, concentration
Without elimination, both a new world
And the old made explicit, understood
In the completion of its partial ecstasy,
The resolution of its partial horror.
Yet the enchainment of past and future
Woven in the weakness of the changing body,
Protects mankind from heaven and damnation
Which flesh cannot endure.
Time past and time future
Allow but a little consciousness.
To be conscious is not to be in time
But only in time can the moment in the rose-garden,
The moment in the arbour where the rain beat,
The moment in the draughty church at smokefall
Be remembered; involved with past and future.
Only through time time is conquered.

        —T. S. Eliot, "Burnt Norton"

The Growth and Loss of the Incorporative Self

In the preceding chapters I have been trying to suggest a rather simple thing: If you want to understand another person in some fundamental way you must know where the person is in his or her evolution. I have been saying that a lifelong process of evolution or adaptation is the master motion in personality, that the phenomena of several developmental theories are plausibly the consequence of this motion. And I have tried to describe a number of plateaus in this adaptive process. I use the word "adaptation" not in the sense of "coping" or "adjusting to things as they are," but in the sense of an active process of increasingly organizing the relationship of the self to the environment. The relationship gets better organized by increasing differentiations of the self from the environment and thus by increasing integrations *of* the environment.

Why is the state of a person's evolution so crucial to understanding him or her? Because the way in which the person is settling the issue of what is "self" and what is "other" essentially *defines* the underlying logic (or "psychologic") of the person's meanings. Since what is most important for us to know in understanding another is not the other's experience but what the experience means to him or her, our first goal is to grasp the essence of how the other composes his or her private reality. The first truth we may need to know about a person, in other words, is how the person constructs the truth. What is self and what is other may be a question of the person's "biology," but it is equally a question of the person's "philosophy": what is the subject-object relationship the person has become in the world?

That question suggests at least two things that have so far received little of our attention. First, subject-object relations *become*; they are not static; their study is the study of a motion. Second, subject-object relations live *in the world*; they are not simply abstractions, but take form in actual human relations and social contexts.

If persons simply remained forever in one or another of these evolutionary truces, then understanding another might only be a matter of grasping their underlying psychologic. But these self-other distinctions are in fact tenuous, fragile, precarious states. They are balances, I have said; they can tip over. They are truces, I have said; chaos and a state of siege hang around the corner. I have been suggesting that we are studying the master motion in personality, but in the last chapter we saw little of motion. The "stages" in their seductive clarity returned to center stage.

In this second section of the book we return the stages to their proper place as markers in an ongoing process. They mark those periods of relative balance in the lifelong process of evolution. We turn now to the *experience* of this process throughout the lifespan. I said the first section of this book brought us to a simple pronouncement: To understand another we must know the underlying psychologic by which he or she makes meaning. The second section of this book moves, like all science, from taxonomy to ontogeny. The person is not static. These "psychologics" change. As important as it is to understand the way the person creates the world, we must also understand the way the world creates the person. In considering where a person is in his or her evolutionary balancing we are looking not only at how meaning is made; we are looking, too, at the possibility of the person *losing* this balance. We are looking, in each balance, at a new sense of what is ultimate and what is ultimately at stake. We are looking, in each balance, at a new vulnerability. Each balance suggests how the person is composed, but each suggests, too, a new way for the person to lose her composure. In this section of the book we look at the experience of defending and surrendering the balances we are, we have been, and we will be throughout the lifespan.

In laying out a series of self-other balances, Chapter 3 also suggested that self-other balancing is something a person does alone, or, even worse, something that a person does "inside himself" or "in her own head." Between the ages of five and seven, for example, the impulses were said to move from "self" to "other." Instead of being embedded in my impulses and subject to them, I am able to differentiate from my impulses, to integrate them into a new self whose control they come under. "Well and good," the reader might say, "but I thought we were going to talk about the self and the other, about organism and environment. The child is said to emerge from embeddedness in its environment, but what is the environment — its impulses? The new embeddedness is said to be the 'enduring disposition' or 'needs.' Are needs an environment? If categories like 'impulses' and 'needs' are to be taken as environmental contexts from which the person differentiates when he evolves, then 'the environment' is at best an internal psychological environment; it doesn't seem to involve a real world of people and social arrangements."

If this section of the book returns the study of subject-object relations to the study of a lifelong motion and its experience, it also returns it to the study of real relations in the world. One of the most powerful features of this psychology, in fact, is its capacity to liberate psychological theory from study of the decontextualized individual. Constructive-developmental psychology reconceives the whole question of the relationship between the individual and the social by reminding that the distinction is not absolute, that development is intrinsically about the continual settling and resettling of this very distinction. The infant, I have said, is embedded in its sensing and moving, but there is a real human environment in which it lives, with which it confuses its own sensing and moving. D. W. Winnicott was fond of saying that there is never "just an infant." He meant that intrinsic to the picture of infancy is a caretaker who, from the point of view of the infant, is something more than an "other person" who relates to and assists the growth of the infant. She provides the very context in which development takes place, and from the point of view of the newborn she is a part of the self. She provides a true psycho*social* context: she is both "psycho" and "social," depending on whose perspective we take, and the transformation by which she becomes for the infant gradually less "psycho" and more "social" describes the very evolution of meaning itself. This psychosocial environment, or "holding environment," in Winnicott's terms, is the particular form of the world in which the person is, at this moment in his or her evolution, embedded. Since this is the very context in which, and out of which, the person grows, I have come to think of it as a culture of embeddedness. "Culture" here is meant to evoke both an accumulating history and mythology and something grown in a medium in a Petri dish.

In Winnicott's view the "holding environment" is an idea intrinsic to infancy. In my view it is an idea intrinsic to *evolution.* There is not one holding environment early in life, but a succession of holding environments, a life history of cultures of embeddedness. They are the psychosocial environments which hold us (with which we are fused) and which let go of us (from which we differentiate). The preschool child is embedded in her impulses, but this takes living form in the triangular dynamics of the family; the school-age child is embedded in the psychological construction I call the "needs," but this confusion is exercised in the role-recognizing cultures of the school, the peer gang, and the family as an institution of authority, and so on. What Winnicott says of the infant is true for all of us, even for you at this moment. There is never "just an individual"; the very word refers only to that side of the person that is individuated, the side of differentiation. There is always, as well, the side that is embedded; the *person* is more than an individual. "Individual" names a current state of evolution, a stage, a maintained balance or defended differentiation; "person" refers to the fundamental motion of evolution itself, and is as much about that side of the self embedded in the life-surround as that which is individuated from it. The person is an "individual" *and* an "embeddual." There is never just a you; and at this very moment your own buoyancy or lack of it, your own sense of wholeness or lack of it, is in large part a function of how your own current embeddedness culture is holding you. Each chapter in this section of the book looks at a different holding environment and its role in the evolution of the person. (These are summarized in Table 7.)

In considering the functions and fortunes of the developing person's cultures of embeddedness we begin here a kind of exploration which Erikson foretold when he spoke of a *sequence* of expectable environments:

> The specific kind of preadaptness of the human infant—namely, readiness to grow by epigenetic steps through psychosocial crises—calls not only for one basic environment, but for a whole se-

quence of "expectable" environments, for as the child adapts in spurts and stages he has a claim, at any given stage reached, to the next "average expectable environment." In other words, the human environment as a whole must permit and safeguard a series of more or less discontinuous and yet culturally and psychologically consistent developments, each extending further along the radius of expanding life tasks. All of this makes man's so-called biological adaptation a matter of life cycles developing within their community's changing history.   (1968, p. 222)

I have already mentioned that Freudian and Piagetian psychologies alike depict the first human development as a move toward differentiation. However different their underlying epistemologies and root metaphors might be, we can hear in Erikson's or Freud's schemes the same emergence of "otherness" which we hear in Piaget's rendition of the infant's discovery of the permanence of objects. Freud speaks of a move from orality to anality, a shift from a wholly incorporative, assimilative orientation in the world to one of expulsion and elimination, or constipation, holding on, refusing to let go. The second orientation is intrinsically about the idea of separateness—that which is, or can be, separate from me, an idea which does not exist earlier.

We can see the same shift in Erikson's characterization of the same period, a move from issues of hope and security, to issues of will and autonomy, shame and doubt. The issue with which the infant is dealing in the first year, Erikson suggests, has to do with a general disposition toward the enterprise of being alive. The phenomenology Erikson suggests for us makes no distinctions between my life and other life, between distress or comfort that has its origins in me and that which has its origins in others, or a world apart from me. Erikson imagines an infant whose bodily needs have been well attended to in the womb—food and oxygen piped in, temperature and pressure cabin-controlled—who now finds himself with longer experiences of stress and discomfort. Does life come to be felt as a basic ground of satisfaction temporarily interrupted by periods of discomfort which are reliably relieved, leading thus to a feeling of trust in and hopefulness about the biological enterprise? Or is life essentially "one damn thing after another" broken up by periods of calm from which no real satisfaction can be taken since one knows that at any moment the basic fact of life's discomfort will reassert itself? The fundamental question here is: Which is to be figure and which is to be ground in the

TABLE 7. Forms and functions of embeddedness cultures

Evolutionary balance and psychological embeddedness	Culture of embeddedness	Function 1: Confirmation (holding on)	Function 2: Contradiction (letting go)	Function 3: Continuity (staying put for reintegration)	Some common natural transitional "subject-objects" (bridges)a
(0) INCORPORATIVE Embedded in: reflexes, sensing, and moving.	Mothering one(s) or primary caretaker(s). Mothering culture.	Literal holding: close physical presence, comfort and protecting. Eye contact. Recognizing the infant. Dependence upon and merger with oneself.	Recognizes and promotes toddler's emergence from embeddedness. Does not meet child's every need, stops nursing, reduces carrying, acknowledges displays of independence and willful refusal.	Permits self to become part of bigger culture, i.e., the family. High risk: prolonged separation from infant during transition period (6 mos. – 2 yrs.).	Medium of 0-1 transition: blankie, teddy, etc. A soft, comforting, nurturant representative of undifferentiated subjectivity, at once evoking that state and "objectifying" it.
(1) IMPULSIVE Embedded in: impulse and perception.	Typically, the family triangle. Parenting culture.	Acknowledges and cultures exercises of fantasy, intense attachments, and rivalries.	Recognizes and promotes child's emergence from egocentric embeddedness in fantasy and impulse. Holds child responsible for his or her feelings, excludes from marriage, from parents' bed, from home during school day, recognizes child's self-sufficiency and asserts own "other sufficiency."	Couple permits itself to become part of bigger culture, including school and peer relations. High risk: dissolution of marriage or family unit during transition period (roughly 5-7 yrs.).	Medium of 1-2 transition: imaginary friend. A repository for impulses which before were me, and which eventually will be part of me, but here a little of each. E.g., only I can see it, but it is not me.

(2) IMPERIAL Embedded in: enduring disposition, needs, interests, wishes.	Role recognizing culture. School and family as institutions of authority and role differentiation. Peer gang which requires role-taking.	Acknowledges and cultures displays of self-sufficiency, competence, and role differentiation.	Recognizes and promotes preadolescent's (or adolescent's) emergence from embeddedness in self-sufficiency. Denies the validity of only taking one's own interests into account, demands mutuality, that the person hold up his/her end of relationship. Expects trustworthiness.	Family and school permit themselves to become secondary to relationships of shared internal experiences. High risk: family relocation during transition period (roughly early adolescence, 12-16).	Medium of 2-3 transition: *chum.* Another who is identical to me and real but whose needs and self-system are exactly like needs which before *were me,* eventually a part *of me,* but now something between.
(3) INTERPERSONAL Embedded in: mutuality, interpersonal concordance.	Mutually reciprocal one-to-one relationships. *Culture of mutuality.*	Acknowledges and cultures capacity for collaborative self-sacrifice in mutually attuned interpersonal relationships. Orients to internal state, shared subjective experience, "feelings," mood.	Recognizes and promotes late adolescent's or adult's emergence from embeddedness in interpersonalism. Person or context that will not be fused with but still seeks, and is interested in, association. Demands the person assume responsibility for own initiatives and preferences. Asserts the other's independence.	Interpersonal partners permit relationship to be relativized or placed in bigger context of ideology and psychological self-definition. High risk: interpersonal partners leave at very time one is emerging from embeddedness. (No easily supplied age norms.)	Medium for 3-4 transition: *going away to college, a temporary job, the military.* Opportunities for provisional identity which both leave the interpersonalist context behind and preserve it, intact, for return; a time-limited participation in institutional life (e.g. 4 years of college, a service hitch).

TABLE 7, continued

Evolutionary balance and psychological embeddedness	Culture of embeddedness	Function 1: Confirmation (holding on)	Function 2: Contradiction (letting go)	Function 3: Continuity (staying put for reintegration)	Some common natural transitional "subject-objects" (bridges)[a]
(4) INSTITUTIONAL Embedded in: personal autonomy, self-system identity.	*Culture of identity or self-authorship* (in love or work). Typically: group involvement in career, admission to public arena.	Acknowledges and cultures capacity for independence; self-definition; assumption of authority; exercise of personal enhancement, ambition or achievement; "career" rather than "job," "life partner" rather than "helpmate," etc.	Recognizes and promotes adult's emergence from embeddedness in independent self-definition. Will not accept mediated, nonintimate, form-subordinated relationship.	Ideological forms permit themselves to be relativized on behalf of the play between forms. High risk: ideological supports vanish (e.g., job loss) at very time one is separating from this embeddedness. (No easily supplied age norms.)	Medium of 4-5 transition: *ideological self-surrender (religious or political); love affairs protected by unavailability of the partner.* At once a surrender of the identification with the form while preserving the form.
(5) INTER-INDIVIDUAL Embedded in: interpenetration of systems.	*Culture of intimacy* (in domain of love and work). Typically: genuinely adult love relationship.	Acknowledges and cultures capacity for interdependence, for self-surrender and intimacy, for interdependent self-definition.			

a. In the construction of this column I am indebted to the thinking of Mauricia Alvarez.

oscillating relationship between comfort and stress? This is not a question that has anything to do, from the infant's point of view, with his own capabilities or the world's timely trustworthiness; no such distinction exists. Neither comfort nor stress is localized in an inside or in an outside. The issue has to do with living itself. The phenomenology of Erikson's second stage is quite different. Issues of autonomy, shame, doubt, and will all imply—in fact, require—the existence of an other: an other whom I can get along reliably well without (autonomy); an other who can see me when I cannot always see me, leaving me vulnerable to attacks from behind (shame), a "behind" I cannot have unless there *is* an other; an other before whom I perform and display myself, creating a kind of self-consciousness (doubt); an other against whom I move and who moves against me (will). The essence of every aspect of Erikson's depiction of the second year of life involves this differentiation. From the point of view of our underlying evolutionary motion, he is capturing something of the transition from the incorporative to the impulsive balance (stage 0 to stage 1).

The infant's first evolution of meaning, then, involves his differentiation from complete embeddedness in the life force. But he does not transform himself; he does not go through this alone. He gets a kind of help that is more than some other separate entity coming to his aid; he gets help from that which is in some way a part of him. Evolutionarily there is a sense in which the infant (and the person throughout life) climbs out of a psychological amniotic environment. Some part of that world in which the infant is embedded nourishes his gestation and assists in delivering him to a new evolutionary balance. I call that part the embeddedness culture, that most intimate of contexts out of which we repeatedly are recreated. I suggest that it serves at least three functions. It must hold on. It must let go. And it must stick around so that it can be reintegrated.

HOLDING ON

When Winnicott says there is never just an infant, he does not mean only that someone has to attend to and take care of this small creature. He means that if there is a thriving infant he or she comes "attached to" another person. The question for a newborn's survival is thus not so much, "Will there be someone to take care of it?", as,

"Will the infant be able to attach itself to the 'uterine wall' of its new amniotic environment?" and, "How securely is it attached?" To continue the metaphor, the unattached child does not receive the nourishment and oxygen of the mother's blood and will begin to suffer. Its life is threatened, psychologically and literally.

In the successful attachment of baby and mother, one sees that the baby is endowed with a host of abilities (at first, a matter of reflexes, a species inheritance to which the organism is staked) that seduce the mother—the baby's grasp of the mother's garment, his orientation to her eyes—and that the mother is able to attend to this beguiling and is won over. Where the attachment does not take place, one or both of these predispositions may be impaired. The baby may lack the normal "sending power" or "hooking ability," a constitutional matter. Or the mother may be unable to respond to it; she may be depressed or disturbed, too involved with the precarious state of her own evolutionary balance to be a good enough evolutionary host.

In a case Margaret Mahler (1968) cites, a mother, age twenty, is herself so poorly held, and for so long has gone without adequate "intrauterine" nourishment, that she is unable to provide even the first function of a culture of embeddedness for her child. She is almost completely unable to "hold" her infant, Violet, almost completely unable to host her, to allow Violet to attach herself to her. Violet's mother had no deep social attachments at any time in her own life; she was raised by a harsh grandmother and felt abandoned by both parents. She had Violet in hopes that the baby would give her a whole new kind of life and associated a child with a doll her father had given her when she was three. She became deeply depressed several weeks after Violet was born. She then had nothing more to do with Violet except during periods of breastfeeding, which she considered the only point to remaining alive. Her relationship to Violet consisted thus of brief, intense periods of closeness and longer stretches of complete separation. Although Violet tried her best to establish the culture of embeddedness she would need for her own wholesome development—crying, eye contact, smiling, vocalizing—Violet's mother could not be drawn in. By fifteen months, at which time an infant would normally be in the midst of differentiating, Violet, still unable to establish a context of embeddedness, appears to have given up: "When Violet made her first appearance with us [age two], she was mute; she had an absolutely blank and unanimated facial expression, and she focused on nothing and nobody. She had no verbal language . . . She showed no response to people and acted as though she did not hear their voices . . . her neurological examination was completely negative" (p. 152).

In some respects Violet presents a picture similar to an undifferentiated newborn, a state of "normal autism." Her state is not so much regressed as it is detained; her fundamental evolutionary organization is in some respects similar to a newborn's. On the other hand, she is not a two-year-old who looks like a healthy two-month-old. Much more research is needed to understand what is really happening in these unsatisfactory embeddedness cultures. One imagines that the conditions of confirmation and contradiction which promote growth must be present at least to some extent in almost any situation, but that in situations of such dramatic insufficiency it is as if the organism must do its growing in an amniotic environment that barely protects it, that provides very little buoyancy and increases its brittleness, that provides very little nourishment and leaves it starved, that provides very little psychological oxygen and leaves its vitality impaired.

There is never just an infant, and even Violet has some kind of holding environment. She is struggling to survive, and it seems as if survival at this point is largely a matter of making the early moments of life survivable under such inadequate conditions of support. It seems as if she is so unready to deal with the next chapter of life, issues of differentiation promoted by the sense of contradiction (between the more perfectly responsive intrauterine environment and the less perfectly responsive extrauterine one) that she has gone into a defense against any information getting through. Information comes by means of interaction, and she seems to feel she would be in danger from any information. This is what is most dramatically different about Violet's autism and the normal undifferentiation of the infant. The picture of developmental detention—a two-year-old unwilling to communicate, a five-year-old unwilling to go off to school, an adolescent unwilling to eat—is, above all, one of an active attempt to resist the motion of life, the motion of evolution, which, to some extent, however attenuated, is proceeding even in these extremely impoverished circumstances. Violet differs most dramatically from a "healthy autistic" child (that is, a newborn) in that she is in pain, and her pain can be understood as the resistance to the motion of life, a resistance to her own life project. Her present psychological state is as much a reaction to this pain—an attempt to screen it out—as it is the cause of that pain. One reason that timely intervention is so crucial is this mutually exacerbating relationship between the causes of pain and the reactions to pain which in turn cause pain. The picture of Violet's circumstance with which we are left is that of a dramatically inadequate culture of embeddedness, one that does not adequately hold the child, and thus one from which she is unable to emerge and meet the next moments of life. As in every so-called psychotic circumstance, she is actively and uncompromisingly set against the motion of her own life.

This will not be our last picture of Violet. She was successfully treated, and the nature of her treatment will be of interest to us in Chapter 9. We will return not only to Violet, but to the whole notion of the naturally therapeutic function of a successful embeddedness culture. We will consider at that time whether there is not here a natural wisdom to guide the "unnatural" therapeutic practices of professional therapy and counseling.

The first function of the culture of embeddedness—its holding function—can be examined with respect not only to the fundamental question as to *whether* the infant is held, but to the question of *how* the infant is held. The radical impairment of the first function, the lack of an attachment, raises the most serious questions for the child's development, questions which often demand an address in the next few years of the child's life. Analogously, how the child is held or "hosted" may raise questions not of whether she will continue to function but of how she will. Among these questions, and following directly upon the discussion earlier in this chapter, one of the most important might be how the child comes to experience anxiety.[1]

How we feel about our feelings is certainly crucial to our life experience. Among the most costly of our emotional experiences, and among the most common of the feelings that counselors and therapists deal with, are the negative feelings we have about our negative feelings, the feelings we have about ourselves because we are feeling unsuccessful or out of control or anxious or confused. The assumption that our attitudes toward our feelings—how we feel about them and how we cope with them—are essentially socially derived gets supported and reconstructed by a constructive-developmental perspective. We learn to comfort ourselves from the way others comfort us, is the

1. I would like to acknowledge here that the discussion which follows owes much to conversations with Kiyo Morimoto.

way the social-derivation hypothesis usually goes. If we take seriously the notion of cultures of embeddedness, the notion of an evolutionary host, then the question is no longer whether the source is the individual or the environment, but how we are comforted by that with which we are "confused," that which we are taking to be a part of ourselves, that which is both organism and environment. Or, more specifically: How does the mother respond to the infant's anxiety?

The reader can engage this question more experientially by recalling those moments when she or he responds to an anxious person—a child crying, or an adult who has stopped in her tracks. The question is: What are we up to when we respond to anxiety? What are we trying to do? Are we trying to make a bad feeling go away? Are we trying to make it so he can go back to feeling the way he did before, so she can go back to what she was doing before? Is our response essentially to the anxiety or to the person who is feeling anxious? This is a subtle but critical distinction. The usual caring response to negative feelings is an attempt to relieve the feelings. This is a well-intentioned, humane, and understandable response, especially when the distressed person is one whom we love and would not like to see suffer for a single moment. It is also an extremely problematic response, and more so when it comes from the person's holding environment.

When a mother responds to anxiety with the intention to relieve it, she brings the culture of embeddedness to the defense of a given evolutionary state (the state of equilibrium) in opposition to another state (the state of disequilibrium). She directs herself to the individual (the current evolutionary organization) rather than to the person (the movement of evolution itself). She responds to the protection of made-meaning rather than to the experience of meaning-making. She contributes to the feeling that the anxiety is "not-me" or an alien experience—when in fact the anxiety is only not-the-me-I-have-been. It reconfirms the me-I-have-been at the expense of the me-I-am-becoming. From such experiences, what is the infant most likely to learn about the experience of being in disequilibrium?—that it is not-me, and that a not-me experience is to be corrected; that it is wrong and bad to be in disequilibrium; that the infant is just not himself.

How we respond to a person in anxiety is a fundamental question because it raises for us the question of who we believe the person to be. Who is he or she most fundamentally? When we respond not to the problem or relief of the problem but to the person in her experience of the problem, we acknowledge that the person is most of all a motion, a motion that neither we nor she can deny without cost, and a motion which includes experience of balance and imbalance, each as intrinsic to life, each a part of our integrity, each deserving of dignity and self-respect. When we respond to the person in her experience of pain rather than in order to relieve the pain, we testify to our faith in the trustworthiness of the motion of evolution, to our faith in the trustworthiness of life itself. At the same time that we enhance the "good-host" quality of the embeddedness culture—providing careful attention, recognition, confirmation, and company in the experience—we do not tighten a grip by creating a dependence on the host to solve or manage the experiences of disequilibrium. When we respond instead to relieving the pain, we communicate a basic lack of trust and move from *holding* the infant to *holding onto* the infant, an impediment to the process of separation.

The ability to remain present for another when he is anxious, to recognize and accept his anxiety, without ourselves becoming too anxious or immediately trying to relieve the anxiety, has long been understood to be a feature of competent professional psychological help. We need look no further than to the naturally therapeutic contexts of support (the cultures of embeddedness) to see why this is so. When a professional is addressing people old enough to mediate their interactions by language, it is the things one says and how one says them that best convey one's address to anxiety. How is this conveyed by the naturally therapeutic mother? I suspect that the infant reads the mother's reaction to his anxiety by the changes in her motions, sounds, and especially the musculature of her body. In the way we can talk literally of infancy themes that all the rest of life we will mean metaphorically—issues of losing and finding the object, issues of being in and out of balance, issues of being seen and not seen—the "holding environment" is here literally a matter of holding and carrying. Speech, after all, is in part a very subtle form of touch, and the naturally therapeutic mother "speaks" most influentially to her infant through physical touching, holding, carrying. The mother who can hold her infant unanxiously when the infant is itself anxious is giving her child a special gift. She is holding heartily at the same time that she is preparing the child to separate from her.

LETTING GO

The second function of a culture of embeddedness is that it must let go. Better yet, it should assist in the timely differentiation by which it becomes gradually less a part of the infant and eventually more that to which the child relates. I have already suggested that the seemingly countervailing demands upon a culture of embeddedness—that it be good both at holding on *and* at letting go—are not really opposed to each other. Healthy holding lays the stage for separation even as it meets, acknowledges, and accepts its guest. All the same, the shift from embeddedness to differentiation must be to some extent as difficult for the host as it is for the guest. Something is leaving, being lost. As with the question of how we respond to anxiety, the infant's bid for differentiation raises the question of whether we feel a stronger commitment or investment in the child's present state of development (the individual) or the motion of the developing child (the person).

In cases where the culture of embeddedness has serious difficulties letting go, some surrender of host-like functions has probably taken place, and the host seems to experience something like the child's experience of a loss of *self*. In such situations the evolutionary host is drawing upon the guest as if the guest were a culture of embeddedness for the host. The host is deriving a kind of support from the guest, as inappropriate to the context of natural therapy as it is in "unnatural" therapy, and as dangerous to the development of the client or guest.

The infant's differentiation—dramatically evident in its new capacities to move itself about, its emerging ability to stand up for itself and walk away—inevitably tests the evolutionary host's capacities for opposition and otherness. Erikson is eloquent on this theme, as he is on so many, in his discussions of the child's autonomy and the parents' reaction to it. "The kind and degree of a sense of autonomy which parents are able to grant their small children," he says, "depends on the dignity and sense of personal independence they derive from their own lives" (1968, p. 113).

Failure to assist the child in the natural "emergency" of its further becoming can take the form of holding too firmly, and of too emphatically or harshly stressing the separation. The latter can paradoxically have the effect of further complicating the tangle between the developing child and the human context in which it is embedded.

A mother whose own lack of nourishment has led her into too intense a nurturance for herself from the experience of nursing may find the prospect of the child's weaning a loss of unendurable proportion. Some part of her becomes invested in keeping the child a baby, and to that extent she is unwittingly moving against the life project of her young in behalf of her own survival. The mother and the baby are both in need of support. It may be that only a third party, fortuitously or designedly, can supply it.

The so-called borderline personality of later life is often attributed to early childhood impairments in what amounts to this second function of the culture of embeddedness. Although my own feeling is that adult "pathology" is as significantly related to the current evolutionary situation—including the performance of one's contemporary embeddedness culture—as it is to past experience, the depiction of the early childhood situation thought to contribute to a borderline character is a vivid example of problems in the second function, and is certainly unsupportive of the child's development at that time. Masterson (1976) considers a dynamic as follows: the mother encourages the child's dependency and discourages his emerging steps toward independence; she uses the baby to help ward off her own "abandonment depression"; the child experiences strongly that being gratified requires remaining fused, that separation is unsafe and ungratifying, that autonomy is about an end to gratification. The implication is that this kind of experience while the child is in the midst of separating, a project to which some part of the person must remain loyal, leaves the young child compromised. He must purchase his differentiation at the price of integration. He comes to experience closeness and being taken care of highly ambivalently—they are his fondest wish and his gravest nightmare.

Such experience in the first years may indeed be contributive to a borderline character in an adult. It may also be that such experience in the first years is more saliently related to ensuing problems in childhood which may or may not be resolved by adulthood, and that the borderline condition in adulthood is more strongly related to a somewhat similar, but developmentally more sophisticated impairment in the contemporaneous adult culture of embeddedness. I discuss this further in Chapter 7, which considers the emergence from embeddedness in interpersonalism.

REMAINING IN PLACE

The third function for the culture of embeddedness is that it remain in place during the period of transformation and re-equilibration so that what was a part of me and gradually becomes not-me can be successfully reintegrated as object or other of my new balance. Growth itself is not alone a matter of separation and repudiation, of killing off the past. This is more a matter of transition. Growth involves as well the reconciliation, the recovery, the recognition of that which before was confused with the self. This is the evolution of meaning, increasingly more encompassing meaning for ourselves and for the others with whom we live. As H. Richard Niebuhr put it, "We understand what we remember, remember what we forgot and make familiar what before seemed alien" (1941, p. 81). But in the early moments of being "made object" the embeddedness culture can experience itself as being "thrown over" (which, as we have said, is just what the word "object" means). It takes a special wisdom for the family of an adolescent to understand that by remaining in place so that the adolescent can have the family there to ignore and reject, the family is providing something very important, and is still, in a new way, intimately and importantly involved in the child's development. This special wisdom is intrinsic to many families, and its source is derived not from psychological experts but from nature itself. In a similar way, successful parents beset by the "terrible twos" understand in a way they probably cannot articulate that their child's negativism is not directed so much at them as at the child himself. The newly differentiating child has to oppose the culture of embeddedness to protect his fragile cleavage and to prevent his reincorporation.

It is exactly because the newly "thrown over" culture of embeddedness is as much the old me as the not-me that it must remain in place for the child herself to gradually redefine her relationship to it. For the culture to disappear at exactly the time when the child is experiencing a loss of herself is to leave the child with a kind of unrecoverable loss, a confirmation of her worst suspicions about the life project. We can call this "unhealthy" or "abnormal" simply because it is unnatural. That is, the normal experiences of evolution involve *recoverable* loss; what we separate from we find anew. What is unnatural is for a culture of embeddedness to "disappear," either through a kind of psychological withdrawal, or through the actual, *physical* loss of the caretaker during the critical period of transition, roughly nine to twenty-one months.

There is a distinguished literature concerning the risk of early childhood separation from the mother (Bowlby, 1973), notably in connection with the effects of hospitalization (Spitz, 1946; Robertson, 1958), war orphanage (Burlingham and Freud, 1942), and the risks of adoption at particular times (Offerd, 1969). The understanding of the child's difficulty, however, is usually couched in terms of the attachment relationship. Yet the evidence seems to indicate that the infant is not at high risk from a temporary separation until around six months. From our point of view, the risks to the infant of separation have to do not so much with issues of attachment as with issues of detachment, specifically the confounding of an *abnormal* detachment on the part of the embeddedness culture at the very period when the infant is undergoing its own *normal* detachment from the embeddedness culture. The result seems to be a sense of unrecoverable loss, the very experience which separates mourning (or grief) from melancholia (or depression). In a beautiful essay, Freud indicates how similar mourning and melancholia are (1917), with the one dramatic difference that the reproaches of melancholia seem to be directed at the self. Everyone agrees that the underlying substrate of depression is loss; from a constructive-developmental point of view it is related to complications in the loss of one's evolutionary balance. What we have lost is not an object but some part of ourselves which we ourselves are only beginning to make object.

When the embeddedness culture disappears at just the moment we are beginning to emerge from it, it may feel as if the evolutionary motion of separation is more a matter of our being thrown from, of our being rejected, of our being made object. The evolutionary valences can get reversed and the customary repudiations of the emerging object are replaced by the more disturbed, and disturbing, repudiations of the emerging self. It may be difficult to live with the negativism and willfulness of the child in her twos; but these are the difficulties of normal growth. A child's "no" to her parents is a declaration of her newly found distinctness from them and a protection against a reincorporation in them. It is a message to her old self which has become object, to that mothering one who before *was* the child and is now becoming someone she *has*. When the new balance is more secure, the child will no longer need to protest so much about what she is not. The image of the other-repudiating child and the difficulties she can cause those in her midst is one we will see again and again in ever more complex forms. Most of all, it is an image of evolution and its experience. Its most striking feature is its depiction of growth as involving more than a new relationship between self and other; it involves a new *construction* of self and other; it involves a redrawing of the line where I stop and you begin, a redrawing that eventually consists in a qualitatively new guarantee to you of your distinctness from me (permitting at the same time a qualitatively "larger" you with which to be in relation).

No "larger relation" can be looked forward to in the presence of a child who is repudiating not the self she has been, but the self she is becoming. Erikson's "tragic case of Jean" (1963) is an excellent example. She is six years old when Erikson meets her. Most of those her age are in the midst of another "natural emergency," which we will turn to in the next chapter. But though she is six, the evolution of Jean's meaning is closer to that of the transformations of infancy, and more than this she herself seems to be alienated from this transformation. Separated at nine months from her mother, who was recovering from tuberculosis, Jean spent the next five months outside her mother's care. Although we cannot know to what extent this loss caused Jean's ensuing inability to thrive in the world, we do know that she lost her mother at exactly the time she could be expected to have begun separating from the culturing of her mother. We know that this development (the emergence from complete embeddedness) *creates* the object world and that most children pursue and actively engage these other things and other people which have now come into being. And we know that Jean's relationship to things and people was tremendously fearful, as if the life movement which brought them into being was somehow against her will. We know that the creation of objects is intrinsic to the capacity to retain an image, to symbolize, and to develop language. And we know that Jean "turned against speech," as Erikson's reporter puts it; that, like most seriously disturbed children, she "repudiates her own sense organs as hostile and 'outside'" (p. 198). Again, it is as if somewhere in the developments of the first year she lost charge of life's motion and became herself its object. The question arises as to whether this is not because she lost herself (the mother confused with self) along the way. We know that in the normal course of this and every developmental transformation the emergence from embeddedness involves the "throwing away" of that in which I have been embedded, that the very word "object" refers to throwing away. But Jean herself feels thrown away; she is "outspokenly self punitive" and repeatedly asks, even literally, to be thrown away.

In one of Ovid's most "developmental" stories, Deucalion and Pyrrha are the only living persons on earth following the great flood. The world is at a new beginning and it falls to them to further its evolution. The gods exhort them to "throw the bones of your mother behind you." Although this sounds to them at first like a horrible desecration, they come to a more palatable interpretation. The gods, they decide, are referring to the earth; the earth is their mother, the earth that has held them, the earth over which they have lately floated. They pick up the boulders of the earth and throw them over their backs, and slowly, gradually, these turn to separate living forms, to persons, like themselves, with whom they will walk the earth.

The infant has survived a flood, lives in a world without separate others, and is responsive to the gods' exhortations to further the development of the world. Like Deucalion and Pyrrha, the healthy infant throws the bones of her mother behind her, and, in unearthing herself, creates others in the world with which she can be in relation. In the process she is especially sensitive to the earth tremors of her mother's brief departure, for these risk her balance. But should her mother actually disappear at this time, as she did with Jean, the very ground on which the child lives can seem to have given out, and the child may feel that it is she, rather than her mother's bones, who has been thrown behind.

FIVE

The Growth and Loss of the Impulsive Self

In the last chapter we looked closely at a major transformation in personality development, one which seems to occur roughly between nine and twenty-one months, and which leaves the person at its end somehow different in fundamental ways. These differences, I have suggested, are a matter of evolution, of the changing relationship of the organism to the "life-surround." The differences are not so much "in" the baby as in the very state of his relationship to his world, including his relationship to us. The differences we experience in our relationship to a growing person have much to do with the different person we ourselves have become in the organizing of the other. The transformations of infancy, and the themes of attachment and separation they evoke, are now well known in psychological literature. What we are about to see, as we begin an exploration of another equally fundamental evolutionary change, is that these themes retain their potency throughout our lives, and recur, not as attenuated reprisals of infancy, but as the next chapter in the life history of evolution (see Table 8).

Anyone who has spent time with both a four- or five-year-old and an eight- or nine-year-old cannot fail to take account of how different they seem, a difference which feels like more than just a child's "getting bigger," or continued psychological growth along the same

TABLE 8. The impulsive to imperial transformation

Diagram labels (helix of stages):

INTERINDIVIDUAL [5]

INTERPERSONAL [3]

INSTITUTIONAL [4]

IMPULSIVE [1]

IMPERIAL [2]

INCORPORATIVE [0]

Psychologics favoring inclusion

Psychologics favoring independence

	Stage 1 Impulsive	Stage 2 Imperial
Underlying structure (subject-object balance)	S— Impulses, perceptions O— Reflexes (sensing, moving)	S— Needs, interests, wishes O— Impulses, perceptions
Piaget	Preoperational	Concrete operational
Kohlberg	Punishment and obedience orientation	Instrumental orientation
Loevinger	Impulsive	Opportunistic
Maslow	Physiological satisfaction orientation	Safety orientation
McClelland/Murray	—	Power orientation
Erikson	Initiative vs. guilt	Industry vs. inferiority

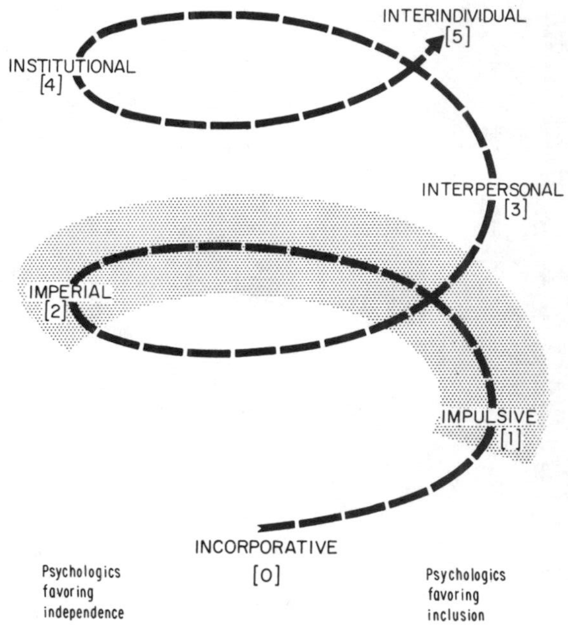

Evolutionary balance and psychological embeddedness	Culture of embeddedness	Function 1: Confirmation (holding on)	Function 2: Contradiction (letting go)	Function 3: Continuity (staying put for reintegration)	Some common natural transitional "subject-objects" (bridges)
(1) IMPULSIVE Embedded in: impulse and perception.	Typically, the family triangle. *Parenting culture.*	Acknowledges and cultures exercises of fantasy, intense attachments, and rivalries.	Recognizes and promotes child's emergence from egocentric embeddedness in fantasy and impulse. Holds child responsible for his or her feelings, excludes from marriage, from parents' bed, from home during school day, recognizes child's self-sufficiency and asserts own "other sufficiency."	Couple permits itself to become part of bigger culture, including school and peer relations. High risk: dissolution of marriage or family unit during transition period (roughly 5-7 yrs.).	Medium of 1-2 transition: *imaginary friend.* A repository for impulses which before *were* me, and which eventually will be part *of* me, but here a little of each. E.g., only I can see it, but it is not me.
(2) IMPERIAL Embedded in: enduring disposition, needs, interests, wishes.	*Role recognizing culture.* School and family as institutions of authority and role differentiation. Peer gang which requires role-taking.	Acknowledges and cultures displays of self-sufficiency, competence, and role differentiation.	Recognizes and promotes preadolescent's (or adolescent's) emergence from embeddedness in self-sufficiency. Denies the validity of only taking one's own interests into account, demands mutuality, that the person hold up his/her end of relationship. Expects trustworthiness.	Family and school permit themselves to become secondary to relationships of shared internal experiences. High risk: family relocation during transition period (roughly early adolescence, 12-16).	Medium of 2-3 transition: *chum.* Another who is identical to me and real but whose needs and self-system are exactly like needs which before *were* me, eventually a part *of* me, but now something between.

plane. The older child seems to be functioning on a qualitatively different plane. She is not only physically larger, but seems physically more "organized," more "tightly wrapped." The younger child has a hard time sitting still for any length of time, is continuously moving into and out of spaces with little predictability, and has a short attention span for any activity involving accommodations to others; the older child seems capable of adult-like forms of physical patience, "motoric propriety," and perseverance. The difference, most palpable and dramatic on a physical scale, is to be seen over and over again on a score of more subtle dimensions. The younger child uses language as an appendage or companion to her means of self-presentation and social intercourse; for the older child, language is the very medium of interaction, central to the social presentation of the self. The younger child's life is filled with fantasy and fantasy about the fantastic (being Spiderman); the older child has taken an interest in things as they are and fantasy life is about things that actually could be (being a doctor). The younger child will engage her parents in the middle of a conversation that she has already started on her own, as if she has trouble keeping track of which portions of a conversation she has actually had with you and which she has only imagined with you, or as if she takes it for granted that her private thinking is as public and monitored as her spoken thinking; the older child never does this, and, indeed, in her cultivation of a sense of privacy and self-possession she seems to have "sealed up" this psychic cavity.

The earlier chapters on Piaget and Kohlberg suggested other examples of the difference. Younger children seem to take their idiosyncratic perceptions of an object as the object itself; this physical plasticity is absent in the older children, who seem to distinguish between a change in their perceptions and a change in the object. Younger children make decisions of right and wrong on the basis of what an outside authority deems to be right and wrong, and orient in their thinking to the consequences of an act; the older children make decisions of right and wrong on the basis of what benefits themselves and orient to the intentions which underlie the consequences. Finally, there are those differences between the younger and older child, which, whatever their meaning, will probably be forever associated with Freud: the younger child is often intensely involved with both the opposite-sex parent (as a favorite) and the same-sex parent (as a rival for the attentions of the favorite); the older child seems to be much less involved in this charged, triangular relationship.

In 1920 a young Swiss psychologist went to an International Psychoanalytic Congress in Vienna and gave a paper with Sigmund Freud
in attendance. The paper discussed a kind of thinking that seemed to
be neither Freud's infantile "primary process" nor the logical, reality-
oriented thought Freud called "secondary process." As far as the Swiss
psychologist could tell, this different kind of thinking occurred right
between the development of primary and secondary thinking, between
infancy and latency, the era Freud called the oedipal period. It was a
highly intuitive, representational, fantasy-filled, imagistic, free-
floating, associationistic kind of thinking, just the kind of thinking
that was encouraged in the practice of psychoanalysis. Since the
therapeutic approach, with its orientation to free association and fantasy and image, was getting people to think in a mode natural to that
of the oedipal-age child, perhaps this was why—the psychologist suggested—oedipal issues were what so often arose. The young Swiss
psychologist, of course, was Jean Piaget, and the kind of thinking he
was talking of he later called preoperational thought. Freud is reported
to have been fascinated by the paper, but there is no evidence that the
meeting led to anything significant for the thinking of either man. It
appears to be one of those numerous crossings in intellectual history
where what would seem to us, in retrospect, to be a fertile match,
turns out not to be. Perhaps this is due in part to the lack of an integrating context, a broader soil in which the insights of both can be
firmly rooted.

In this chapter I want to consider to what extent these apparently
universal and disparate phenomena of childhood might find a unified
accounting in an understanding of a specific transformation in the
evolution of meaning. It is the transformation in which the person
emerges from an embeddedness in the impulses and perceptions, and
from a special adult-child relationship which cultures that embeddedness.

If the earlier transformation (from stage 0 to stage 1) is about the
birth of the object, this next transformation (from 1 to 2) might be
called the birth of the role. Certainly both cognitive-developmental
and psychodynamic understandings of this shift center on an acquisition of "role," although they seem to be speaking of two quite
different phenomena. Cognitive-developmentalists point to the emerging capacity to "take the role" of another, to see that others have a
perspective of their own. Psychoanalytically oriented theorists point to

the processes of oedipal resolution and identification by which the child gives up its impossible hopes for the opposite-sex adult and takes on the social role of a child—a child who will grow up to be an adult, a child in relation to parents. Both of these reconstructions of the self may be the consequence of a single motion in personality development, the evolution of meaning. Among the most striking themes emerging from the specific instances of this childhood transformation is a sense of the young person taking himself in hand, a move toward a kind of cognitive, affective, interior, and behavioral self-sufficiency which was not there before. An evolutionary association that comes to mind is the move from an exoskeletal form to an endoskeletal one. The child's structure seems to "come inside," to be covered over, rather than being constantly open and somehow shared with the world. What would psychodynamically be referred to as "internalization" is, from the constructive-developmental point of view, the evolutionary process by which that which was subject gets taken as object and integrated into a new subjectivity. This new subjectivity can "internalize" perceptions, can coordinate one perception with another, and can thus see that an object has not changed its physical properties just because it looks different to us; it can integrate two different impulses at the same time and so experience ambivalence; it can integrate the same impulses across time and so construct "enduring dispositions" (needs and interests), "ways I tend to be"—that is, a notion of myself. As a toddler, in conquering the object and in filling my language with "me" and "mine," I am expressing my sense *that* I am; but as a seven-year-old, in conquering the role, I am developing a sense of *what* I am, a self with properties that persist through time.

Central to this evolution, as to all, is a specific loss. At the time that we can say the child's transformation involves the creating of a self-sufficiency, we must also say it involves the discovery of the "other-sufficiency" of the world. The physical object which before had so much to do with me that my changing perception of it occasioned its very change is now seen to have an existence of its own. A human being who before had so much to do with me that I imagined his vantage point on the world was the same as mine is now seen to have a perspective of his own. Viewed from the outside the child is moving from a fantasy orientation to a reality orientation; the child is growing; the evolution of meaning is the career of the truth; it resolves qualitatively better guarantees to the world of its distinct integrity.

But the evolution of meaning is also experienced by the evolving person, and the same process involves the loss of a very special involvement with the objects and others which the child himself discovered only a few years ago as a result of the last great upheaval in his evolution of meaning.

What we speak of descriptively as the process of differentiation may involve for the child a growing disappointment and disillusionment with an object world which, the child comes to see, does *not* have so much to do with him that its very poses and purposes are a function of his own. An infant discovers that there is a world separate from him; but not until years later does the child discover that this separate world is not subject to him. In bringing his impulses and perceptions under his own regulation, the child creates a self that he sees as distinct and in business for itself; in its fullest flush of confidence this is the bike-riding, money-managing, card-trading, wristwatch-wearing, pack-running, code-cracking, coin-collecting, self-waking, puzzle-solving nine- or ten-year-old known to us all. But in its first fragile moments on the scene, this is as likely to be a six-year-old who is more struck by the reciprocal reality—that other people, too, are in business for themselves, have "enduring dispositions" of *their* own, and, however much they love him or seem to, are not regulated by, indeed are not even perfectly attuned to, his longings for satisfaction, comfort, relief, embrace. The cognitivist's "learning to take the role of the other" and the analyst's "giving up the oedipal wishes" both find a reading in this same evolutionary transformation.

From a constructive-developmental point of view, the oedipal drama—its intense parental relationships, rivalrous and romantic; its disappointment; and its resolution—is chiefly about the experience of an even more fundamental relationship than that of parent and child. It is about the investment in, and reconstruction of, an evolutionary truce; about the growth and loss of *oneself* (with whom the parents have been confused) and one's fundamental relatedness to the world. Like the infant's attachment and separation from her mother, the oedipal drama is the era-specific enactment of a process which continues throughout development. When that process recurs, as it will in most lives, it may not be the oedipal drama that is recurring but the next act of the drama of evolution itself. Like the anxiety of the twelve-month-old infant, which may be about the loss of his balance with the world more than it is about the loss of his mother, the five-year-old's anxiety may be about more than the ungovernability of his impulses (monsters, nightmares, and phobias); it may be about the very separation from himself which raises the possibility of impulses being governed in the first place.

Freud's famous scene, then—about which he said modestly, "Were my work to have given nothing to mankind but knowledge of the oedipal period, this alone would be enough to insure its place in the history of civilization"—turns out to be neither an inoperable relic of Victorian Vienna nor primarily about the vicissitudes of childhood sexuality. What Freud seems to have located is the *second* extrauterine amniotic sac, or holding environment, or embeddedness culture; a human medium which carries the evolutionary "subjectivity"—in this case the embeddedness in the impulses—and more or less assists in the birth of the new personality which issues from it.

Unlike the infant who confuses the working of his own reflexes and sensing and moving with that of his culture of embeddedness (the mothering one), the young child recognizes there is a world separate from him, but confuses the workings of his own impulses with that of *his* culture of embeddedness—a family of other people. The child is now able to see others as distinct from him, but his conception of an "other" is still radically different from an adult's conception. One of the most hard-to-keep-hold-of pictures this framework presents is that a person's evolution *intrinsically* creates anew "the other" with which the person can be in relation, that as a person evolves those of us around him become something fundamentally different to him. Crucial to the change is that the person confuses us less with himself—and not quantitatively less, but qualitatively less. For the young child, other people are confused with the satisfaction or thwarting of his impulses.

While it seems to benefit us little to think of the young child as wanting to have a parent as a lover, it is edifying to consider that the only social context available to a small child in which to be embedded in his impulses *is* the family; that his mode of loving, like anything else, is a function of his meaning-making; that his ability to get his impulses satisfied must in some way be thwarted, at least in part, by the reality that he is not getting all the attention; and that by this means the culture of embeddedness naturally performs the twin functions of confirmation and contradiction, which both securely hold, and, in timely fashion, assist in the emergence of, the developing person.

While from this point of view it is misleading and backward to imagine that a child's impulse life springs from an attraction to the opposite-sex parent, it is plausible to consider that, in fusing with the embeddedness culture, she finds one parent the more likely vehicle by which to satisfy her many impulses than the other, and, as she experiences the imperfect fate of this wish, to identify the other parent, or, indeed, siblings, as a rivalrous thwarter of her satisfaction. Despite the popular penchant for notions of "splitting" in infancy—the baby's presumed sense of a good and bad mother, eventual resolution of her into a single object neutralizing erotic and aggressive impulses — it is simply not developmentally justified to presume this complexity in a newborn. (Clearly *some* psychodynamic speculation must be adjusted in light of what is now known about the timetable of the developmental processes which that theory addresses. For example, the oedipal period cannot be placed in years three to five, as the old wisdom would have it; it reaches its peak during these years, but its "resolution"—that is, the evolution which resolves it—goes on in the next two to three years.) Indeed, the young child's orientation to one parent as her means to impulse satisfaction and the other (or others) as impulse inhibitors is a direct consequence of even a three-year-old's inability to successfully integrate hero and villain in a single person. The result is a feeling for a single person that she can never quite feel again—a feeling of unmediated, unqualified, unbounded yearning to be completely cared for in the company of this other person who is distinct from her and yet knows her completely—body, mind, heart, and soul.

Although this feeling can never be satisfied (a central Freudian theme), it demands respect and nurturance; it defines who the person *is* at this moment in her evolution, and—perhaps most important—it is in a way no *more* "impossible" than any of the subjectivities at the heart of later evolutionary truces. The capacity of the favored parent to receive this love (and of the unfavored parent sympathetically to play an unsympathetic role) is crucial to the first function of the next culture of embeddedness—to hold securely. In recognizing, enjoying, and confirming the young person's displays of closeness, the favored parent is not so much fanning the flames of an inappropriate love affair (the unfortunate sexualized inheritance of the Freudian legacy) as he or she is fanning the flames of the life project itself, nurturing the vitality of the organism's very activity of knowing and meaning, as much a support to its mind as to its emotions. As the organism grows, its culture of embeddedness becomes more complex, involves more people in ever more complex arrangements, and sets new tests and challenges for those persons and institutions which would sponsor the evolution of the species. If the infant tests the capacities of a mothering one to hold and let go of someone who has been so dependent, the young child puts strains on the marriage itself, for the culture has widened to the family. Of course, the arrival of a newborn is itself a test for a couple, but the greater complexity of the young child intrudes on the couple's dynamics intrinsically, not secondarily. Hurtful as it might feel to the unfavored parent, especially to a mother who has enjoyed so close a relationship to this young person when she was more baby than girl, it is important for the unfavored parent to understand that he or she is not without a crucial role; it is just a different role. And in the end this "carrier of contradiction" represents the protection to the child against an overholding, an eventual support for that slowly emerging side which will ultimately let the child parent himself or herself.

The early years of childhood have enormous appeal to most grownups. We often find ourselves lamenting the passing of the fantasy-filled child for the more stereotypic responses of the older child who has become concerned with the correspondence of his productions to "reality." Even physically we find the older child less cute. It is possible that what we mourn most of all is the passing once again of a yearning, ever reawakable within us, to be perfectly cared for and protected, comforted and held by a bigger and stronger presence than ourselves. The two greatest yearnings of human life, I have suggested, may be the yearning for inclusion (to be welcomed in, next to, held, connected with, a part of) and the yearning for distinctness (to be autonomous, independent, to experience my own agency, the self-chosenness of my purposes). These yearnings are in obvious tension, and the history of development is a succession of temporary resolutions in favor first of one side, then the other. Every evolutionary truce sets the terms on differentiation and integration, which is only a cold way of saying the same thing. The impulsive balance (balance 1) is a temporary resolution on behalf of integration; its central hopes and yearnings are hopes about the other. The balance to come, on the other side of the five to seven shift, on the other side of the oedipal crisis, is a temporary resolution on behalf of differentiation. The sealed-up, self-sufficient, competency-oriented child is a function of a balance whose central hopes and yearnings are about the self. This shift from an overly integrated balance to an overly differentiated one is repeated later in life, usually in late adolescence or early adulthood (the shift from the interpersonal balance to the institutional one, balance 3 to balance 4); again, it is not that adolescence is a replay of the oedipal relationship, as psychoanalytic theory would suggest, as it is that the two periods have common evolutionary features.

How the small child navigates this first growth and loss of a full-blown yearning for inclusion must certainly have consequences for its future orientation to this side of life's motion. What is learned at this juncture in development about allowing oneself to have apparently unfulfillable hopes and longings, for example? Surely this allowance is crucial to the future exercise of creativity and originality, to an experience of vibrancy, brilliance, adventure about life. In undergoing this transformation, the person is faced with the need to take leave of his or her young child; the question is where the child goes. Do we differentiate without ever successfully reintegrating, in which case the child may get lost and an overdifferentiated, over-adult, "realopathic" quality may take over? Do we never successfully differentiate, in which case an overintegrated, loose-boundaried, "pretend adult" style may get its start?

And how the small child navigates this evolutionary growth and loss, as with every period, must surely be related to how he is received, nurtured, and contradicted by the culture which holds him. In a moment we will look more particularly at specific functions and dysfunctions of this culture of embeddedness, but I would like to say a word first about its important male-female nature. Although I will not take the reader through the thorny topic of sex-role identification (Miller and Dollard, 1941; Sears, Rau, and Albert, 1965; Kohlberg, 1966; Maccoby, 1966; Bandura, 1969; Mischel, 1970; Kaplan and Sedney, 1980), it is of course no accident that the time when the developing child comes to have a sense of itself as male or female is the same time the culture which holds it has become ambisexual as well. The issue I do want to raise here is not so much about the child's sex-role development as that of the parents who provide its culture. It is arguable that the roles parents play at this time in the child's development are in part human embodiments for the child of each of the two fundamental yearnings which the child itself experiences. Certainly in the impulse-embedded state it seems reasonable to consider that the favored parent is the very representation of inclusion/integration. And it seems possible that as the agent of differentiation, and the model upon whom the self-sufficiency of the next balance is set, the formerly unfavored parent is an embodiment of differentiation. By such an analysis fathers and mothers are called upon to personify both sides of this enduring tension, depending upon whether their child is a boy or girl. And yet if anything can be safely said about personality differences between men and women, it is that, in our present state of evolution, neither sex is well equipped to play both roles. Men have tended toward overdifferentiation and women toward overintegration, a tendency which may reproduce itself in the very amniotic environment we are presently exploring. By such an analysis young girls are calling upon their fathers to be representatives of their yearning for inclusion, a role in which many men are disappointing; and upon their mothers as models of differentiation, a role in which many women may be disappointing. When it comes to identification with the same-sex parent, boys are likely to be overserved and girls underserved in support of the autonomy-oriented self-sufficiency of the imperial balance. We will return to the implications of this line of thinking for a new conception of wholesome male and female adulthood later in this chapter and again in Chapter 8.

While Freud's oedipal drama captures some of the important features of this second culture of embeddedness, it is misleading to imagine that it captures all of them. Not all impulsive activity is conveyed through the family romance; siblings as well as the same-sex parent serve as the harbingers of contradiction; the opposite-sex parent is not solely involved with holding and the same-sex parent is not solely involved with assisting in letting go. Indeed, one of the most important functions of this culture is to set limits on the child's behavior, a task best performed by both parents who in joining ranks assist the child in the gradual recognition of the appropriate boundaries between himself and his parents, eventually between himself and his own impulses. A couple which cannot close ranks—which, for example, is fraught with its own discord, one side of which tends to take on the child as an ally—inevitably makes a greater investment in whom the child has become than in the child as a growing and changing process.

Limit-setting, so crucial in this period, is a classic instance of a culture's necessary communication of contradiction, in this case contradicting the confusion of the child's impulses with those around her. "Without contraries," William Blake said, "there is no progression." But the contraries which a successful culture of embeddedness provides must reflect the internal contradictions in the developing person's own meaning-making. The best limit-setting (at any stage in development) is not merely about prevention, control, or the application of authority; it is about the exercise of just those preventions, controls, or authorities which we can reasonably assume the developing person to next take over on her own. In this way, effective limit-setting both recognizes who the child is and who the child is becoming, embracing an ambivalence which at the moment is "projected" (the subjectivity of any evolutionary balance) and which eventually will be "internalized" (the integrated object).

I felt myself the recipient of this graceful form of limit-setting recently when trying to avoid a visit to the University Health Services. I had a sore throat and "knew" that all I needed was some penicillin. I didn't want to march down to the Health Services building, sit in a waiting room with a bunch of other miserable people, and finally see a doctor, only to get a prescription which he or she could have phoned to my neighborhood druggist without my getting out of bed. The Health Service, of course, frowns on laymen phoning in requests for their own medication. Our conversation went something like this:

Me:	. . . so I wonder if you could just phone the prescription in.
Nurse:	Yes, I see. Listen, I hope you don't mind my asking, but, are you a doctor?
Me:	No, I'm not.
Nurse:	But you'd really like to avoid the hassle of coming down, and waiting, and stuff like that? [Question X]
Me:	Exactly.
Nurse:	Well, let me ask you one more thing: Why are you settling for such amateur medical attention? [Question Y]

Of course, there is something about this that is too cute, but its structure is illustrative. In her questions X and Y she is really addressing two quite different sides of me. In the first speech she recognizes the side which is presenting itself, the side that wants to take care of this and be its own doctor. So she does not simply ignore this side; she lets me know she sees this. But in the last speech she speaks to another side of me which I have not presented—not the side that is trying to do the doctoring, but the side that is the patient. And, of course, however much she respects my first side, she is quite clear that her primary loyalty is to the patient side and seeing that this side gets the best care it can. While she is exercising her authority and, if I do not get the message, will more bluntly control and prevent, she is taking pains to recognize all of me, and to champion one side which she feels is being ignored. And to the extent that that side is my developmental leading edge, her limit-setting is not authoritarian but authoritative. Whether in fact we can really push this example so far as to say it speaks to my own developmental predicament is not clear.[1]

As the young child begins the differentiation from her old impulse-bound self, she fairly cries out for the support of a culture which will bridge the self-she-has-been and the self-she-is-becoming. One day when my daughter was five or six, she came into the house after she had been playing with an older girlfriend who lived across the street. I was in the living room, which is not in the line of sight between the front door and the stairs leading up to the bedrooms. Although I heard her come in I could not see her, and if she had wished she could very easily have gone straight up to her room. Instead she sought me out, though since I was involved in something I was reading, I did not engage her and took her quiet shuffling around my chair as aimlessness. In fact, she was trying to initiate a conversation of the most difficult sort, and when I finally tuned into it, unaccustomed, I suppose, to a kind of talk from her that did not make its little hungers explicitly and insistently known, she was saying something like this: "You see this toy? I—uhh—found it right in the street between Janie's house and our house. Some kid must have just lost it. [The toy, some kind of interesting-looking puzzle, did not look at all as if it had been lying in a street.] Since it's lost and there's no way of finding out who it belongs to I guess I can just keep it. I mean, I guess, it can just be mine. Ahh—isn't it strange that it was just lying there in the street? And that it doesn't belong to anybody, and, ahh—"

She went on this way, standing by my chair, not really looking at

1. Though, as I look at it now, a case could be made that in inviting me to shift my focus from the continued smooth-running of the supposedly self-sufficient psychological organization that is my (old) self, to a focus on caring for that organization both by myself (to come) and by others, it is essentially an address to stage 4; see Chapter 8.

me, turning the toy around in her hands. She did not seem at all eager to end this interaction and looked like she would have gone on for as long as it would take for me to figure out what she was really saying, and what she was really asking for, which was, of course, that she had stolen the toy from her girlfriend, and that she wanted me to know about it and help her with the turmoil she was feeling over it. I take this as classically transitional behavior for a child moving out of the impulsive balance. Had she been firmly embedded she would have had no trouble acting on her impulse like the good little cookie monster she had for so many years been ("Want cookie! Take cookie!"). (The Cookie Monster on "Sesame Street" is a brilliant character for the balance 1 and 1-2 transitional children at which the show is aimed, because he embodies the raw impulsiveness which they are just beginning to differentiate themselves from, and while they can take a sneaking comradely satisfaction in his uncontrollable urges, they can also practice publicly the condescension and scoffing that is directed his way. The key is that he is both monstrous and unterrifying.) Had my daughter been firmly embedded in her impulses, she would not be directing my attention to how she got the toy and the legitimacy of her keeping it; she would just be playing with it. Had she been firmly embedded in the *next* balance, she would not be engaged in such a conversation either. She would be able to *have* the impulse rather than *be* it, and experience herself as jealous, which might be enough to keep her from having to take it; or she would purposely and planfully steal it (not as an exercise of impulsiveness but need-embedded self-sufficiency), and she would quite intentionally get herself upstairs to hide her booty away before I saw her. But she neither played with the toy nor hid it away. Instead she came to look for a parent, and sought to initiate what I suggest is the hardest kind of conversation, because rather than meeting the first requirement of human interaction—the presentation of a coherent self—her conversation is about the very inability to be any longer coherent; she is presenting instead two selves, not because she is crazy, but because she is evolving. Some part of her no doubt wanted me to confirm her ruse, to celebrate with her in her good fortune at finding so attractive a toy. But when we were able to share together that she had taken it, and talked about how much she wanted it, and how jealous she felt, and about how embarrassing it was going to be returning it, she seemed to experience the kind of relief a person feels when a private emergency has been recognized by another. Children need limits, we say; but what they need most of all is a kind of intimate participation in their personal experience of evolution, an experience which at times involves a natural "emergency"—the emergence from the self I have been.

Many of the most common psychological problems in this age seem related to the natural evolutionary circumstances of emerging from an embeddedness in the impulses. Enuresis, encopresis, masturbation—all quite natural and unconcerning in early childhood—are problematic in a seven-year-old, but generally *not* because the child is still embedded in the old balance of early childhood. Were the seven-year-old still there in his development, he would not be bothered by his inability to control his bladder or bowels. The picture seems more commonly to be one of a child who has begun to separate from the impulses, but lacks sufficient capacity to integrate them (coordinate or control them) into a new balance. Thus the child is faced with the fundamental inability to keep his own balance or make his relationship to the world cohere. Nightmares and fears of bogeymen in the dark may also be a function of having loosed oneself from one's impulses, only to have them now uncontrolled and capable of coming after one. The particular monsters and agonies may reflect specific unruly, unacceptable feelings, or they may reflect on the frightening side of the evolutionary predicament in general. What must be most frightening, having begun the emergence, is the risk of losing oneself, one's new fragile, emerging self, through reincorporation or captivation by the impulses. The theme of being eaten alive is particularly salient, as in the story of one small child whose particular image may betray her capacity to take the role of the monster as much as its victim: she feared a monster "with a thousand eyes in its throat so it can see you when it eats you!" What is most important, by this analysis, is to see that nightmares or fears of the dark or a recurrence of problems with toilet control are not in themselves cause for alarm; they are a part of the natural phenomenology of evolutionary change. It is when they persist, are particularly intense, cause the child prolonged discomfort, or impair his or her capacity to interact with the world that we would begin to be concerned. But again, our concern would be expressed in terms of an understanding of normal processes of development. Why aren't they proceeding? Why are the impulses experienced as so unmanageable? Why does the fear of them seem to be so great? These questions often direct us to that human context which cultures the child's evolution.

The classic clinical problem of this age period—school phobia—gets a new reading in light of just this kind of analysis. School phobia, among the most common difficulties of children who find their way to clinics and mental health practitioners, is a fear of going to school, an unwillingness to leave the home during school hours. According to Waldfogel, Coolidge, and Hahn:

> It is invariably accompanied by somatic symptoms, usually involving the gastrointestinal tract, but sometimes including such diverse symptoms as sore throat, headache, or leg pains. The somatic complaints are used as a device to remain at home, and often disappear once the child is assured that he does not have to attend school. The most typical picture is that of a child nauseated and vomiting at breakfast or complaining of abdominal pain, resisting all attempts at reassurance, reasoning, or coercion to get him to school. Often other phobic symptoms may accompany the fear of school—fear of animals, fear of noises, night terrors. (1957, p. 754).

When a culture of embeddedness fails to perform what we said was its second basic function (timely letting go), it evokes negatively the three central themes which we saw in infancy. We said that the transitional infant (balance 0–balance 1) physically experiences the tension of being seen or unseen (worked out, for example, in peekaboo), being in balance or feeling unbalanced (as in learning to walk), and finding or losing the object (as in countless games with hidden toys). These themes, here experienced physically, may actually be manifestations of evolutionary transition itself and seem to be raised, in an abstracted way, at every fundamental renegotiation of the evolutionary truce. An embeddedness culture which fails to serve as a bridge in time of transition leaves the emergency one has become dangerously unseen and out of balance, and—perhaps of most importance to the matter of school phobia—it leaves one with the experience that growth involves an unrecoverable loss. The family has been the stuff of the old embeddedness (of my impulses, and, even more, the very self I have been). The family's failure to let itself become the object of a new balance (and its unwitting collusion in defending the old balance) raises the specter that growth must involve the very loss of myself (and my family with which that old self is entangled).

Modern American institutional life forces a physical separation of the child from the culture of the family at around the age of five or six by its regulation of schooling according to chronological age. A physical separation *can* assist a psychobiological separation, and the quasi-familial nature of kindergarten, for example, can serve as a gradual diversification of the culture of embeddedness. But a physical separation is not to be equated with a psychobiological separation, and some children of the appropriate calendar age are unready for the move, just as some families are unready to relinquish an exclusive role in the culturing of the child's evolution.

The case of Elizabeth (Waldfogel, Coolidge, and Hahn, 1957) may be illustrative of a family which has become entrenched both in culturing the child's impulse embeddedness and the romantic triangle in which such embeddedness often results:

> . . . Elizabeth plunged into the seductive relationship with her father, and her pleasure in taking mother's place, and gave indications of being under a high degree of strain. The mother, who was still dealing in her interviews with the daily tribulations about school, was confronted quite directly with our belief that Elizabeth was under considerable sexual tension. With this as an aid and with implicit permission, mother proceeded to deal with this area and gradually revealed an important part of her own past and present. It quickly became apparent to her that Elizabeth's difficulty in falling asleep seemed related to father's early bed hours. Elizabeth remained awake until father retired and then, complaining of being lonely, would climb into bed with him, where she was readily received. Mother, sitting downstairs alone, also felt lonely. She felt her husband could stay downstairs a little longer with her, but was powerless to express her wishes. She heard Elizabeth and her father laugh and giggle upstairs but could recognize neither the seductive relationship between them nor the mounting sexual tension in her daughter.
>
> Although mother could discuss sexual matters with adults in a matter-of-fact way, she felt confused and anxious with Elizabeth and was unable to give her any sex education. Once having recognized what was taking place and how sexually aroused Elizabeth became, she began to assume more authority as a mother and effectively put a stop to the acting out in which all three were involved.
>
> Miss Gray, Elizabeth's unsympathetic teacher, openly blamed Elizabeth and another girl for making her sick with a skin rash. Elizabeth told how upsetting this had been and mentioned how furious she often had felt toward Miss Gray. Although she could not accept the interpretation that she had been fearful that Miss Gray's ill-

ness could have resulted from her thoughts, she did concede that she sometimes wished mother to be the victim of a minor catastrophe, such as breaking her ankle. It was suggested that this was why, then, she needed to remain close to mother, so that she could be sure nothing would happen to her as a consequence of her hostile thoughts. Elizabeth again denied this connection but immediately changed the subject, the new topic itself obviously associated with the root of her hostility toward mother. "There is something going through my mind. It was a trick I played on father. I sneaked up and unfastened his suspenders. He chased me and we had a lot of excitement and a lot of fun." She finally agreed with the therapist that she and her father were sweethearts, but hastened to add that he could get angry, too, and she wasn't sure she preferred father to mother.

The next week Elizabeth was reluctant to come and needed to be reassured by her therapist before she would join him in the interview room. She then reported a dream. The atom bomb dropped in bed. She awoke terrified, calling for mother. She felt afraid of being alone and mother quickly came into her single bed. It was crowded. Elizabeth complained to mother, who reportedly told her she could take mother's place in father's bed. This Elizabeth did. "Father and I talked and did all sorts of things and had a real good time." The doctor echoed her frequent wish to exchange places with her mother. Elizabeth agreed, "Oh yes, I would tell her," and gesticulating violently with her fists, "and when I have children, I'll make them go to school. If they don't, I'll march them there and make them stay." It was interpreted that she was angry at mother for not being firmer, as well as for standing in her way. The theme that something might happen to mother as a consequence of these thoughts was again broached. The next week Elizabeth proudly announced she had returned to school. (pp. 768-769)

The general picture of the parent-child relationship when a child is afraid of going to school is one of overinvolvement on the part of one or both parents. Rather than any communication of contradiction or facilitation of differentiation, one finds an incapacity to set limits, a refusal to punish, an inability to acknowledge or express feelings of anger at one's child. More than this "nondifferentiating" stance, one finds, as in Saxon's cartoon (see Figure 5), an overinvested "integrating" stance that expresses itself in a kind of child-centeredness gone wild: "The entire pattern of child rearing in this group reflects the mother's subservience to her child. She is determined that there

"Christopher has never been treated unkindly by adults. He trusts us implicitly. I hope, Miss Forbes, you won't in any way betray that trust."

Figure 5   Drawing by Saxon; © 1975 The New Yorker Magazine, Inc.

shall be no deprivation of either his physical or emotional needs and constantly sacrifices her own comfort and convenience to his. Thus, one mother, who had to sit with her son every day in kindergarten, stated resignedly that she did not mind as long as it was for his good" (Waldfogel, Coolidge, and Hahn, 1957, p. 757). In the same study, fathers, too, are seen as overinvolved, either joined with the mother or competing with the mother for primacy in the nurturant role.

Although both the psychoanalytic and the constructive-developmental perspectives view this parental picture as contributory to the school-phobic child's difficulty, the two perspectives have somewhat different notions as to why that is so, and what a more wholesome picture would look like. Waldfogel and his colleagues find the children in their study confused about their own sexual identity, and the researchers attribute the children's bisexual conflicts to the failure of the parents (especially the fathers) to provide clearly distinct parental roles. The implication is that mothers should stick to their role as the supporter and model of the yearning for inclusion, connection, and integration; and fathers should stick to theirs as the champions of agency, autonomy, and differentiation. But it is arguable that the child's bisexual confusion and failure to make a distinction about himself or herself are not primarily a reflection of the parents' failure to differentiate their roles from each other, as it is their failure to deal with both sides of the fundamental tension within themselves. Children may be less confused about their sexual identity when parents clearly polarize themselves (vis-à-vis the inclusion/autonomy tension), but it is arguable that such polarization at precisely the time in the developmental life of the child when he or she is becoming able to integrate various facets into a single construction of self or other, encourages the overdifferentiated and overintegrated quality of modern masculinity and femininity, respectively. Psychoanalytic theory argues for a clear role difference between parents as if sexual identity is tied to role performance. Among the characteristics of mature adulthood from a constructive-developmental point of view (see Chapter 8) is the capacity to see oneself as a man or woman without fear of acknowledging fully one's yearning for inclusion or autonomy, respectively. By that account the most developed parents would both be champions of both sides of this fundamental human tension, and their parenting roles might each reflect confirming *and* contradicting, nurturing *and* limit-setting. It is an empirical question whether such sameness of role performance would inhibit the clear development of a child's sexual identity (the psychoanalytic prediction) or enhance the possibility of a more well-balanced masculinity and femininity.

From a constructive-developmental point of view, it is too simple to think the inadequacy of the phobic child's parents is their inability to balance each other. The mother's overinvolvement is not due primarily to the father's neglect of his differentiating role; the mother is herself underdifferentiated and is therefore unable to modulate her own yearnings for closeness and connection to her child. By such an account, the mother's yearnings do not get denigrated as inappropriately large; there is something beautiful and wholesome about those yearnings. It is not those yearnings that are suffocating the child; they represent a strength and gift for the child just as many mothers themselves experience it. Rather, it is the mother's own undeveloped or unacknowledged *competing* yearning—the absence of its influence—which is suffocating the child. Similarly, the father's contributions to the difficulty are not best understood as his capitulation of his role as champion of differentiation, as if his involvement with the problems of child care and rearing is itself inappropriate. His involvement is itself a resource; it only becomes a problem when it is unmodulated by his own access to his competing yearnings for distinctness, personal initiative, and the exercises of self-declaring boundaries. In the context of the current re-examination of sex roles in American life, the father's situation here points up the difference between new roles for fathers which may promise a healthier development (for fathers, their children, and their wives) and new roles which really seem to promise a new form of developmental difficulty. The invitation which this cultural re-examination creates for men to turn to their longings for inclusion (or women to their longings for independence) can be accepted in various ways. It is important to bear in mind the distinction between *abandoning* the old longing on behalf of the new, and integrating the new with the old, a distinction essentially between the dichotomous and the dialectical.

Despite the contradictions between psychoanalytic and constructive-developmental understandings of the school-phobic child's embeddedness culture, it is important to see that they share similar understandings of the problems the child is facing. The psychoanalytic understanding of the processes and costs of the child's maladaptation are informative and meaningful to an exploration of the evolution I suggest is the central motion of personality development. Waldfogel, Coolidge, and Hahn (1957), for example, talk about (1) "impairment of ego autonomy," (2) "inflated need for narcissistic gratifications," and (3) "the impairment of the repressive process." Let us consider each of these.

Lacking solid external controls, the child has not experienced the comfort of relief of even auxiliary impulse control, let alone begun to develop confidence in his own ability to regulate his impulses. It is interesting, as is pointed out in the Waldfogel study, that school-phobic children are *not* usually found to have had some unusual degree or number of early traumatic experiences. The phobic child's posture on life is thus not a matter of a learned disposition toward a frightening and dangerous world; rather, we assume, it is due to the frightening and dangerous proportions one's impulses can take on when one is deprived of the opportunity to experience their real consequences and susceptibility to control. Unable to control these impulses (to "have" them), the child is safer "being" them, or trying to be them, which means remaining embedded in that context with which the impulses are confused—that is, the family. All developmental transitions are about a new form of "ego autonomy"; all problematic or arrested transitions threaten that autonomy. In holding onto the parents this way, it is not so much that the child is "giving up" autonomy to external agents, as that he is settling for the autonomy of old (the autonomy over the reflex) rather than the autonomy to come (the autonomy over the impulse). The child is not so much remaining dependent on his parents, as detaining the process of his own evolution so that the distinction between himself and his parents-as-impulses is not yet made.

"Coupled with his deficiency of autonomous ego functioning," say Waldfogel, Coolidge, and Hahn, "is the inflated need for narcissistic gratifications, which he achieves mainly through the continuous exploitation of his subservient parents. Their inability to limit his demands, which at times assume tyrannical proportions, nurtures his omnipotent fantasies, supporting the tendency toward magical thinking, where the wish becomes equivalent to its realization" (1957, p. 757). All of this makes perfect and simpler sense understood in the context of the evolution of meaning. Because the child does not successfully differentiate from her impulses, she is quite naturally at that developmental place where fantasy is still not reflected upon and her construction of reality is as labile as her wishes; "magical thinking" is the natural evolutionary state of the balance 1 child. The child's exercise of the powers her parents inappropriately give to her are "exploitative" only from some perspective other than the child's. The child must achieve precisely the self-sufficient "ego autonomy" of the next balance (2) before her behavior can properly be called "exploitative" or "manipulative." The phobic child is merely availing herself of an embeddedness culture that is overconfirming and undercontradicting of her confusion of her impulses with her parents.

Similarly, what is referred to as an impairment of the "repressive process" is, from a constructive-developmental point of view, the very lack of that integration of the old structure so that it neither disappears nor is the very structure by which we are defined, but is mediated by the new structure which we have become. Every development involves such "repression," the passing of the immediate to the realm of the "mediate." At this point in development it is the impulses and fantasies-as-reality that are due to be integrated. What it may mean to find "the conscious expression of oedipal fantasies ordinarily repressed at this age" is that the child has not successfully made the evolutionary move appropriate to his age. Latency is not a matter of "hiding" the impulses or "dampening" them, but integrating them into a new organization. Similarly, the behaviors and "symptoms" of the school-phobic child are not regressive in the sense of developmental ground being lost; they are delayed or detained.

The consequences of a child's unsupported emergence from embeddedness appear to be manifold and deleterious. It is like growth without the protections of the amniotic shield. We can speculate that the child feels deeply torn between the seductive, "conservative" attractions of the control he has (over the family) to satisfy his impulses, on the one hand, and his longing for differentiation, terror at reabsorption, and rage at the parents for smothering him, on the other.

Above all—beyond an inability to go to school, an inability to separate from the family, an inability to resolve the Oedipus complex—what the child cannot do is either separate from herself or recover herself; she can neither separate from nor recover the balance she has been. She has lost her fundamental balance; she does not know; she cannot make meaning; she cannot adequately mediate, regulate, coordinate, organize her own impulse life; she can neither hold herself together well, nor the world in which she lives.

School phobia is a work disturbance par excellence. The child cannot go to work. The problem is not with work as a *content,* with a particular kind of work; the problem lies with work as a *structure,* the underlying evolutionary psychologic of work, which, as Freud said, is about impulse control. In a far-fetched but colorful parable, Freud told the story of human evolution into a species capable of industry. The secret to industry was the fashioning of tools, and the secret to their fashioning was the exploitation of fire. Man's basic impulse in the presence of fire, so the parable goes, is to urinate upon it and extinguish it. In order to *use* fire—and so become "industrial"—man had to learn to control the impulse to extinguish it. If ontogeny recapitulates phylogeny, this is the moment—roughly between the ages of five and seven, as the child is marched off to school—when that bit of phylogeny is being recapitulated. It is not for nothing that Erikson calls the latency years the era of industry. I am suggesting that we are looking here at the deep structure of the child's new orientation to work, competency, skills, and tools. When the child is marched off to work but is psychologically unready to work, the mismatch between social task and personal evolution is bound to be painful—to the child and to anyone who cares for him or her. The response in the child does not have to be school phobia; any number of responses are possible, including the brave attempt to do what is asked of me by those who love me and the complete bewilderment at why what I am doing is somehow displeasing to those around me. Whatever the mismatched child's reaction, the picture, if we can look through the surface particulars, is always that of a young person being asked to do more than he or she is capable of doing. Anyone who has seen such a picture knows that what must happen first is that such pressure must stop.

Among those new providers of the next culture of embeddedness into whose partial care the parents pass their child is the peer gang, which in its own way is as confirming and celebrative of the life of rules and order, self-sufficiency, competency, and personal display as the public institutional life of the school. A child must have evolved to the next balance to take her place in a peer gang; she must be able to take the role of the other; she must be able to recognize the other as a distinct person with purposes and intentions of her own. I consider the peer society further in the next chapter, but it is of note here that it is interesting and troubling to watch the way eight-year-old children discover and deal with those of their age peers who are not their evolutionary peers. They do not announce to themselves or their friends or the subject of their analysis that "This person is still in balance 1 while the rest of us have moved from the impulsive to the imperial balance," but they do make a diagnosis—that the person is "weird"—and cease extending a "holding" presence in his or her direction. Robert Selman and his colleagues at the Manville School of the Judge Baker Child Guidance Center work with children who are referred for "problems in interpersonal relations," and their research supports the premise that these children tend to be at balance 1 or in the 1–2 transition, while matched "normals" (same age, sex, I.Q., social class) tend to be at, or moving out of, balance 2 (Selman, 1980).

And, as we have said, when a child is not ready for the psychological tasks of school-going, we look to that intimate context—the embeddedness culture—which is both a part of the child and a supporter of its growth. As with every embeddedness culture, we can distinguish three primary functions: it must hold securely (confirmation and recognition); it must let go in a timely fashion (assist in differentiation, contradiction); and it must remain for recovery during that delicate period when the child is leaving behind what seems still like itself and which the child must recover as part of its new organization. We have considered in this chapter the exigencies of the first two functions; perhaps a word on problems in the third function is in order. The classic failure of the culture in the third function at this age is, of course, the dissolution of the parental unit—death, divorce, or separation. While divorce is a crisis for every member of a family at every stage of development, it is particularly risky for a child in the 1-2 shift, because it represents a blow to the very heart of the culture which holds the child—a culture which earlier focused on a single parent and will later extend beyond the parents. But right at this moment the essence of the culture is the couple itself. Its separation from the child at just that time he or she is separating from it recalls the picture of Spitz's hospitalized infants whose life projects seem to come to a halt when they lose contact with their mothers during the period of their own differentiation from them. There may be as many ways to be divorced as there are to be married, and it would seem that if the separating partners can each continue to play a role in the child's life, especially during the critical period of the child's own differentiation from the marriage, the risks to the child's life project can be considerably reduced.

Another aspect of the third function (continuity) is the provision of a bridge from the old culture (now increasingly becoming other and separate rather than a medium of embeddedness) to the new culture to come. When the child of school-going age *is* psychologically ready to work, it must be due in part to the parents' willingness to themselves undergo the transformation from near-exclusive sponsors of the child's development to a sharing of that role with an other—an other which is not only quantitative (more "people," teachers, and so on) but qualitative (they are known differently by the child and take a place in a whole new evolutionary balance), an other of which the parents are themselves about to be a part. If the new balance is about industry, then, it is facilitated by the parents' willingness to permit the differentiation of labor (in the culturing role) which evolves from a cottage craft to a public industry.

When the child undergoes this evolution and takes upon herself that authority which before had to be exercised by others, she displays a remarkable self-sufficiency. Perhaps the classic (and classically comedic) expression of this self-sufficiency—symbolic of so much that has gone before in this chapter—is the young child who decides to run away from home. And perhaps the classic expression of a culture performing successfully its third function is the patient waiting of the parents and their permitting the child to find her own way back when she discovers she cannot run away. A true story, with which I bring this chapter to an end, conveys for me something of a perfect marriage between the parents' recognition of the sensitivity of that moment when the child returns and the child's new capacities to attend to his own dignity and integrity.

An eight-year-old boy decided late one afternoon that he had had it with his parents and announced his intentions to leave home. The parents sympathized and watched him pack a few things into a bag. They told him how much they would miss him and bid him farewell. They watched discreetly from a window as their son walked away from the house and fell into playing with some friends from the neighborhood. Before too long it was dusk and dinnertime and the boy's friends headed off for home. The parents watched their son as he stood for a long while by himself, then stood for a long while by his little suitcase, and then slowly, dejectedly began to walk back home. The parents were concerned about what would happen at their reunion. They saw the shame on their son's face and they did not want to humiliate him further; and so they ended up making what is often a wise choice when one is not quite sure what to do. When their son returned they remained seated, kept their mouths closed, and offered the boy a quiet undemanding attention. They watched as he sat down in a chair opposite them, and then he too was quiet, pensive, self-absorbed. No one said a thing. Finally the family cat ran across the middle of the room. The boy looked up and said to his parents, "I see you still have that old cat."

S I X

The Growth and Loss of the Imperial Self

I left you, in the last chapter, with the picture of a little boy preserving his dignity. His attempt to run away from home failed, but his new evolutionary balance did not. It was as if he said, "Okay, I've returned; but not to have you rush in and take care of me, not to depend on you. I am still in charge of myself. I was away for quite a time and now I'm back." "I see you still have that old cat," he said. Years of evolution and hard-won differentiation stood behind the "you" in that sentence.

This new balance, taking the impulse and perception as object, brought into being the impulse across time, the perception across time, the enduring disposition, a continuing sense about things and people. A most important continuing sense is the one the child comes to have of herself. With the evolution of the balance the child develops a self-concept. The overdifferentiated issues of self-esteem, competence, self-display, and personal aggrandizement are as central to the life of the school-age child as the overintegrated issues of intrafamilial impulse satisfaction are central to the preschool child. The environments the child now finds himself in—family, school, peer culture—are all potentially a part of the next evolutionary culture of embeddedness, the first function of which is to recognize and confirm the displays of the new meaning which the child has become. In this chapter we consider the workings of this new holding environment, both as it cultures its host and as it assists in the evolution of personality *beyond* the imperial balance. As with every chapter in this section, we are looking at the phenomenology of the subject-object relation, the experience of its transformation, and the psychosocial environment in which it takes place. Our story in this chapter is the voyage along the helix from the overdifferentiated imperial to the overincluded interpersonal (see Table 9).

What makes the school, the peer culture, and a reconstruction of the family all part of a common psychosocial environment is that each is potentially able to culture the *role*—to support not a particular role so much as the organization and exercise of what a role itself is. In differentiating from his impulse confusion within the family, the child grows out of an undifferentiated adhesion to these older people with whom he lives, and into the role of "child" in relation to "parents." This role construction is part and parcel of the more general evolution which makes the child, rather than his parents, the master of his impulses in every aspect of his life. This maturity requires recognition on the part of the parents who can remain a part of the child's culture of embeddedness only by reconstructing their attention in keeping with the child's own new *form* of embeddedness. Whether it takes expression in increased respect for the child's privacy and private space in the home, the gift of a wristwatch, or the conferring of an allowance, one way or another the family is called upon to "make allowance" for the qualitative changes in their young. This, as always, is the first function of the culturing environment: recognition, confirmation of who the person has become. A holding environment must hold—where holding refers not to keeping or confining but to supporting (even "floating," as in an amniotic environment) the exercises of who the person is. To hold without constraining may be the first requirement of care.

In taking over the controls and authority which were formerly exercised by the parents, the child, in her family life, is bidding for recognition of her new organization in the very arena of her old (possibly shameful) immaturity—a risky business for the child and a difficult task for the parents. Fortunately for all concerned, the parents are no longer the sole providers of the culture. The salutary effect of the increasing differentiation of the embeddedness culture is that the old support is always accompanied by a new player who can modulate and correct the inevitable distortions of the veteran player. Thus the mother remains a player in a three-year-old's culture of embeddedness but, lest she be overly guided by her sense of the child as an infant, she is accompanied by the different perceptions of her husband, who now becomes an intrinsic part of the new culture. Similarly, the worlds of school and peer relations join the parents—whether they like it or not—to assist and correct their own developing vision of their young, when the child evolves to the imperial balance.

Harry Stack Sullivan (1953), who calls the imperial balance the "juvenile era," considers two dynamics to be the hallmark of this period: competition and compromise. Both can be given ample opportunity for display in the cultures of the formal school and informal peer relations, and both are about the exercises of the role. However much school reformers or liberal parents may decry the spirit of competition they feel the schools are instilling, it is arguable that such behavior is in large part a natural expression of the child's meaning-making. And while the sometimes interminable argument, comparison, and devaluation one finds in the informal interactions of children of this age can be so grating to the ears of adults, it is arguable, too, that these serve the same developmentally appropriate needs to establish, test, measure, and esteem an "enduring disposition" toward the self. The pragmatic compromises to which Sullivan refers are equally an exercise (or test) of the new competence, the ability to take the role of another, to see that one has to take turns for one's own benefit.

These competencies are central both to school and to peer environments for the child of this age and evolution. Whatever other kinds of learning one might be told the primary grades are about, what they are most centrally about is learning to *go* to school, learning to live in a world of rules and roles where egocentric behavior is less and less tolerated. For most children there is a good match between the (often unwitting) developmental demands of the school's hidden curriculum and the evolutionary level of the child. The school is ready to hold exactly the individual the child has become. Children's love of ritual, order, bargain, making things, receiving the information that their manner of conducting themselves is correct, successful, or praiseworthy, is a love born of nothing less than the love for life itself, that ceaseless, creative motion which they are. It is a sacred celebration of the meaning they are. A school that is sensitive to the shame of failure

TABLE 9. The imperial to interpersonal transformation

	Stage 2 *Imperial*	Stage 3 *Interpersonal*
Underlying structure (subject-object balance)	S— Needs, interests, wishes O— Impulses, perceptions	S— The interpersonal, mutuality O— Needs, interests, wishes
Piaget	Concrete operational	Early formal operational
Kohlberg	Instrumental orientation	Interpersonal concordance orientation
Loevinger	Opportunistic	Conformist
Maslow	Safety orientation	Love, affection, belongingness orientation
McClelland/Murray	Power orientation	Affiliation orientation
Erikson	Industry vs. inferiority	[Affiliation vs. abandonment?]

Evolutionary balance and psychological embeddedness	Culture of embeddedness	Function 1: Confirmation (holding on)	Function 2: Contradiction (letting go)	Function 3: Continuity (staying put for reintegration)	Some common natural transitional "subject-objects" (bridges)
(2) IMPERIAL Embedded in: enduring disposition, needs, interests, wishes.	Role recognizing culture. School and family as institutions of authority and role differentiation. Peer gang which requires role-taking.	Acknowledges and cultures displays of self-sufficiency, competence, and role differentiation.	Recognizes and promotes preadolescent's (or adolescent's) emergence from embeddedness in self-sufficiency. Denies the validity of only taking one's own interests into account, demands mutuality, that the person hold up his/her end of relationship. Expects trustworthiness.	Family and school permit themselves to become secondary to relationships of shared internal experiences. High risk: family relocation during transition period (roughly early adolescence, 12-16).	Medium of 2-3 transition: chum. Another who is identical to me and real but whose needs and self-system are exactly like needs which before were me, eventually a part of me, but now something between.
(3) INTER-PERSONAL. Embedded in: mutuality, interpersonal concordance.	Mutually reciprocal one-to-one relationships. Culture of mutuality.	Acknowledges and cultures capacity for collaborative self-sacrifice in mutually attuned interpersonal relationships. Orients to internal state, shared subjective experience, "feelings," mood.	Recognizes and promotes late adolescent's or adult's emergence from embeddedness in interpersonalism. Person or context that will not be fused with but still seeks, and is interested in, association. Demands the person assume responsibility for own initiatives and preferences. Asserts the other's independence.	Interpersonal partners permit relationship to be relativized or placed in bigger context of ideology and psychological self-definition. High risk: interpersonal partners leave at very time one is emerging from embeddedness. (No easily supplied age norms.)	Medium for 3-4 transition: going away to college, a temporary job, the military. Opportunities for provisional identity which both leave the interpersonalist context behind and preserve it, intact, for return; a time-limited participation in institutional life (e.g. 4 years of college, a service hitch).

at this age, especially public failure or public incompetence, is responding to something more than a peripheral, albeit humanizing, dimension of school life. It is dealing with an ultimate issue—a matter that impacts the child's very disposition toward the life project—and it is giving the issue the respect it is due. On the other hand, the school cannot be expected to meet the child wherever he or she is evolutionarily, and if the child is not ready to begin, however tentatively, the exercises of the imperial balance, if the child cannot play a role and take a role, then the school is left holding the child-to-come rather than the child-who-is, a situation costly for both and in need of intervention.

The peer culture of the elementary school years seems less formal than the school itself, but in a sense it is not. There is an astonishing regularity to the practices of these child cultures, not only in form but even in content, a veritable oral tradition. Parents are taken aback to hear their children engaged in the same word play and elaborate rituals which they themselves employed a generation ago. These countless rituals, games, and understandings are also about the exercise, even the celebration, of role. Although their content may seem perfectly meaningless—for instance, if two people say the same thing at the same time they must link fingers, recite the proper incantation, and remain silent until a third party asks a direct question—the child's investment flows from the very heart of its meaning-making, for the *form* of the ritual is itself its function and meaning. The idea is that each party does have a prescribed role; each can display to the others his ability to exercise it; each can predict the behavior of the others. On far more subtle levels, as well, children's interactions, including their exercises of competition and self-interested compromise, permit the opportunity to display themselves, the selves they have become.

To the extent that children of this age and evolution can provide something of a culturing environment for each other, something quite new in the history of the evolution of meaning is now taking place. For the first time, the human context of embeddedness is, in part, peopled by age mates, or actually more than age mates—"developmental contemporaries." These are the first moments of a remarkable development in the evolution of meaning, for at this time the organism, which for so long has been cultured, begins itself to assume the function of culturing, a function crucial to the continued survival and enhancement of that greater life community of which it is a part.

The child's capacity to culture, nurtured over many years by the manner in which it has been cultured, is still minimal at this age, and so it is well-modulated by the culturing of adults at home and in school. It can hold, but it is fickle, a consequence not so much of the unselfconscious nature of its holding (for, in a way, most culturing, where it operates most powerfully, is probably unselfconscious) but of its self-centeredness. It can hold, but it can be very inconsistent. The celebration of running a self that draws the child in to these pragmatic peer associations, and which creates cooperative rituals and rules, can as easily ostracize a peer on behalf of the same celebration. Witness these clubhouse rules of a gang of ten-year-old girls (*New Yorker,* September 18, 1954):

1. Do not tell a white lie unless necessary.
2. Do not hit anyone, except Ronny.
3. Do not use words worse than "brat."
4. Do not make faces, except at Ronny.
5. Do not make a hog or pig of yourself.
6. Do not tattle, except on Ronny.
7. Do not steal, except from Ronny.
8. Do not be a sneak.
9. Do not destroy other people's property except Ronny's.
10. Do not be grumpy, except at Ronny.

This particular decalogue is not exactly a triumph of the Golden Rule, but, as we now know, the organism is exactly one evolutionary transformation away from making any sense of the Golden Rule. But when the time comes, the organism will construct a world of mutuality and reciprocity, and it will look to a holding environment that cultures its interpersonalism. At that time adults will still be needed, and will support the adolescent's growth (to the extent they are able to reconstruct their attention yet another time). But, in contrast to the division of labor in culturing the imperial balance, in the interpersonal balance it will be the peers who share the greatest responsibility. Thus the appearance of the ten-year-old peer gang—however shaky a holding environment it is—is a debut. It is the debut of a culturing medium which, in keeping with the need for continuity between one culture and the next, is readying itself for a more reliable kind of caring in evolutionary balances to come.

We do not begrudge an infant its symbiosis with its mother, or a young child its romance with a parent. We do not imagine that these connections when the child is ready for them should be tentative in order to make it easier to give them up when it comes time. We imagine that a strong, robust connection, when connection is called for, is the best support for the process of evolution which is no less itself when it is embedded than when it is emerging from embeddedness. We imagine that strong, robust connections are actually easier to separate from than conflicted, tentative, or ambivalent ones. In the same way, then, we might confirm the imperial child in full bloom, even in the midst of her mercantile morality, her advertisements for herself, her scratching to be scratched—features as true of the ten-year-old as her more benign forms of self-sufficiency. Such strong confirmation only paves the way, rather than inhibits, the effectiveness of the contradiction to come. The same organism, now so invested in itself, will, upon successful navigation of the transformation to come, begin to take its place as a giver of care as well as a receiver. Is its future capacity to care for another in some way related to the extent it has been permitted, even encouraged, at this earlier time, to care for itself?

And what is the contradiction to come? The admirable self-sufficiency of the eight-year-old is not as attractive in a sixteen-year-old whom others are expecting to be not only self-sufficient but interpersonally trustworthy. The contradiction which invites an end to the imperial balance is a contradiction to overdifferentiation, just as surely as the contradiction to the impulsive balance was a contradiction to overintegration. Earlier the culture (the parents) made it known that the child did not belong in the parental bed, did not belong at home during school hours—invitations to the yearning for independence. Now the culture (family, school, friends) begins to make it known that it expects the adolescent to be able to take other people's feelings into account even when the adolescent is considering himself or herself; to be able to keep agreements, meet expectations, and independently construct the reasons for doing so—invitations to the yearning for inclusion. The parents who help their five-year-old become the master of his jealous feelings (interceding, for example, in his overly aggressive play with his baby sister), and the parents who call their fourteen-year-old to account when she breaks curfew on a Saturday night, are both involved in limit setting. But I think it is clear that they are limits in an opposite direction. The first is limiting a kind of overinvolvement, the second a kind of underinvolvement.

This helps us to consider the specific experience of loss which can attend this natural emergency. Evolutionary activity, we have said, gives rise to constructions of balance, to truces, but what is at stake in these truces? Viewed from the outside, it is what shall be taken for "self" and what shall be taken for "other." Will I, in other words, continue to know? Hence equilibrative activity is naturally epistemological. But what is at stake in maintaining the balance when viewed from the "inside" is whether I (this constitution of "I") shall continue to *be*. Hence equilibrative activity is also naturally ontological. Viewed with respect to the experience of being one who equilibrates, we open ourselves to the study of feeling, from which the traditional Piagetian orientation to stages must necessarily exclude us. For we are not our stages; we are not the self who hangs in the balance at this moment in our evolution. We are the activity of this evolution. We compose our stages, and we experience this composing. Out of this evolutionary motion, which we are, we experience emotion (this is what the word means—*ex* + motion: out of, or from, motion). Any theory of emotion must begin by naming that motion it regards as the source. I have named my candidate. Feeling may be the sensation of evolution; more complexly, the phenomenology of personality in its predicament as self-constituting meaning-making.

Nowhere is that predicament more painful than those times in our lives when the specter of loss of balance is looming over the system. These are the moments when I experience fleetingly or protractedly that disjunction between who I am and the self I have created; the moments when I face the possibility of losing my self; the moments that Erikson refers to hauntingly as "ego chill." The chill comes from the experience that I am not myself, or that I am beside myself, the experience of a distinction between who I am and the self I have created.

What seems to be happening in the emergence from the imperial balance? The self's embeddedness in its needs, interests, wishes, becomes vulnerable. That is, the organization of meaning in which I am my needs (and other people are presumed to be theirs) is threatened. I sense that it is not working. I am meeting up with experience in the world that cannot be made sense of according to my present way of organizing reality. For a time I "test" my "theory" (my way of making meaning) according to the principle that if the facts do not support the theory, so much the worse for the facts: this is what is meant by assimilation, and, psychodynamically, by defense. The defenses, so pejorative a category from most theoretical points of view, are first of all a sign of the integrity of an overarching system of meaning; they are what make the system a system. It is only in the face of those experiences which cannot be assimilated or accommodated by adjustments within the system (the recognition of further *implications* of my meaning) that the system finds itself threatened with the possibility of a limitation or inadequacy to its basic *presuppositions.* It is in the self's marshaling of a defense against this possibility—its attempt to reduce or confine the impinging environment—that assimilative integrity can become the clinical defensiveness so dramatically characterized by increasing social isolation, or even, in the more extreme exercises of control, by delusions. Psychotic delusions represent the most costly of victories over a threatening environment, because in the creation of (rather than interaction with) an environment, the person has largely cut himself or herself off from the "informing complexity" which nourishes development.

In the defensive posture the evolution of meaning has become overidentified with its present organization; the world has become threatening, an enemy of the established order. Those defending the imperial balance may tend to feel that others are persecuting them, holding them too close, not giving them their freedom, trying to make them "feel guilty." But whatever the balance that is being defended, the sense is that *I* work okay, if others would just shape up—and the shape I would like them to shape up to is the one I have known and loved so long but no longer can make work—my own.

But life gets more disequilibrated before it can become balanced again, and this involves the actual reconstruction of the relationship between self and other. My recognition of the subjectivity of my embeddedness in my needs begins to move them over from self to other. When this process is complete there will be a new self which, rather than being its needs, has needs—that is, is able to take them as an object of attention. The new self is able to coordinate its needs (which it has separated itself from) with other people's needs, and so constructs originally the interpersonal relationship, of which prior it had no understanding (and so drove everyone—including clinicians who regularly report their frustration with so-called sociopathic adolescents—wild). But the new truce does not come into being immediately. Between the old, need-identified truce and the new "need-coordinating" one there is a period of being me and not-me simultaneously, of feeling that I have lost one self with no new self that at least *is* a self, only to discover again its untenability (but this time with the added knowledge that its abandonment does not lead automatically—ever?, I must ask myself—to a new consolidation). For the imperial-interpersonal transition the loss of my self means the loss of the effective prosecution of my own needs, interests, wishes. It is not yet clear that what is being lost is not "my needs" but my ultimate orientation to them.

I want to consider the problematic negotiation of this evolution in three contexts where it commonly appears: (1) a clinician's consulting room or psychiatric ward (where many adolescents who seem to be overembedded in the imperial balance or stuck in the transition are diagnosed "sociopathic" or "adolescent adjustment reaction"); (2) the prison or correctional institution (where the most frequent evolutionary balance seems to be the imperial); and (3) Youthwork and CETA projects with so-called unemployable persons (whose unemployability seems related to their evolution of meaning).

Remember Terry, the fifteen-year-old girl we met in Chapter 3? Her parents had taken her to the hospital because they could no longer put up with her behavior. She had been skipping school, lying, and fighting constantly with her parents about the controls they tried to put on her behavior. On the ward she claimed she had no psychological problems ("My problems aren't mental; they have to do with getting along with my family"), a heresy in milieu therapy where progress through the ranks requires an ability to speak with some internal reflectivity. She was seen in community meetings by the staff as trying to divine what an acceptable formulation of her "problems" might be, so that she could appear to be on the right wavelength. In this she never really succeeded. She said that what she wanted most was to be accepted by others but what she feared most was that in being accepted she would have to "submerge my personality." She said she no longer felt like "a whole person: it's like others are woven into me." When she violated agreements about confidentiality and not using drugs during weekend passes she was discharged on grounds that she would not do "the work of the ward," was "argumentative," "disruptive," "inciting to other patients," and "a staff-splitter."

Phillip is a sixteen-year-old boy who is admitted to a psychiatric ward after his mother decides she can no longer deal with his behavior: frequent running away, walking out of school, pretending to go to school but being elsewhere, setting fires in backyards, petty thieving. The mother describes her son as a "professional liar."

He presents himself in meetings with the family as a poor, wounded boy who is constantly being hurt and battered about by the world. This characterization is not altogether incorrect, but it is decidedly nonmutual, as is, for example, his orientation toward his own "improvement" as he conveys it to the family and therapist: he will go back to school but only to X Academy, an expensive private school he knows it would be impossible for his family to afford; he will go back to school and behave if his parents give him a VW bus as a sign of independence. Nonetheless, he begins meeting his responsibilities on the ward and progresses on the ladder of increasing personal freedom (status changes are approved democratically by vote of the whole community, patients and staff), including passes outside the hospital for family visits. Due to a slip during therapy it gets discovered that he has been lying to the community and his parents as to what he has been doing on his passes. (He had several times been smoking marijuana with friends.) The community withdraws his privileges and he goes into a week-long depression of some intensity. He becomes isolated, withdrawn, and self-absorbed. When he starts to come out of it he says he has realized that he has been "screwing myself for the last six years" and wonders if he can do anything to stop it. Staff notes indicate that Phillip, during the entire course of his hospitalization, had difficulty "identifying" with staff members or other patients, and that he was "unsuccessful in forming an intimate interpersonal relationship." Planning for discharge involved the preparation of "mutual expectation lists" by both himself and his parents.

Roxanne is an inmate in a woman's correctional institution (Blakeney and Blakeney, 1977). She has prostituted herself, shoplifted, picked pockets, stolen other people's welfare checks, used other people's credit cards. She feels that stealing is generally wrong ("stealing is the worst thing I do") except when it is necessary to meet one's needs ("stealing is okay when you need the money for yourself"). On the other hand, she feels that people who shoplift for the fun of it are definitely wrong, and that people who sleep around a lot are "whores." ("It's wrong if you're not getting paid for it.") She defends another's check-stealing on the grounds that "if she didn't steal the money she woulda got put out, right? So that made it fair to her, then. I wouldn't have thought about jail then. I'd have stole it and it would have been fair 'cause it was for my needs. It would be right to steal it at the time and you don't think about coming to jail. When you're cashing checks, you don't think about getting caught." The only thing that makes it not right, in other words, is that one is sure to be caught for it and sent to jail, but she can understand how, under the pressure of need, one would not exercise what is implicitly one's "best judgment" — that is, don't steal in situations where you are likely to be caught. When she is asked if it would be fair for someone else who faced the same kind of needs to steal her check, she says, "No. That wouldn't be fair." As Blakeney and Blakeney say, the logic seems to be that "it is right for me to take someone's check *because I need it*, and it is wrong for someone to take my check *because I need it*," a position that is at least consistent if it is not reciprocal.

I met Richard in the CETA program. He was twenty and out of work. He had held a series of jobs in factories which he either walked out of or was asked to leave. After a few weeks in the CETA program he established himself with the staff as "one of those with an attitude," "a conman"; and with the other workers, especially those who had been in the program quite a while, as someone who "doesn't care about the program," "is just in it for the money." The program, which seeks, in the context of job training, to engage the workers in cooperative decision-making and to promote personal responsibility, made little sense to Richard. He could not describe its purposes other than job training, could not specify the explicit rules or implicit codes of the group. He felt he was often unfairly in trouble, and that many of the expectations others had of him (which he only became aware of in violation) were unreasonable. For example, he tended to arrive late or irregularly, to which his employers and co-workers objected. "I think they were complaining a little too much. My thought is, well, one of the mornings I didn't come in, my ride didn't show up. I could have thumbed, but I didn't call. I have the habit of not calling anyway. So I didn't think — if I couldn't make it I couldn't make it. I don't see why I was holding anything up." In his initial interview he presented himself as centrally concerned with the pursuit and satisfaction of his own interests, others being viewed almost exclusively in terms of either facilitating or thwarting that goal. He had no objections to the disorganization and lack of clarity in the new program, one suspected, because such a state made it easier for him to take care of himself. Asked in the interview what kind of person he admired, his immediate response was, "Someone who's doing exactly what he wants." Asked what prevents people from doing what they want, he answered, "Other people." Asked what is important to him, he said,

"Money." Asked why this is important: "You can be free." Asked why that is important: "Don't have to listen to people, follow their orders, live in places where you can't do what you want."

Every development seems to require its own culture; every renegotiation of the evolutionary contract seems to require some bridging by that culture to a new one of which, in some new way, it becomes a part. If we consider some of the "treatments" designed for persons like Roxanne, Terry, and Richard, we might begin to consider the relationship between what they need and what they get from their "cultures."

A popular form of treatment in "correctional institutions" (prisons) is behavior modification, modeled somewhat on such successful boasts of B. F. Skinner as that pigeons can be taught to bowl. Behaviorists put pigeons in miniature bowling alleys and allow them to behave as they wish. Eventually they happen to stand where the bowler rolls the ball, and at this moment they are rewarded with food. They then go about their business but eventually return to the bowler's position, where they are again rewarded. Before too long they begin to hang around at the bowler's spot, and eventually in their random body movements they lower their heads toward a miniature bowling ball; at this moment they get an even bigger reward. Before too long they not only spend most of their time where a bowler stands, they also have their heads down ready to push the ball. Eventually, of course, they actually push the ball, and—well, you get the idea. As Skinner said, "Getting them to bowl *strikes* takes even longer, but is no more complicated."

The pigeons in correctional institutions are moved through a set of behaviors in a somewhat similar fashion and can probably be expected to come to know as much about social relations as the birds come to know about bowling—essentially, that certain behaviors will lead to certain payoffs. The inmates, upon admission, are usually confined to a cell and nothing is asked of them. They have no freedoms, but they have no obligations either. They may rise at whatever hour they wish, for example. Eventually, though, an inmate happens to have her eyes open at the "rewardable hour" (say, 7:00 A.M.) and finds someone thrusting a token in her direction. She usually takes the token and falls back into bed. But before long she is regularly waking at 7:00 A.M., even if only for a moment to collect her token. A while after that she decides, "What the hell, I'm awake, I might as well get up," whereupon she is given even more tokens. Eventually she is rising at the regular hour and participating in the simplest of prison routines; and she is amassing a large enough token fortune to be transferred to another level in the hierarchy of increased freedoms and responsibilities. Now she not only has to keep to the simple routine, she may have to assume a chore in order to be rewarded. Eventually, she may have to take part in group activities, talk about herself and her plans for release, and so on.

Now I am not intending here a sophisticated analysis of the theory that underlies behavior modification. Nor in considering what such a treatment "means" from a constructive-developmental perspective do I believe I am providing ample basis for ruling it out of court. I simply mean to consider such an approach in light of those issues which I see as most important, and to the extent that those issues seem in some way valid, such a consideration must raise questions for the behavioral approach. What the behavioral treatment amounts to is a kind of polyester version of an imperial culture of embeddedness. Geared entirely to the quid pro quo, it provides a perfectly clear environment for one whose meaning makes central the ability to predict the actions of others consequent to one's own behaviors. As a synthetic culture it is reminiscent of the scientist in Saul Bellow's *Augie March* who had created a life form in his laboratory; it lacked two features of natural life forms—the capacity to move and the capacity to reproduce—but other than that it was perfect. The polyester culture lacks the capacity to move with, or foster the movement of, the organism it cultures, and it lacks the capacity to reproduce itself at the next level of evolution. It is not merely geared to, but locked on, the imperial balance, neither recognizing nor inviting the emerging capacities for internalized mutuality. In this respect it is little different than a sanitized version of the dog-eat-dog street culture which is the natural milieu of many persons who become detained in this balance. While it is more orderly and less violent, it is as unresponsive to an interpersonal psychology as the street, where it is "every man (certainly every man with any sense) for himself." In shaping the superficial behaviors of good citizenship without any self-conscious attention to the organization of the person giving rise to these behaviors, the behavior modification approach comes close to the notion that the living of one's life is comparable to an activity like bowling where the behavior is identical to the thing itself. That inmates in such programs return to their former lives, former crimes, and sometimes even their former prisons with no less frequency than other inmates (Hickey and Scharf, 1980) is testimony either to the greater complexity of a game like life or to the possibility that, however different the discharged inmate's behavior has come to look, he or she remains in some fundamental way unchanged. Although it would be foolish to say, "Yes, he *appears* to be a fine bowler, what with his 250 average and all, but he actually has no understanding of the game," it does not really seem at all strange to say something comparable about a human being or the extent to which our own distinct identities are guaranteed and preserved by his or her way of knowing us. Like the school tracking programs of the 1960s, the individual is found to lack a certain ability (to reason abstractly or to live within the strictures of the law) and is thereby placed in a learning setting which by not inviting the development of that ability (rote learning or behavior modification) only assures that the original diagnosis will be truer at the program's completion than at its inception. The least attractive feature of the behaviorist approach, as I see it, is its deaf ear to those in any group of offenders who are themselves beginning to emerge from an embeddedness in the "needs." The street culture which will only see the emerging recognitions of interpersonalism as the exposure of a soft underbelly is so disconfirming of the reality of this new possibility as to lead a person to feel they were not only going out of their mind, but going crazy as well. I don't mean to romanticize socially disorganizing behavior, but it may be that some among the offending population are as much as anything taking actions to secure their escape from a culture which is disconfirming their own bids for growth. Taking actions which land you in a psychiatric hospital or a prison are costly, though they may feel less costly to you than taking your life or losing your grip on reality. Especially in consideration of the cost, one might hope that the new environment the person finds is more recognitive than the one from which he or she has escaped.

If a treatment program can fail to replicate a wholesome culture by refusing to evolve, it can also do so by insisting on an evolutionary state that does not yet exist. When we first met Terry, I asked a question which I have still not tried to answer. I said that we could see her in group meetings struggling unsuccessfully to talk about herself in a way the staff would approve; that she would say in different ways, "My problems are not mental; they have to do with getting along with my family"; that the staff, however gently and indirectly, was unsatisfied with this formulation and took it as resistance to dealing with herself, her feelings, her responsibilities; that the staff grew more exasperated with her and when they discovered that she broke agreements about confidentiality and drug use they discharged her. And I asked why it was that such a concerned and competent professional staff was unable to engage or be of help to Terry.

I think it is fair to say that no one — not her parents nor an outstanding professional staff — was drawn to Terry at sixteen in a way they might have been moved by her struggle to walk at one or read at five. It would *not* be fair to say that no one loved her. I believe her parents love her very much, and that some people at the hospital stood ready to pay her a kind of attention I would not be uncomfortable calling a species of love. But love comes in shapes as well as intensities; it has a way of seeing or not seeing, which can never be made up for by the depth or sincerity of caring that accompanies it. It is this seeing, this paid attention, that is the hidden treasure. Terry's parents love her, and the hospital was ready to care for her, but she was unhelped because no one could feel moved by or attracted to her. On the contrary, people found her revolting. People are moved by heroic and vulnerable expressions of dignity and integrity, and no one could see these qualities in the way Terry lived her life.

But on the basis of Terry's interviews researchers agreed that she was only just beginning to emerge from an embeddedness in the imperial balance. It is as important to an understanding of her predicament to know that she was undergoing the throes of transition as to know that her most familiar organization of reality was imperial. Although, as analyzed in Chapter 3, much of her interview was solidly imperial, one could detect material in which the beginnings of a new organization appeared. Her reasons as to why a promise should be kept oriented to no one party but to the shared context, "a bond of feeling between two people," as she put it. The answer to what it is that makes a person feel bad when a promise to them is broken is analogous to the first standing steps of the infant who is tentatively moving from the accustomed equilibrium of the crawl to the new, not-yet-integrated equilibrium of walking. Listen to her reflecting back and forth between parties as she seeks to describe the dynamics of a "bond of feeling between two people," rather than orient to the needs of any one party exclusively:

Because they put their trust in the person who misused it. I guess that person has broken promises, but it is always different when the shoe is on the other foot. She gave a promise and it was important to her and it was broken. She felt hurt. It might make her more understanding of other people if she ever breaks their promises, it is just important to that person, it really is. It should take first priority, but then again, you can't feel like this unless you have been through it and it has happened to you, if a promise of yours has been broken.

If one listens to Terry in light of the experience of transition, one begins to hear the familiar themes which first appeared physically in infancy and keep recurring in each transition—the themes of meaning in the process of transforming itself: not being seen, losing the object, being out of balance. In only beginning the differentiation from her own needs and wishes that would eventually permit her to invest her loyalty in the strictures and benefits of interpersonal relationships, the feeling of losing others as satisfier and guarantor of her own needs was still so staggering that the possibility that she might recover others again as partners in an interpersonal world was at the moment beyond her ken. High I.Q. notwithstanding, Terry's developing "psychologic," the evolution of her meaning-making, was poised at a precipice more familiar to persons three and four years her junior. In fact, her I.Q. and verbal dexterity only exacerbated her predicament, since other people felt justified in counting on Terry to know them and herself in a fashion appropriate to her age.

A girl's body can begin to take on the shape and features of a woman. She can speak with the sophistication associated with adolescence or even adulthood. Social and legal arrangements can permit new freedoms simply because a person reaches a certain age. But until the evolution of meaning becomes interpersonal, there is a very real sense in which the person is not yet an adolescent. If those around him or her should mistake physiology, calendar age, or verbal ability for psychological age and expect the person to function interpersonally, they create a situation which is dangerous both for them and for the developmentally delayed teenager. The costs to a person of being unseen, of been seen as the person-one-might-become rather than the person-one-is have already been weighed in the case of the six- or seven-year-old who is unready for "real school." In some sense there must be a similarity at any moment across the lifespan to all these bewildering experiences of being unfairly demanded of. In the case of the not-yet-interpersonal adolescent, the situation seems more vulnerable to negative reactions on the part of the unsuccessful holding environment. Any evolutionary balance can be viewed with respect to its constraints, the way the self confuses the other with itself; to that extent it fails to guarantee to the other its distinct identity. The preschool child smuggles the other into the very workings of his impulse life; the interpersonalist adolescent or adult requires the other to complete a context out of which he derives a self. Both of these "subjectivities" represent a kind of violation to the other, and if the other is expecting to be seen as more separate, it will come as a surprise to be treated otherwise (we usually experience this surprise as a kind of smothering). But because both subjectivities are of the "overly included" variety, they have a different quality than the experience of the overly independent imperial balance, which others might experience as manipulation. When we are welcoming an interpersonal balance and discover that this is not what we are involved with, the holding environment can come to feel as if it is holding the bag. Such a surprise can be infuriating, especially if we look at it in terms of the other's betrayal rather than our faulty diagnosis. It is not parents or teachers alone who find themselves so enraged; psychologists and psychiatrists, mental health workers of all sorts—persons who are trained to attend to their own reactions to the people they work with—regularly evidence, in subtle and not-so-subtle ways, this kind of hostility to so-called sociopathic or acting-out adolescents.

Having only just begun the "moving over" activity which will lead to the recovery of her needs as an object of attention, it may now feel to Terry as if they are being ripped from her. She seems to speak of this kind of experience in her sense that she is going to have to submerge her personality, her sense that she is no longer whole, and, most poignantly accurate of her particular state, that, strangely, "others are woven into me." It is this weaving, which now feels so alien, that constructs the shared psychological context that is the hallmark of the new balance.

In the absence of the new balance, and this sharing, Terry's relation to her emotional life—and her emotional life itself—does not allow the kind of psychologizing of her interior states that make her reachable through a therapy that depends on such reflectivity. Without the internalization of the others' voices in her very construction of "self," how she feels is much more a matter of how actual external others will react, what they will or will not do in consequence of what she does. Her emotional situation is thus always changing, depending on the actions and reactions of others who are not easily decipherable since their interior life cannot be constructed by the subject any more complexly than she can construct her own. Thus she is left looking "out there" in her construction of her problems, which are therefore "not psychological but have to do with getting along with my family."

Seen in this light, I wonder if Terry's behavior, so inciting to those around her, does not begin to take on a different cast. I wonder if her "manipulation" is not, at the same time, the universal effort of all organisms to order and regulate their relations to the environment. The limits of Terry's regulating make it impossible for her to hold "the other" interiorly or imaginatively (the shared reality, the essence of mutuality), so she must seek to hold and regulate the other externally. I wonder if her violations of group rules are acts of defiance and hostility (which presumes that she shares a sense of their rightness and defies them) or whether the benefits and purpose of meeting the other's expectation when it interferes with her own interests are lost on her. I wonder whether her inability to speak about her problems in group in the acceptable fashion, viewed by staff as strategic manipulation to find out the right thing to say, is some kind of resistance, or whether it is more accurate to say that when she describes her problems as "out there," or "social problems," she is as accurately locating the arena of her "mental" or "psychological" life as the patient who talks about her guilt. I wonder if her lack of guilt is due to a "mental disease" called sociopathy, or whether, subject to her own needs and unable to locate the self in the coordinating of needs that constructs the mutual and the shared, she is left at the mercy of whether her mother knows she lied in order to know what her own "feeling" can be—in other words, the "socio" is the psychological. And I wonder if the exasperation of Terry's parents and the staff does not spring from their disappointment at not being known (not being held, grasped, seen, found, balanced with) in the way they expect. And I begin to wonder if a form of treatment for Terry which presumes at the outset that very capacity (to be a member of an interpersonal community), which is actually her growing edge, is not in the end an unwitting form of cruelty.

This is not to suggest that Terry's behavior should go unassailed. It is to suggest that before someone deals with her behavior, someone must see her. It is to suggest that her behavior is the vulnerable and heroic exercise of her integrity. "Integrity" seems the perfect word here, as it has a biological as well as a psychological meaning, and both are intended. When I feel recognized and have a sense that you understand how I am experiencing my experience (whether this is how you experience it or not), I can find your limit setting tolerable and even a relief; if I do not feel recognized, I resent it as a violation of who I am—which is just what it is. (In Chapter 9 we will visit Terry a final time when we consider the implications of the framework for therapy.)

Richard's story does not turn out like Terry's. Richard is still in the CETA program a year later. He has begun to learn a trade, and the people around him feel that he himself has somehow changed too. It is not just that they find him more reliable and cooperative; the staff feels that, in some way they cannot quite name, he *understands* them now. Richard himself feels he has changed but is not sure why or how. He now thinks he used to have "a bad attitude." He talks about how he "never used to share with other people what I think." He says, "It used to be, when I screwed up I worried that I was gonna get it; now when I screw up I worry that other people are going to worry."

Terry is called sociopathic, and Richard, at first anyway, unemployable. One is regarded as in some way "ill," in need of a quasi-medical attention; the other as "untrained," in need of some kind of educational attention. But the constructive-developmental perspective would suggest that they are in a similar psychological predicament and that neither a health-and-illness model nor a learning deficit model best captures that predicament.

The lesson in the differing outcomes of Terry's and Richard's "treatments" is not that psychiatric wards are bad places, or doomed to failure, or even inappropriate. The differences in outcome seem to be reflected in the unlucky match, in the one case, of a young woman with a program developmentally ahead of her, and the happier match, in the other case, of a young man with a program that was developmentally attuned to him. In the CETA program the values of cooperation, mutuality, joint decision making, taking responsibility, and sharing are *not* placed in the foreground. What Richard saw when he first arrived was a half-finished boat in a boatworks; a letter from a buyer offering several thousand dollars for the boat when it was done;

competent adults who knew how to finish the boat and who were willing to teach people like himself how to build them. Richard was engaged by the program, the constructive-developmental perspective would suggest, because he was first of all communicated with at the most fundamental level of his meaning-making, which was, at this point in his development, oriented to personal control, personal enhancement (even aggrandizement), and the display of, and acquisition of, personal competence. At the powerful, subtle levels his inability to be *inter*personal was not only *not* being tagged as a problem, but the strengths and motivations of his noninterpersonal instrumentalism were being recognized. Once hooked, of course, it was only a matter of time before he came to see that there were limits to his way of making meaning. Learning to build the boat eventually became quite a different matter than he first surmised, involving not just new acquisitions for the person he has "always" been, but an actual reconstitution of who he is. This is the dynamic of development that constructive-developmentalists see in every domain they study, what Perry (1970) calls the Trojan horse phenomenon: tempted from the fortress of our established habit of mind by an intriguing figure on familiar ground, we engage it, only to have it explode upon us; a whole army spreading out, captures the fortress, and establishes a new ground. The CETA project seems to work because it provides a version of the bridging function we find in natural evolution. It both recognizes and holds securely the imperial balance, *and* it assists in the emergence from this embeddedness, welcoming the capacity for interpersonalism through the nurturance of a cooperative community which is ready to receive the evolving person when he or she is ready to see it for what it is.

The movement from the imperial to the interpersonal, which enables a person to regulate his working with another, to construct the meaningfulness of shared agreements, to integrate his own authority with that of an employer's, may be more crucial to an individual's employability than any set of trade-related skills. What is the possibility that the constructive-developmental framework offers a basis for goal-setting and evaluation in youthwork programs, such as CETA and others, of considerably greater sophistication and promise of durable effect than the customary orientations to changes in situation-specific behavior or job skills?

One program was a luckier match than the other, I said. But of course the most important lesson in the stories of people trying to be helpful to Terry or Richard or Roxanne is that the outcomes do not need to be a matter of luck at all.

SEVEN

The Growth and Loss of the Interpersonal Self

Eric was a college freshman who brought himself to a counselor because he was depressed and had stopped working. It was the middle of his first semester and he said he was feeling "terribly insignificant." He was living alone in a dormitory room away from home. "You could die in there," he said, "and no one would know it till your body started to smell." He missed his parents terribly. He would call them and write to them frequently. In his communications with them he said he felt he was wasting his opportunity and their money; he was here to study and learn but he wasn't studying and he was not learning; he was letting them down.

Eric's parents told him he owed them nothing, that they felt college was a time for all kinds of learning and that this included learning to live through difficult experiences. "What is happening to you right now," they said, "is a real part of college life, too. We are sorry that you are having a rough time, but we don't think you're wasting it; you're doing it. And you aren't letting us down."

Eric felt tremendously betrayed and rejected by this apparently understanding and sympathetic response from his parents. "It's like you've been a good agent of the home office all these years," the counselor suggested. "You've met your quotas and reported in regularly, and—" "And now," Eric said, "I've been fired."

As Eric continued to meet with the counselor he decided that his real longing, in the things he said to his parents, was that they would say to him, "Come home. Give it up and we'll take you back." He kept up the pressure on them with his complaints and despair, but his parents would not rise to his bait and welcome him back home. Finally, when he was home for Christmas and had them at close range over a longer period, his mother finally told him that if he wanted to quit he could, and both parents told him they would understand if his grades first semester were not first rate.

In counseling, after returning to campus, Eric found he felt quite hurt by his parents' willingness to lower their expectations of him. He seemed to feel somehow that with their reduced expectations he was himself reduced. And also — and he himself found this strange — he felt terribly let down by what he saw as his mother's collapse through her willingness to let him come home. He started to feel that in his complaints he was not only hoping to be taken back, but that a part of him hoped they would *not* take him back, hoped they would help him by standing firm. Once he recognized this he became a lot firmer himself.

Over his next several sessions he began to talk about pleasing himself, about making decisions on his own that reflected his own wishes. He found — paradoxically, he thought — that as he began to think more about "deciding for myself" he also began to feel less lonely. He stopped writing home and calling home so frequently, and at his last counseling session he told a story about running into a fellow student on campus who was from his home town. The student had recently been home and had run into Eric's father. Eric's father had said, "If you ever see that bum of a son of mine, tell him to drop us a line; we haven't heard from him in weeks." Eric told the story with pride and joy.

Whatever excitement, adventure, and joyous emancipation may be associated with a young person's going off to college, it is as true that it is a time of vulnerability and high susceptibility to depression. George Goethals (1978) speaks of such unhappiness as grief over the loss of a home, by which he refers to something more than family and familiar surroundings. From a constructive-developmental view, it may be grief over the loss of balance, the loss of feeling at home in the world (*Heimlichkeit*). For the young person who has begun to emerge from an embeddedness in the interpersonal, the experience of going away to college can provide a new evolutionary medium that recognizes and cultures the moves toward self-authorship and psychological autonomy which characterize the new balance. The subtle and overt messages a college freshman gets that he is on his own in the conduct of his academic and private life can serve to honor that newly emerging voice in the development of personality. But for a person who has not yet begun this emergence, the same messages—which professors and advisers may think of as confirmations of the student's adulthood—can be experienced as an abandonment, a refusal to care, and a disorienting vacuum of expectation. This new embeddedness culture is not yet called for, and the old one has been lost. It is as if the amniotic fluid has been drained from the holding environment, and everything which suspends or supports life, giving it its characteristic glide and buoyancy, disappears. This buoyancy and glide is taken for granted until it vanishes, and then buoyancy is replaced by leaden heaviness and glide by the inability to get out of bed. At the risk of overworking the metaphor, it may be well to remember that embeddedness cultures do burst their waters before passing the organism to a new evolutionary state, so the rude shock of college to an interpersonally embedded freshman can itself potentially provide just the experience which may lead him or her out of the current evolutionary truce. But for this to happen there must be some context which recognizes the student's predicament and does not consider a sustained acknowledging of his or her grief as precious hand-holding. Providing a bridging environment that both recognizes the old interpersonalism but refuses to be swept into it is actually more than hand-holding (as certain stern folk in every college community love to refer to psychological or advisory services); it is a holding of the whole life enterprise. But what those who are uncomfortable with such an engagement might consider, is that, in kind, their own independence-oriented engagement is *no less* a holding of the identical life enterprise.

Of course, the evolutionary unreadiness of some eighteen-year-olds to leave home for college brings to mind the picture of the school-phobic six-year-old who is unable to leave home for elementary school. This continuity of life themes is celebrated in a famous story about a mother who was getting breakfast for her son. She noticed that he not only had not appeared but he seemed to be making no sounds of preparation upstairs. She went to his room and, finding the door closed, asked if he was okay. He said he was fine but that he was just not going to school today. The mother, being of the modern sort, decided to engage her son in reasonable conversation, and asked him to provide three good reasons why he should not go to school. The son obliged: "Number one, I don't like school; number two, the teachers don't like me; number three, I'm afraid of the kids." "Okay," said the mother. "Now I'm going to give you three reasons why you *are* going to school. Number one, I'm your mother and I say school is important. Number two, you're forty years old, and, number three, you're the principal!"

Although adults and children, or adolescents and children, both experience difficulties in separating (even difficulties separating and going off to school), and although a college freshman's difficulties may bear some relation to the nature of his or her separations in childhood, it would be misleading and unclarifying, I believe, to see the former *in terms of* the latter. Although the picture of Eric when he first comes for counseling is of a young man too enmeshed in his family, the evolutionary distinctions of constructive-developmental theory help us to recognize how very different his enmeshing is from that of the impulse-embedded child. The task that lies before him and through which he struggles involves a separation of himself from his parents vis-à-vis the very source of judgment about, and expectations of, himself. Eric is not just leaving home or leaving his parents; he is reconstructing the relationship between self and other, a relationship which in some respects is only deceptively similar to the self-other relationship of impulsive child and parents.

The helix of subject-object relations (see Figure 4) suggests the way in which Eric's predicament is both similar to and different from early childhood. In acknowledging the similarity, the constructive-developmental view is consistent with the psychoanalytic perception that adolescence rearouses the themes of the "Oedipal period," but it suggests a rather different explanation for why that might be. The emergence from embeddedness in the interpersonal balance does involve the loss of a special inclusion and does bring into being a new, sealed-up self (the institutional balance of ideological adulthood), but this development is no more determined by, or a reprise of, the oedipal drama, than the institutional balance is a recapitulation of the imperial childhood. What goes on in these earlier truces may have important influences on our experience and resolution of similar themes in later life, but the connection between, for example, the impulsive balance and the interpersonal one is presumed to be categorical rather than causal; these two balances belong to the same group of inclusion-favored resolutions to the evolutionary quandary.

An oversimplified (but I think not unreasonable) account of the psychoanalytic understanding of personality development between five and fifteen might use a metaphor from cryogenics—the notion of cold storage. The overincluded impulsive era of early childhood is brought to a temporary halt by the refrigeration of repression; the impulses are still alive but frozen, hidden away, latent. At adolescence, the impulses are defrosted, they break out again into the body politic which has meanwhile been developing on its own during the freeze. Such a conception struggles and fails to recognize simultaneously both the similarity and the difference of the adolescent situation to that of childhood. The whole notion of latency—of a Dark Ages in personality development—is one of Freud's least preservable constructions. As many students of personality have since pointed out, and as I have tried to suggest in Chapter 6, there is a great deal going on during these years, and it is not at all hidden. But most problematic about the conception is the way it excludes from development for several years a whole domain of personality— the impulses—and then seeks to reintroduce them when new phenomena seem to require them for explanation. Lacking a modern evolutionary model it fails to consider the possibility that the intellectual development and self-sufficiency of middle childhood (which it recognizes) are actually in part those same impulses integrated into a more complex organization. And thus, even though psychoanalytic theory knows that the yearnings for inclusion in an adolescent have a whole different character than those of a three-year-old, it must still see the former as an outbreak of the child's impulses which do battle with, rather than naturally grow out of, the juvenile's order and self-sufficiency.

While constructive-developmental theory is less inclined to perceive an identity between childhood and later lived phenomena, it is more inclined than psychoanalytic theory to see the unity and continuity of such phenomena. The evolutionary model permits one to observe recurring phenomena of similar color and tone throughout the lifespan without having at the same time to regard such similarities as regression or recapitulation. In the face of so much evidence that these later phenomena, while similar on the surface, are also far more complex and importantly different than their earlier cousins, psychoanalytic perspective inevitably renders them as regression.

From a constructive-developmental view, "impulse" is not an un-changed phenomenon throughout life which is merely differently managed by more complex defenses as the person develops. Impulse, rather, evolves into imperium, and imperium into interpersonalism; now the interpersonal is evolving into a kind of psychological home rule or public governance which I have characterized as "institutional." The institutional and the imperial both involve a kind of self-possession and sealing up; they favor differentiation over in-tegration, the theme of agency and independence over that of inclu-sion. But they are different, just as the ability to direct oneself in the absence of another's expectation is different from the ability to resist pushing someone down the stairs when one is angry at him. The efforts by Eric's parents to be helpful are the important communica-tion of contradiction, the second function of a culture of embedded-ness (see Table 10); but what they are contradicting is not his impulse confusion but his confusion as to who it is that defines his purposes and directions. From his point of view they are firing him after years of obedient psychological employment; but his parents are speaking to the point of view to come and contradicting the first point of view. They are saying, "We're not firing you so much as declaring that you can be self-employed, work for yourself, be in business for yourself." The triumph in Eric's relating of the story about being a neglectful son is that in the end he is parenting himself and has become his own pride and joy.

I have met a number of young men who sought help because they were terrified they might be homosexual. Their world had come to a complete halt and nothing could proceed until this matter was re-solved. They often had no homosexual experience (and, as important, almost no heterosexual experience); they rarely felt physically attracted to men; nevertheless, for one reason or another they began to consider the possibility that they were homosexual and became immobilized, filled with dread. I do not want to generalize across a number of human dispositions and predicaments; there were important dif-ferences. The origin of one fellow's fear was as apparently accidental as a dormitory discussion in which a perfectly decent, thoroughly ad-mirable young man openly discussed his preference for sex with other men. My client began to think, "My God, if this guy's gay, anyone could be—why, even I could be"—an impermissible but undispatch-able thought. At quite the other end of the spectrum, another's con-

INTERINDIVIDUAL [5]

INTERPERSONAL [3]

IMPULSIVE [1]

INSTITUTIONAL [4]

IMPERIAL [2]

INCORPORATIVE [0]

Psychologics favoring inclusion

Psychologics favoring independence

TABLE 10. The interpersonal to institutional transformation

	Stage 3 Interpersonal	Stage 4 Institutional
Underlying structure (subject-object balance)	S— The interpersonal, mutuality O— Needs, interests, wishes	S— Authorship, identity, psychic administration, ideology O— The interpersonal, mutuality
Piaget	Early formal operational	Full formal operational
Kohlberg	Interpersonal concordance orientation	Societal orientation
Loevinger	Conformist	Conscientious
Maslow	Love, affection, belongingness orientation	Esteem and self-esteem orientation
McClelland/Murray	Affiliation orientation	Achievement orientation
Erikson	[Affiliation vs. abandonment?]	Identity vs. identity diffusion

Evolutionary balance and psychological embeddedness	Culture of embeddedness	Function 1: Confirmation (holding on)	Function 2: Contradiction (letting go)	Function 3: Continuity (staying put for reintegration)	Some common natural transitional "subject-objects" (bridges)
(3) INTER-PERSONAL Embedded in: mutuality, interpersonal concordance.	Mutually reciprocal one-to-one relationships. *Culture of mutuality.*	Acknowledges and cultures capacity for collaborative self-sacrifice in mutually attuned interpersonal relationships. Orients to internal state, shared subjective experience, "feelings," mood.	Recognizes and promotes late adolescent's or adult's emergence from embeddedness in interpersonalism. Person or context that will not be fused with but still seeks, and is interested in, association. Demands the person assume responsibility for own initiatives and preferences. Asserts the other's independence.	Interpersonal partners permit relationship to be relativized or placed in bigger context of ideology and psychological self-definition. High risk: interpersonal partners leave at very time one is emerging from embeddedness. (No easily supplied age norms.)	Medium for 3-4 transition: *going away to college, a temporary job, the military.* Opportunities for provisional identity which both leave the interpersonalist context behind and preserve it, intact, for return; a time-limited participation in institutional life (e.g. 4 years of college, a service hitch).
(4) INSTITU-TIONAL Embedded in: personal autonomy, self-system identity.	*Culture of identity or self-authorship* (in love or work). Typically group involvement in career, admission to public arena.	Acknowledges and cultures capacity for independence; self-definition; assumption of authority; exercise of personal enhancement, ambition or achievement; "career" rather than "job," "life partner" rather than "helpmate," etc.	Recognizes and promotes adult's emergence from embeddedness in independent self-definition. Will not accept mediated, nonintimate, form-subordinated relationship.	Ideological forms permit themselves to be relativized on behalf of the play between forms. High risk: ideological supports vanish (e.g., job loss) at very time one is separating from this embeddedness. (No easily supplied age norms.)	Medium of 4-5 transition: *ideological self-surrender (religious or political); love affairs protected by unavailability of the partner.* At once a surrender of the identification with the form while preserving the form.

cern arose out of a consideration of his friendships and his long-standing history of being more invested in relationships with other men. But whatever the origin of the concern, there did seem to be some unavoidable similarities among most of these young men—the most striking of which was that their concern nearly always had less to do with sexuality than they thought.

The possibility of their homosexuality had become the only issue worth considering in and out of therapy. They nearly all came wanting to know "the answer." "Even knowing that I *am* gay would be better than this, better than the suspense; at least then I would *know* and I could go shoot myself." The therapist, of course, knew neither the answer nor even if there was one, and, in his own peculiar way, soon lost all curiosity. What *was* a question for the therapist, though, was why the possibility of being homosexual should seem to be the absolute and incontrovertible end of the world. Here we were certainly dealing with the powerful forces of ultimacy at risk. And when the therapist would attend to the young man's experience, to the terror of not knowing, to the sense of impending doom and completely unacceptable reversal, it would usually emerge that what was really at risk—more even than the young man's sexuality—was a particular evolutionary truce, the very balance which composes the self and the world. The powerful forces of ultimacy at risk seemed to be evolutionary, and, more particularly, the evolutionary truces of interpersonalism. Imagine what the meaning of homosexuality can be for a person whose balance is embedded in the interpersonal. "Here I have lived for years as a person worthy of others' approval and affection; I have met their expectations and seen myself through their eyes. And now, through absolutely no fault of my own, I discover that there may be something about me which would make me unacceptable and disappointing to all those persons. It seems so terribly, so horribly *unfair*." Because it is out of this very confusion of the self with these other persons that the interpersonal self emerges, the inability to meet their expectations and be acceptable in their eyes is nothing short of the ultimate inability—the inability to make *myself* cohere. I have turned against my self. I have become riot.

This is just the kind of experience that, with the proper support, can facilitate development. After several weeks of therapy in which the issue of "Am I or am I not gay? How can I find out?" crowds every minute, the nature of the personal reflection slowly begins to give way to the deeper stirrings which shape the whole issue of where one derives one's self-image. The question moves from "Am I gay?" to "Who's in charge? Who is it that admits me to the human race?" The young man comes to find that whatever the answer is about his sexuality, the self that discovers the answer is a new one.

There is yet one aspect to the lostness of many a college freshman that we have not considered. This is the poignant lostness of not even knowing what it is one has lost. Because American culture as a whole tends to favor and recognize the yearning for agency and independence to the exclusion of the yearning for inclusion and connection, we can sometimes fail to recognize this latter yearning in ourselves. Being admitted to college is often experienced as confirmation of my individual ability and achievement, testimony to the success of my initiative. It is much less often experienced as confirmation of the quality of my supports, the security and integrity of how I am held. And yet the latter is certainly as true as the former. Our well-being (or lack of it) is as much as anything a reflection on the quality of those most intimate "supports" which, from the point of view of our current evolutionary truce, are confused with ourselves. Not being aware of this makes us vulnerable to unforeseen losses when we make choices, however wholesome such choices may be, that cost us these supports. Any move which disrupts our supports—and especially to a place where such supports are not likely to be easily replaceable—is bound to be painful. It can be even more painful and bewildering when we are not even aware of the price we have paid. The proud young freshman, wearing at least a psychological beanie as if it were a laurel to personal achievement, frequently runs into an immobilizing depression that is most of all a bewilderment to himself or herself. Frequently the student cannot work, and one usually hears, "It's not that it's too hard or that I can't understand it; it's just that I can't get myself to do it. I don't *want* to." Of course, from the young person's view, getting into college—and life itself—is about personal, independent achievement, so this failure is a blow to the only recognized yearning. The only problem here is that depression is terribly hard to "solve" through the exercise of personal agency and independence, especially at a time when such exercise has inexplicably (often for the very first time) lost its appeal. Without some way of recognizing that the satisfaction of one yearning (here, for example, through academic achievement) really requires the satisfaction of the other (feeling connected and supported) in order for either to feel worthwhile, the person is left to wander around in the worst sort of lostness—the kind that does not even know what is missing.

We first met twenty-year-old Diane in Chapter 3. She tends to meet a man and become dependent upon him; she gradually withdraws from other friendships and involvements until her whole life is built around him; he eventually finds the relationship too burdening and moves to end it or reduce its intensity; she then becomes despondent and tries to kill herself. After her third suicide attempt she admitted herself to the psychiatric ward of a local hospital.

In Chapter 3 we asked what was happening to Diane. From the little we saw of her structural interview we began to consider whether she tended to construct the world interpersonally. But Diane's interview, like Terry's, contains a second voice which comes to struggle with the first. After orienting in the first part of the interview to the interpersonal context, the interviewer introduces the legal system to which Diane does not spontaneously refer. "Heinz is apprehended and brought before the judge. Should the judge give him a sentence?" This begins a fascinating section of the interview, for Diane does not assimilate the legal system to the ultimacy of altruism, as is ordinarily the case when the equilibrium of stage 3 is reigning comfortably. In such a state, a person is likely to nest "the judicial system" and the "judge" within the interpersonal; the judge, for example, might "put himself in the place of the husband" and see that he would do the same thing. But Diane explicitly rejects such a perspective:

> I could see an argument for it of it being this man is not a thief in the extreme sense of the word, he is not going to go out and steal, this was a specific situation and he won't do it again, unless this specific situation comes up again and his wife is now cured and it probably won't. I could give an argument for it, but I don't personally believe in that argument.

What does she believe in? Letting Heinz off "would show disrespect for what we live by." But what she lives by, at the moment, is in a state of flux. In trying to reconcile her earlier interpersonalist point of view with the societal perspective she now finds herself taking, she advocates a "flexibility" for "the law"; but notice the disequilibrated nature of this reconciliation:

In dealing with Heinz's case, the law should also be flexible to include individual situations.

Why?

Because as humans we do value our lives. We are individuals and every situation is different and if that is not reflected in the official code, then it's wrong for the populace. It is doing more harm than good.

So you're saying that is what the judicial court has to reflect, the individuality and uniqueness of situations?

But you can't make laws for individuals.

One can see, particularly in company with the earlier excerpts indicating her construction of the argument she rejects, that this is not an instance of 4-5 disequilibrium. The value of the law is never relativized. The pleas for a recognition of individuals and uniqueness do not go on from a perspective that establishes the priority of persons to the social arrangements they agree to (the so-called out-of-society perspective that is the hallmark of the rebalancing out of 4); they come from the interpersonalist perspective whose regard for the differing "investments," attachments, circumstances of distinct interpersonal relationships, is feeling wrenched by the emerging rebalancing which has not yet recovered "the interpersonal" as object, but leaves one feeling "the interpersonal" is going to be abandoned, or sacrificed upon the altar of "social order." ("I think the law is made, the stealing law anyway, for the majority of the people and it has to be upheld, it has to be respected as a law to live by, which is why I feel that he should have some sentence—but then no rule is good if it is entirely flexible.") She has not yet come to the new balance, which moves over the interpersonal from subject (or structure of knowing) to object (or content of knowing). But she demonstrates that she is in the midst of this rebalancing in her final defense of the law as having "to remain for the majority of the people, it has to be a generalized thing." She says: "I was just thinking if the law did make allowances for that, I guess that I don't trust people enough, so that I think it would be abused." Trust, the foundation stone for the interpersonalist balance, has been found wanting as an ultimate good. She is caught between one way of making meaning and another—and she knows it:

Is there anything you want to say about these situations or after thinking it through?

Yah, I feel on a very personal level, they mentioned to me before, in my therapy, that I have a great deal of trouble making decisions, pointing them out as right more than anything.

When you say you have a hard time making decisions, that that is a bad thing?

Well, it is a harmful thing, because I then have to look toward others to make the decision for me. Here you have me on the spot where I can't turn around and say, "Hey, you make the decision."

In the hospital, Diane was at first afraid to talk about her problems, because "others may not like me." She discovered a parallelism about her feelings toward her father and her boyfriend: in both cases, despite her subjective experience of being rejected by the man, she persisted in trying to please him and shelter him from what she perceived to be his fragility in the face of any direct confrontation. She began dealing with the conflict she felt in relation to her family: a desire to be loved, and cared for, and approved of, versus a desire for independence. She felt a similar conflict in relation to her boyfriend, complicated by an emerging fear of sexual intimacy: it felt to her like there was no way to hold him and be with him without losing herself to him in the relationship. She began to feel, and deal with her feelings of, anger toward her father, anger toward the hospital staff, anger toward her boyfriend. Toward the end of hospitalization, she had put controls on the pattern of her father's visits, and prepared for discharge to a living and working situation which would put into effect her decision to continue her career and separate from her boyfriend. She expressed her apprehension on leaving in terms of being afraid of whether she "can accept responsibility for myself."

I wonder to what extent the disruption, pain, and restoration in Diane's life is not a function of the loss and emerging reconstruction of her present subject-object relating. I wonder if her story is not that of the gradual and harrowing disidentification by her evolutionary activity from that invented self founded on the interpersonal. Prior to hospitalization, the loss or threatened loss of the relationship seems to raise the question of the loss of her very being; by the time of discharge a newly emerging self takes into its own hands the future of that relationship. Taking a relationship into one's hands means moving over the very structure of "relationship" from subject to object. But that "going over" (*Ubergang*) phenomenologically amounts to, first, the relativizing of what was taken for ultimate, a loss of the greatest proportion; and second, a period of not-knowing, of delicate balance between what can feel, on the one hand, like being devoured in the boundarilessness of the old construction, and the selfishness, loneliness, or coldness of being without "the interpersonal" on the other. The quality of the loss and the desperate coldness and isolation before recovery are both reflected in an early recurrent dream of Diane's: "I am in water as red as blood. There is an island on the water. On the island there are people whom I have known in the past. I cry for help but feel myself drowning." Drowning in water as red as blood my gaze is upon the departed: solid and familiar ground, peopled with those I knew before. Yet, viewed from the perspective of the new transitional self (the self "at sea"), even the familiar world, as Diane's later hospital course suggests, can feel like a place to drown in. The newly emerging institutional balance constructs the self-conscious self-system, an intactness that brings "inside" the conflicts which earlier were located between oneself and another (since between oneself and another was where the "self" resided), a kind of self-sufficiency reflected in the expression, "In order to get yourself together, you first have to get yourself apart." The new self moves from being a fragile presence—as in her powerful and terrifying image of a tiny self struggling against ingestion by the giant plastic head—to a more reliable context which places limits on a relationship the termination of which had earlier raised the specter of annihilation. Diane's hospital diagnosis, of course, is "borderline." To what extent is this a matter of her earliest object relations, and to what extent a matter of her present ones, a matter of walking the fearful border between two ways of making the world cohere, one left behind, the other not yet clearly evolved?

Consider Alice. She is recently divorced, lives with her children, and is concerned about her new sexual life vis-à-vis her nine-year-old daughter. The following are excerpts from her initial therapy session.

> And one of the things that bothered me the most is especially men, and having men to the house and how it affects the children. The biggest thing I want—the thing that keeps coming to my mind I want to tell you about is that I have a daughter, nine, who at one time I felt had a lot of emotional problems. (I wish I could stop shaking.) And I'm real conscious of things affecting her. I don't want her to get

upset, I don't want to shock her. I want so badly for her to accept me. And we're real open with each other especially about sex. And the other day she saw a girl that was single but pregnant and she asked me all about "can girls get pregnant if they are single?" And the conversation was fine and I wasn't ill at ease at all with her until she asked me if I had ever made love to a man since I left her Daddy and I lied to her. And ever since that, it keeps coming up to my mind because I feel so guilty lying to her because I never lie and I want her to trust me. And I almost want an answer from you. I want you to tell me if it would affect her wrong if I told her the truth, or what.

* * *

I feel that in time she will distrust me, yes. And also I thought well, gee, what about when she gets a little older and she finds herself in touchy situations. She probably wouldn't want to admit it to me because she thinks I'm so good and so sweet. And yet I'm afraid she could think I'm really a devil. And I want so bad for her to accept me. And I don't know how much a nine-year-old can take.

* * *

I don't know if she can accept me the way I am. I think I paint a picture that I'm all sweet and motherly. I'm a little ashamed of my shady side too.

* * *

I have a feeling that you are just going to sit there and let me stew in it and I want more. I want you to help me get rid of my guilt feelings. If I can get rid of my guilt feeling about lying or going to bed with a single man, any of that, just so I can feel more comfortable.

And I guess I'd like to say, "No, I don't want to let you just stew in your feelings," but on the other hand, I also feel that this is the kind of very private thing that I couldn't possibly answer for you. But I sure as anything will try to help you work toward your own answer. I don't know whether that makes any sense to you, but I mean it.

Well, I appreciate you saying that. You sound like you mean it. But I don't know where to go. I don't begin to know where to go. I thought that I had pretty well worked over most of my guilt, and now that this is coming up, I'm disappointed in myself. I really am. I like it when I feel that no matter what I do, even if it's against my own morals or my upbringing, that I can still feel good about me. And now I don't. Like there's a girl at work who sort of mothers me and I think she thinks I'm all sweet, and I sure don't want to show my more ornery devilish side with her. I want to be sweet and it's so hard for me to.

*   *   *

Like I want to be a good mother so bad, and I feel like I am a good mother, but then there's those little exceptions. Like my guilts with working. I want to work and it's so fun having extra money. I like to work nights, but the minute I think I'm not being real good to the children or giving them enough time, then I start feeling guilty again. Then, that's why it is—what do they call it—a double bind. That's just what it feels like. I want to do this and it feels right, but after all I'm not being a good mother and I want to be both. I am becoming more and more aware of what a perfectionist I am. That is what it seems I want to be—so perfect. Either I want to become perfect in my standards, or not have that need any more.

*   *   *

. . . In the meantime, I can't stop these desires. I tried that also. I have tried saying, "O.K., I don't like myself when I do that so I won't do it any more." But then I resent the children. I think, why should they stop me from doing what I want and it is really not that bad.

*   *   *

What you'd like to do is to feel more accepting toward yourself when you do things that you feel are wrong, is that right?
Right.
It sounds like a tough assignment.
I feel like you are going to say, "Now why do you think they are wrong?" and I have mixed feelings there too. Through therapy I will say, "Now look, I know this is natural. Women feel it—sure, we don't talk about it lots socially, but all women feel it and it's very natural." I have had sex for the last eleven years and I am, of course, going to want it, but I still think it is wrong unless you are really, truly in love with a man, and my body doesn't seem to agree. And so I don't know how to accept it.

*   *   *

Right. I really know you can't answer for me, and I have to figure it out myself, but I want you to guide me or show me where to start or—so it won't look so hopeless. I know I can keep living with this conflict and I know eventually things will work out, but I'd like feeling more comfortable with the way I live—and I am not.

One thing I might ask, what is it you wish I would say to you?

I wish you would say to me to be honest and take the risk that Jenny is going to accept me. And I also have a feeling if I could really risk it with Jenny, of all people, that I'd be able to say, "Here's this little kid who can accept me, and I'm really not that bad." If she really knows what a demon I am and still loves me and accepts me, it seems like it would help me to accept me more—like it's really not that bad. I want you to say to go ahead and be honest, but I don't want the responsibility that it would upset her. That is where I don't want to take responsibility . . . I don't want to quite take the risk of doing it unless an authority tells me that . . . I do not want to feel like I have caused any big traumas in the children. I don't like all that responsibility. I think that's it. I don't like it, feeling it could be my fault.

*   *   *

And you know, I look at it two ways. I like to see myself as being so honest with the kids, and really being proud of myself so that no matter what I told them or no matter how bad they might think I was, I was honest and down deep it is going to be a much more wholesome relationship, and yet you know, I get jealous of like when they are with their Daddy. I feel he is more flip, he is not quite as real, he is not quite as honest, but nevertheless they see a sweet picture of their Dad. You know, he is all goodness and light, and I am envious of that too. I want them to see me just as sweet as they see him and yet I know he is not quite as real with them. So it seems like I've got to swap the one for the other, and I know this is really what I want the most, but I miss some of that glory.

You sort of feel, I want them to have just as nice a picture of me as they have of their Dad and if his is a little phony, then mine will have to be too. I think that's putting it a little too strongly.

But that is close. That's what I mean. But I know she can't have that neat a picture of me, if I were honest. Besides that, I do feel that I am a little more ornery than their Dad anyway. I'm likely to do more things that they would disapprove of.

Then do you really find it quite hard to believe that they would really love you if they knew you?

That's right. You know that's exactly it. Before therapy, I would have definitely chosen the other area. I am going to get respect from them no matter what—even if I have to lie.

I see.

But right now, I know that's not true and I'm not positive they'll accept me. Something tells me they will. I know they will, but I am not positive. I want reassurance. I keep wanting these things.

And now you are kind of in a no-man's-land of probably shifting from one point of view toward them to another, but boy you'd sure like somebody to say, "That's right, you go ahead and do it."

Yes. That's why I get encouraged when I read in a book from somebody I respect and admire, that this is the right thing no matter what—honesty will win out. Well, then that keeps giving me confidence . . .

* * *

I do feel like you have been saying to me—you are not giving me advice, but I do feel like you are saying, "You know what pattern you want to follow, Alice, and go ahead and follow it." I sort of feel a backing up from you.

I guess the way I sense it, you've been telling me that you know what you want to do and yes, I do believe in backing up people in what they want to do. It's a little different slant than the way it seems to you.

Are you telling me . . .

You see, one thing that concerns me is it's no damn good to do something that you haven't really chosen to do. That is why I am trying to help you find out what your own inner choices are.

A therapy transcript, and a brief one at that, is not a comprehensive source of information about a person's meaning-making. While an interview format that permitted probing and follow-up questions would be a good companion to the therapy transcript in understanding Alice, the transcript itself has a number of its own advantages: it shows us the person's real-life conflicts and how she frames them; and, in her relationship to the therapist, it shows us something of the real-life way she constructs the "other."

The overwhelming impression I get from Alice's presentation is of someone who wants to be approved of. She wants her daughter to accept her, her co-worker to think well of her, her therapist to confirm her. These appear to be ultimate matters; more than concerns she has, they seem to *be* her. I say this because it seems that anything which threatens this approval (like her sexual behavior) strikes at her core, throws her whole system out of balance; that is, being approved of does not appear to be relative to anything (for example, to a self which continues to be, whether or not it is approved of). How she *appears* to others seems to be paramount. Appearances are ultimate, we might say. We might even be tempted to say "mere appearances," but that is to relativize them, and to lose what seems to be Alice's perspective.

How things appear can be the ultimate issue if meaning is derived from how others see us. While some part of us may want to taunt a person who worries about what the neighbors will think (probably the part of us that is uncomfortable with our own former ways of making sense), we might have more compassion for such a worry if we considered that it was really about holding oneself together.

When I look at the way Alice constructs her therapist, I find myself thinking about power or authority, an issue which must always be in the air in a therapy situation: one person has gone to, or been sent to, another in order to get help. How will the client construct the authority dimension of the relationship? Does Alice seem to see the therapist and his authority as a kind of threat or obstacle to her own separate authority which she has to vie against or manipulate? Does she see his powers as something she might bend to her own control, or which she might in some way take advantage of without surrendering any of her own control? This would be the typical picture of the imperial (balance 2) approach; people who make meaning in this way, such as Terry, Richard, and Roxanne from Chapter 6, are typically designated as having "authority problems." Actually their "problem" is that they are unable to integrate their own authority with another's — hence in each case there are really two authorities bumping against each other. But Alice's relation to her therapist does not seem to be at all like this. While her behavior may be said to be "manipulative," it is not of this authority-preserving type (actually *all* behavior is in some sense manipulative), and while she may be said to be trying to meet her needs, she is not "need-embedded" (balance 2). (Actually, everyone is trying to meet some need.) She is not need-embedded because her "needs" are intrinsically interpersonal, and she is not manipulating the therapist in an imperial fashion because she is trying above all to avoid independent control. Rather than trying to preserve her authority, she is trying to fuse with his authority, to get him to let her live in his authority.

On the other hand, we can ask if Alice's fundamental stance toward her therapist seems to reflect the importance to her of his respecting, recognizing, and helping her protect her independent judgment and internal self-government. Is she asking to be taken seriously as a grown-up and an equal, making it clear that while she needs help she is not asking to be taken care of, to be taken over, to be patronized; that she recognizes she can and will "do" this herself, just not necesssarily alone? This would be a typical picture of an institutional (balance 4) construction of the therapist and the initial therapy situation. And, again, Alice does not appear to see him in this way at all. On the contrary, she explicitly desires him to take over and is somewhat girlish rather than adult in her demeanor. ("I don't want to take responsibility unless an authority tells me. I don't like feeling that it could all be my fault.")

Thus Alice's construction of her therapist and the therapy situation seems as consistently interpersonal as her presentation of herself and her concerns. But not all is well with the interpersonal balance. Indeed, from a constructive-developmental perspective, this is the sine qua non of the therapeutic situation: behind everything else, the reason persons summon the extraordinary courage to come and talk with a stranger about the intimate details of their lives is that they are experiencing an evolutionary upheaval. Usually it is a matter of collapse in the foundations that hold and culture one's evolutionary balance, or it is a matter of one's own evolutionary leave-taking of the balance which has been "me," and which, in part, struggles to remain so. Something is the matter with the balance in which "I" hang. For Alice the problem does not seem to be so much a matter of others refusing to keep their end of the balance, as it seems to be internal: "I have an 'ornery' side, a part of me I don't know what to do with." How are we to understand this?

"Ornery" is an important word in Alice's vocabulary, and a curious one. Our understanding of it brings us directly in front of the kind of choice I mentioned at the beginning of this chapter — a choice between the psychoanalytic understanding of a regressive replay of early childhood and the constructive-developmental understanding of an era-appropriate expression of themes which have a similarity to an earlier era but could only come about precisely because the childhood construction has passed through two fundamental evolutions. "Ornery" evokes the unruly child. When Alice uses the word, it may help to know, it is usually accompanied by a devilish smile and a wriggling in her seat. She is referring, of course, to her sexuality, but in her use of a word more appropriate for a child, in her general presentation of naughtiness, she reminds us more of the sexuality of the impulse-embedded oedipal child.

While it is tempting to view all this in light of a model of regression in the service of the ego, and a replaying of a childhood issue, we risk losing the sense in which Alice is *not* four years old, the possibility in which her orneriness is actually a *forward* edge (rather than a regressive one) in her evolution. While we are undeniably witnessing a replaying of the theme of overinclusion, this is an evolutionary theme, not a childhood one, and we risk losing the difference between overinclusion in the impulses and the parents who are confused with them, on the one hand, and overinclusion in the interpersonal and all the important interpersonal partners (including the parents) with whom one is confused, on the other. Alice's "ornery" side, from a constructive-developmental view, could easily be the specter of any feeling (in this case sexuality) which is not completely mediated by the interpersonal. While most of Alice is still firmly invested in the interpersonal balance in which she has lived for many years, her experience of difficulty and upheaval could have to do with the fact that some part of her has begun the emergence from this embeddedness. Being largely invested in the interpersonal balance, and knowing the world this way, that part of her which seems determined to have its own rule—to enjoy sex for itself, for example—is going to be seen as an alien and an enemy. Sexuality, no less than any other aspect of human activity, is experienced differently when the meaning I have become is different; and sexuality, perhaps as much as any other human activity, being the adult form of play par excellence, is a kind of affirmation of that meaning. What is most sexually satisfying is the sexual celebration of evolutionary balance (my way of being joined to the world); and what is sexually threatening is that which threatens this balance. Interpersonally embedded sexuality can amount to an ethic of "my pleasure is your pleasure," "what satisfies me is that you are satisfied." This does not look like a position of subservience or self-abnegation until the institutional balance, when the notion of an independent selfhood is paramount. Indeed, in the first flushes of the new institutional balance it may be necessary to avoid sexuality entirely, lest one be reabsorbed in the old embeddedness; or it may be necessary to elect an autoregulative sexuality—masturbation; but again, certainly a very different sexuality than early adolescent masturbation. Certainly the ideological appropriation of masturbation among women at one point in the women's movement seems a good example of a hard-won evolutionary gain. "A woman without a man is like a fish without a bicycle," is the slogan delivered as much to an old evolutionary balance as to the world at large.

But Alice is not in the new balance, not even in its first attempts at balance, so that that part of her which seems governed by a new ethic ("my pleasure is *my* pleasure") may feel naughty, selfish, guilt-worthy—in short, ornery. It is a part of her, but it is not the "real me"; it is out for itself, but the real me takes others into account. It is only the real me which speaks to the therapist and listens to him. In her initial presentation to a therapist, it is as if it is only the real me that is in the room. The "ornery me" is a problem outside the consulting room and perhaps the real me and the doctor can find out how to take care of the ornery me.

In this stance Alice is reminiscent of the college students who come to a college counseling center saying, "I've just lost my motivation; I can't get myself to work." Frequently they are persons who have worked hard in school all their lives and done quite well. Yet somehow, inexplicably, they have come to a halt. This is often expressed as a loss—a loss of concentration, energy, purpose, fire. Something is gone. Often persons in this predicament describe themselves as lazy or having become lazy. The side of the person who talks initially in the consulting room is the side that is not working, the side which has been invaded by "laziness." The side that does *not* speak its own voice is the side that has decided not to work. Sometimes after several meetings and several invitations to that side ("Sounds like some part of you has gone on strike . . . ?"), that side begins to speak. Its voice is often angry. Sometimes the student discovers that she stopped working because she was mad, because she wanted to do one thing and was tired of taking orders from the "real me," who at this very moment is beginning to feel less like the real me and more like the me-I-have-been. Sometimes the me-I-have-been starts to look more like the expectations of *other* people, often one's parents, who are just now gradually being separated from oneself. This is the disembeddedness at the heart of the shift from the interpersonal to the institutional balance, a separating out of a confusion which raises the classic question of this shift—"Who is in charge around here, anyway?"

Possibly Alice's future course in therapy would involve the welcoming in of that side of herself which is only being looked at from the old embeddedness. What is presently only a "growth" (in the sense of a tumor, a problem for the host organism) is potentially the source of her own becoming. How a therapist, acting on these hunches, might address her is a subject I will take up in Chapter 9. But for now, perhaps it can be seen that any resolution of Alice's concerns must involve something more than a better resolution of the old impulsive balance or a better resolution of the oedipal conflict. It must involve a resolution of the limits of an evolutionary predicament far in advance of childhood, a resolution of the limits of interpersonalism. Alice's "problem" can be seen, in part, as an inability to integrate into a single self-organization the relationships of nurturant parenthood and passionate womanhood. This is a meaning-evolutionary problem which can be artificially managed (if not really solved) by the social convention of marriage.

Marriage may provide an external structure by which one can see oneself less conflictedly as both affiliative mother and sexual wife; it subtends both roles and provides something of a boundary between the investments in a child and the investments in a lover. With the conclusion of her marriage, Alice loses that external structure, and because she "is" her relationships rather than "having" them, she is unable to provide the structure internally. At the point in the life history when a person, in addition to needing a culture of embeddedness, may be regularly called on to *provide* one, the single parent embedded in the interpersonal may have difficulties providing the contradictory or differentiation-oriented side of that culture which his or her child needs. Such may have an inhibiting effect on the "sealing up" of the child in his or her move from the impulsive to the imperial balance, at the same time the interpersonally embedded parent is in need of a qualitatively different kind of sealing up. Rather than needing to unconfuse her impulses with others, she needs to unconfuse the very source of her judgments, expectations, and obligations from others (the impulse twice evolved). Alice provides a beautiful example of this too permeable boundary when she talks to the therapist about controlling her sexual desires:[1] "In the meantime, I can't stop these desires. I tried that also. I have tried saying, 'O.K., I don't like myself when I do that so I won't do it anymore.' But then I resent *the children*. I think, 'Why should *they* stop me from doing what I want?' " (Emphasis added.) What begins as a judgment by the self (I will stop) ends up as an external judgment (they make me stop). Because the source of judgment and expectation is confused with the other (in this case,

1. Ann Henderson showed this to me.

Alice's children), guilty feelings must implicate someone else, some other whose expectations are not being met; in the institutional balance, guilt is a matter of violating one's own standard, irrespective of the other's expectations. Once again, such an account is consistent with the notion that this period (not necessarily chronological adolescence, so much as the era of the growth and loss of the interpersonal balance) evokes early childhood themes of oedipal resolution, internalization, and superego formation; but such an account also makes clearer, I think, the sense in which what is similar in color and tone is also different in its psychological complexity.

Thus, the interpersonal balance, while resolving the conflicts of the former stage's need-embeddedness, is vulnerable, in its own embeddedness, to another sort of conflict. Once again, the shift from one self to the next can be painful, protracted, and life-disordering. The threat of the loss of my most important relationships is the precipitating experience par excellence for the crisis of the 3-4 shift. For a self that is derived from interpersonal relationship, it can be experienced as the threat of the loss of the self itself. The neediness, fears of abandonment, wish to be cared for that characterizes the depressive picture at this transition is a grasping for more than any given individual; it is a grasping to keep the self afloat lest it drown in this sudden incapacity to maintain its buoyancy or balance. This threat need not be occasioned only by the rejection or betrayal of another; it can be occasioned by termination at my own initiation as well. If the expectations or obligations of the relationship—the very connective weave in which I locate myself—become excessive, or conflict with the expectation of another equally valued relationship, this too can throw the interpersonalist system into disequilibrium. If such an experience persists or recurs, it is difficult to keep assimilating it—a problem with *this* or *that* relationship—and the possibility arises for the system's "recognition" of the problem of making the interpersonal the ultimate context in the first place. Ultimacy is the issue in every shift. Phenomenologically, it seems that our way of making meaning is, to us, not merely an adequate way of construing the world, but the most adequate construction; and it is this feeling that makes the crisis-inducing discrepancy so threatening. It raises the possibility of making relative what I had taken for ultimate.

Although I have suggested that American culture tends to favor the side of independence over the side of inclusion (and I would extend that to Western culture in general), it is not a generalization that seems to apply uniformly to men and women in our culture. Indeed, although I have no idea why it may be, it seems to me that men tend to have more difficulty acknowledging their need for inclusion, tend to be more oriented toward differentiation, and that women tend to have more difficulty acknowledging their need for distinctness, tend to be more oriented toward inclusion. Whether this is a function of social experience throughout the lifespan, the effects of parenting, anatomical (even genital) destiny, or some combination, I do not know. Whatever the source of this distinction between men and women, I believe it is also the case that this very distinction is to be found within any one person as well. In this respect constructive-developmental theory revives the Jungian notion that there is a man in every woman and a woman in every man; saying so is both a consequence of considering that all of life is animated by a fundamental evolutionary ambivalence, and that "maleness"/"femaleness" is but one of its expressions. Similarly, I believe that while Western and Eastern cultures reflect one side or the other of this ambivalence, they project the other. Western cultures tend to value independence, self-assertion, aggrandizement, personal achievement, increasing independence from the family of origin; Eastern cultures (including the American Indian) value the other pole. Cheyenne Indians asked to talk about themselves typically begin, "My grandfather . . ." (Strauss, 1981); many Eastern cultures use the word "I" to refer to a collectivity of people of which one is a part (Marriott, 1981); the Hopi do not say, "It's a nice day," as if one could separate oneself from the day, but say something that would have to be translated more like, "I am in a nice day," or "It's nice in front, and behind, and above" (Whorf, 1956). At the same time one cannot escape the enormous hunger for community, mystical merging, or intergenerational connection that continually reappears in American culture through communalism, quasi-Eastern religions, cult phenomena, drug experience, the search for one's "roots," the idealization of the child, or the romantic appeal of extended families. Similarly, it seems too glib to dismiss as "mere Westernization" the repeated expression in Eastern cultures of individualism, intergenerational autonomy, or entrepreneurialism as if these were completely imposed from without and not in any way the expression of some side of Eastern culture itself.

Evidence of a recessive pole notwithstanding, the differing emphasis among cultures and sexes seems to me quite powerful, enduring, and beyond question of noncomparable dignity and stature. There should be no question of one emphasis being any "better" than another, certainly not on developmental grounds (indeed, it is as true to say that each is equally limited to the extent it denies its other side). And yet, it is easy for a given group to make its persuasion the standard. The cross-culturalists' claim of ethnocentrism (even the accusation that Western psychology is no less a "folk psychology" than that of any other culture's) (Fogelson, 1981; LeVine, 1981) is analogous to the feminist psychologists' claim that the definitions of growth which developmental psychologists esteem are male-biased (Gilligan, 1978). And both claims would seem to be more true than false. Wherever one looks among developmental psychologists, from Freud at one end of a spectrum to Carl Rogers at the other, one finds a conception of growth as increasing autonomy or distinctness. The yearning for inclusion tends to be demeaned as a kind of dependency or immature attachment. Only a psychology whose root metaphors intrinsically direct an equal respect for both poles (and orient to the relation between them) can hope to transcend this myopia.

But however real the differences between cultures or sexes, and however vulnerable to imperialization one is by the other, I do not believe, as many cross-culturalists do (LeVine, 1981), that we must rule ourselves out as having any capacity to judge, or even think about, another culture unless we expunge ourselves of our own origins. Nor do I believe that the possibility of profound communication and understanding between the sexes is denied us. Our differences do not radically separate us, because there *is* a single context we all share and from which both sides of the tension spring—namely, meaning-constitutive evolutionary activity, the motion of life itself. I believe East *can* talk to West and West to East, that man can talk to woman and woman to man—if neither makes its particular pole-preference ultimate; if neither forces the other to be known in its language; if each recognizes that its language is only relative to the ultimate language they both share.

The struggle of the sexes to know each other, to see each other, and to communicate deeply—a struggle which may be more a feature of adult life in the West than at any time in the past—may rest in the capacity of men and women to learn the universal language they share, an evolutionary esperanto, the dialectical context in which these two poles are joined. It may rest in their recognition that neither differentiation nor integration is prior, but that each is a part of the reality of being alive.

Even in the midst of charged and often irritable relations between men and women, East and West, we have the opportunity to drop back to consider the whole of which we are a part. When we do, something quite beautiful and moving appears: a single community of people who together give expression to the full complexity of being alive; a universality which each of us can find reflected in ourselves (the woman in every man, the Easterner in every Westerner). I am reminded of the story of the infant Krishna, taken to the beach by his mother, who did not yet know he was a god. Krishna ate some sand (as infants will), and when his mother went to him and looked into his mouth, it is said she saw the entire universe. Who among us is not in this way a god?

But if there is something intrinsically differentiation-oriented about maleness and inclusion-oriented about femaleness, it is possible that despite the way the evolutionary truces move back and forth in their emphases, a man may tend to move through all of them in a more differentiated way, and a woman in a more integrated way. Whether the orientations are intrinsic or a product of acculturation, it seems true that as long as they exist we will tend to see men spending somewhat longer times in those evolutionary truces tilted toward differentiation (the imperial (2) and institutional (4) balances), and women spending somewhat longer times in the truces tilted toward integration (the interpersonal (3) and interindividual (5) balances). Put another way, women can be expected to have more difficulty emerging from embeddedness in the interpersonal, men more difficulty emerging from the embeddedness in the institutional. From research on sociomoral development (an analysis closest to the framework we are considering here), there is recurring evidence in the study of adolescents that girls are developmentally beyond their boy cohorts. More particularly, they seem to get to interpersonalism faster (Selman, 1969; Turiel, 1972). There is also evidence that they seem to stay there longer (Haan, et al., 1968; Kramer, R., 1968; Holstein, 1969, 1976; Kohlberg and Kramer, 1969; Gilligan et al., 1971; Hudgins and Prentice, 1973). If women are more vulnerable to fusion (balance 3), it is also possible that they are more capable of intimacy (balance 5). If men find it easier to reach the psychological autonomy of ideological adulthood (balance 4), it is also possible that they find it harder to evolve to mature, postideological adulthood (balance 5).

However much a man or a woman's evolutionary style might predispose him or her to favor a particular evolutionary truce, the radically different nature of traditional supports for men and women for just this kind of evolution is so overwhelming that it is hard to avoid concluding that the greatest source of difference in evolutionary level lies with the differing embeddedness cultures available to men and women. The interpersonalist balance, after all, with its orientation to nurturance, affiliation, and the organization of the self around the expectations of the other, conforms to the traditional stereotype of femininity. Although such an evolution of meaning-making is essentially adolescent in the psychological issues with which it deals (and cannot deal), it is probably safe to say that before the 1960s and the women's movement this was the only culturally supported construction of adulthood for women. The relation between the culture at large (what we ordinarily mean by "culture") and the more intimate cultures of embeddedness which hold and support the evolution of personality is obviously not random. The consequences of the traditional cultural conception of female adulthood could only be a kind of evolutionary double-whammy: it both overholds (undercontradicts) the interpersonalist balance *and* fails to recognize or hold the emergence of a self-authoring identity. To act in any way on one's emergence from an embeddedness in the interpersonal in the absence of any confirmation of its reality is to risk feeling profoundly disloyal and selfish, at best, or to feel like one is going out of one's mind, at worst.

Although the notion that many people who are chronologically adult are psychologically adolescent is controversial or irritating, and risks blaming the victim, its central purpose is to indicate how devastating can be the impact of a lack of those most intimate supports which a person needs to grow. Because the kinds of support a person needs in the fourth evolutionary balance—recognition as an independent person in one's own right, admission to a societal arena, adult participation in a group, opportunity for publicly recognized personal achievement, support and entry to the world of work, especially the notion of "career" rather than "job"—are essentially a matter of social arrangements (looked at externally) and ideology (looked at internally), the deprivation and blindness of the culture at large will have rather *direct* consequences for development in the years normally associated with adulthood.

The results of several constructive-developmental studies indicating that women have tended more frequently than men to remain in the interpersonal balance (Haan et al., 1968; Kramer, R., 1968; Holstein, 1969, 1976; Kohlberg and Kramer, 1969; Gilligan et al., 1971; Hudgins and Prentice, 1973) have turned some people who are concerned about women against the constructive-developmental framework. It would make sense, however, not only to spare the head of the bearer of bad news but to use such news as further support for the position of those concerned about women: cultural deprivations *do have* palpable effects on human development. The constructive-developmental framework ought to be the most important psychological ally of any systematically excluded group because its notion of "pathology" is the least related to adjustment or coping and the most capable of detecting an unwholesome situation even when everyone seems to be functioning in ways that do not make others uncomfortable. Although readers who are strongly wedded to a psychiatric orientation have probably been driven to distraction in this book by the way I have grouped persons who look quite "sick" together with persons who look much better (for example, Diane and Alice, respectively, in this chapter), it is not because I am blind to the differences between them. I bring them together because I think they share something that a psychiatric or pathology orientation would tend to miss and something that I think is of prior importance— namely, they are in a similar evolutionary predicament. After their own meaning-making and fundamental relatedness to the world is understood, the state of their balancing, and how well they are able to preserve their balancing (defenses), can be considered.

It would be a mistake to conclude that because my orientation is fundamentally toward processes of growth rather than processes of health and illness, it is unable to sound a psychological alarm. On the contrary, an orientation to processes of growth is equally an orientation to processes which thwart or retard growth, and an evolutionary approach to meaning-making (as opposed to a purely existential one) establishes a basis for evaluation and judgment which is not as likely to be co-opted by the partialities of custom or convention. The kinds of distinctions a meaning-evolutionary perspective makes does not require a person to show signs of distress, social maladjustment, or "psychopathology" or to make others uncomfortable in order for us to be concerned about them. Individuals can develop at quite different rates, and slow development is not in itself a cause for alarm. But when a whole subpopulation of a culture—whether or not each member needs or seeks psychiatric attention—seems to have developmentally delayed constituents, one has a way to begin analyzing the possibility that the cultural arrangements are themselves deleterious. One has a way that is not defined by the dominant culture and its possibly self-serving notion of health and illness. A good psychological theory protects the least favored members of a culture from having their status preserved by a psychology which is unwittingly the agent of the privileged.

Fortunately, the picture of female adulthood today is no longer monolithically that of interpersonally embedded hyperfeminism. Indeed, the most dramatic and publicly moving demonstrations of the evolution out of the interpersonal balance in the culture today are probably those of women. Among the most important functions—perhaps *the* most important function—of the women's movement has been to provide that culture of embeddedness—a *counterculture*—which recognizes and holds the emergence of a personally authored identity. Consciousness-raising groups, books about a woman's life changes, and story, song, and slogan do far more than mutually confirm one's experience or let one know one is not alone. They actually do raise consciousness (which is what evolution is about) exactly because they sponsor a qualitative reconstruction of the self and the world. The women's movement offers the invitation to women to see the very fact of their womanhood as entry to the ideological participation which is essential to the institutional evolutionary balance. The exercises of ideology—which, for example, provide a system of explanation subtending interpersonal relations; make everyday life political; give one a feeling of control over the present, an understanding of one's collusive role in one's constraining past, and a program for the future; draw and preserve lines of differentiation between the group of which one is a part and groups of which one is not a part—are all expressions of a fundamentally new evolutionary truce which makes the self an organization or an institution, its constituent parts public to itself, its successful internal maintenance and control its ultimate concern.

American culture quite naturally provides these ideological supports to those it favors and elects as fellow participants in the social and psychological institutions which regulate its established arrangements.

Essentially, these favored persons have been middle-class white men. A middle-class white man's evolution out of embeddedness in the interpersonal is not a moving spectacle in our culture precisely because there is no spectacle—you cannot *watch* it (unless you look closely at a given individual over time). It will stand out in the private relations of the person's immediate network but it does not stand out as figure on the cultural ground precisely because it is embedded in the tacit ideology of the culture. This is one reason the tacit ideology is so powerful and insidious for those it excludes: it cannot be seen; it is not held up for examination. What may be the most important consequence of the upheavals of the last fifteen years—largely through the attention these upheavals brought to the arrangements between blacks and whites (the "civil rights movement"), men and women (the "women's movement"), and the government and the governed (the "antiwar movement")—is that the ideological nature of American life was made explicit. (Evolutionarily, if I were to apply my scheme to the culture at large, I should have to say the upheavals of the sixties and early seventies represented the transitional angst of the emergences out of "institutional" embeddedness; of course, from the point of view of the old world not yet left behind, this same upheaval must look like a collapse of our basic institutions, which is just what popular analysis says.) For persons excluded from the tacit culture of ideology to make this move, it is necessary for them to construct their own ideological support which will necessarily stand out. Whether the ideology is feminism or black power or gay rights, it will have common features which serve the absolutely crucial function of supporting the evolution of meaning. It holds and recognizes the group-extensiveness of the new differentiation ("black pride," "I am woman") and protects against reabsorption into the old embeddedness (whether by moratoria from intimate relations with men, say, or turning to women—one's comrades—for intimate relations; or the adoption of a strident language which can be as much an effort to hold off an old self as it is an address to others).

I am not suggesting, of course, that feminism, for example, is *only* ideological, or is incapable of an expression which transcends ideology (we will see what this would mean in the next chapter). I am only saying that it serves the function of nourishing and culturing ideology. Most of all, it should be clear that ideology itself is not a negative category in my vocabulary. On the contrary, I am suggesting that the development of an ideological construction of self and world, tacit or explicit, is a necessary and natural feature of development toward maturity. It may be worth pointing out that the last several pages of this book have only *seemed* to abandon what had thus far been a psychological discourse for what now appears to be a political one. Actually, this more "political" discussion has been no less psychological. Our consideration of the ideological nature of American culture is not at all different from our considering how a family supports a four-year-old, or how a peer gang supports a ten-year-old. The distinction between the personal or psychological and the political or social is quite arbitrary, the inheritance of theories too narrowly drawn in their root metaphors. The last several pages sound political only because the evolution of meaning has become political at this stage in a person's history. That which cultures the evolution has become a matter of wider and more complex social arrangements. Just as the constructive-developmental perspective offers the possibility of resolving the split between affect and cognition by recognizing that each is an expression of a more fundamental phenomenon which gives rise to both, so too it offers the hope of a less bifurcated consideration of the psychological and the social through the same recognition. Neither the psychological nor the social has priority; meaning-constitutive evolutionary activity gives rise to both.

All growth is costly. It involves the leaving behind of an old way of being in the world. Often it involves, at least for a time, leaving behind the others who have been identified with that old way of being. The two-year-old's "No" is really a repudiation of his own old way of being. Seen from the point of view of his evolution, his declaration is really to his old self, which had been embedded in the world. But what the world has largely been for a two-year-old, at least the human world, is its parents, and viewed from *their* perspective the child's "No" is a repudiation of them. The six-year-old's evolutionary "recognition" (not conscious, of course), which enables her to separate her impulses from her parents, involves the disillusioning of a kind of perfect closeness and synchrony which is not to be. To discover basic limitations in one's whole way of knowing can be by itself an anxious and difficult experience; but it is the creation of the new other in the process which makes it also a potentially shameful experience. Shame involves the recognition that others have been aware of vulnerabilities in me that I am only now coming to see. Before, I was naked; now I see that I am uncovered. But "am uncovered" becomes "was un-covered" as soon as possible, shame creating history, a "developmental backside," as Erik Erikson might put it. Shame always carries this retrospective dimension, an attack from behind, a re-seeing of the past through one's new eyes (more able now to see through the eyes of others), a greater participation that may be for a period more humil-iating than enlarging. It is not uncommon for children to go through a period of feeling they have been betrayed or lied to, which is really only an expression of what now seems the falseness of one's own embeddedness. The accusations—often about fantasies now seen through, such as Santa Claus, in which the parents have colluded—are as much at the old self which had been embedded in those who are now being accused. Jung (1954) gives an example of just such behavior which follows a child's gradual discovery that the fairytale accounts of childbirth her parents have given her cannot be true:

> Mother: Come, we'll go into the garden.
> Anna: You're lying to me. Watch out if you're not telling the truth!
> Mother: What are you thinking of? Of course I'm telling the truth.
> Anna: No, you are not telling the truth.
> Mother: You'll soon see whether I'm telling the truth: We are going into the garden this minute.
> Anna: Is that true? You're quite sure it's true? You're not lying?
>
> (p. 14)

Although I believe it is advisable to tell children the truth about childbirth when they ask for it, I doubt very much that even a parent's perfect vigilance against any collusion in the fantasies of early childhood—refusing to endorse the reality of Santa Claus, for ex-ample—will prevent the child's sense of having been betrayed or lied to when he or she moves the fantasies (and the parents-as-impulse) from subject to object in his or her meaning-making. It is only testimony to the parents' successful culturing of the impulsive balance that they are for a time repudiated when the balance itself is repudiated. When the child discovers that his or her parents can be reappropriated in the new balance, that it is not one's parents so much as one's old construction of one's parents that one is rejecting, then the parents can be reknown and reintegrated.

The repeated rejection and recovery of the parents is historic, adaptive, and inevitable, if painful for the parents. "Parenthood," Kiyo Morimoto once remarked, "is the experience of inevitable defeat." Or as Mark Twain put it from the other side, "My parents were so dumb when I was seventeen and so much smarter when I was twenty-one; I can't believe how much they learned in just four years." The parents' role in the culture of embeddedness is repeatedly modulated and augmented as the child moves into new balances, but the parents remain the single most important resource for continuing recognition throughout childhood. Although the relationship is fraught with crises and never more vulnerable to collapse than in those periods of repudiation, its continuity is preserved by the stark reality of the child's ongoing needs for shelter and care. The eight-year-old can run away from home—but only for a few hours. There is something very graceful about this arrangement: at those times when much of the child would like to have nothing more to do with the parents, he or she is forced to return and hang out and make the best of it. Eventually the situation improves because the parents, in the child's meaning-making, become different people.

Although the same phenomena attend transitions at any stage, the situation is not at all so graceful after childhood. The highly elaborated network of relations and anchorings that we associate with preindustrial America may have provided a somewhat similar prophylaxis in times of post-childhood transition, but such extensive supports over time or space are no longer usual. These supports are so integral to the experiences of genuine community that one discovers their form and function more in their absence than in their presence. One of the grimmer features of modern American life is that many people (perhaps most people) live today without this community context. Among its most important benefits is its capacity to recognize a person, a marriage, a family, over time, and to help the developing system recognize itself amid the losses and recoveries of normal growth. Without this support—without the pressure to remain at those times when we want to repudiate real people along with old constructions of these people—we may "run away from home," and unfortunately, given our adult abilities to provide for ourselves, we are not forced to return when it gets dark. Without these supports during times of adult development, left to ourselves, we often negotiate our transitions by separating ourselves not only from our old meaning but from the actual persons who (and commitments which) have come to stand for those meanings.

Modern American life is characterized not only by this decreased support for integration but also by an increased support for differentiation. The present culture provides a kind of sponsorship for personal growth and realization that extends somewhat more broadly across social class, ethnic, and sex categories than ever before. While this may foster more fundamental evolution in adulthood than ever before, the culture has not found a way to respond to the disruption such growth entails or to support the new integrations such growth demands. Our current situation is characterized thus by a lack of once-available supports and the inability of the existing supports to engage completely the phenomena of fundamental change in adulthood.

We live in a time when separation is virtually celebrated as a sign of growth in adulthood—notably in marriage (that is, divorce) but also, more subtly, in movement into and out of communities, work roles, and a host of commitments persons make. It is possible that this phenomenon is a function of our inability to work out the anger and shame attendant on evolutionary development in the context of the relationship or environment that provoked it. It is possible that we turn to the new community and new relationships with a relief that "here, only the new me will be known," and that these new others, in their not knowing, will help me leave my old self behind. If we live at a time when there is more fundamental change in adulthood than ever before, we may be faced with a task that is also historically unprecedented, at the growing edge of our culture's evolution: how to fashion long-term relationships, even "long-term communities" (the term should sound redundant), which are the context for fundamental change rather than ended by it. Serial relationships and serial communities are much in vogue these days, but we might consider at what price we elect them. Long-term relationships and life in a community of considerable duration may be essential if we are not to lose ourselves, if we are to be able to recollect ourselves. They may be essential to the human coherence of our lives, a coherence which is not found from looking into the faces of those who relieve us because we can see they know nothing of us when we were less than ourselves, but from looking into the faces of those who relieve us because they reflect our history in their faces, faces which we can look into finally without anger or shame, and which look back at us with love.

Just as a person is not a stage of development but the process of development itself, a marriage contract is not, ideally, a particular evolutionary contract but a context for continued evolution. If it is not, the marriage may give out at the same time the evolutionary truce gives out. The reconstruction of a marriage is an enormously difficult feat, and, as is the case with all such evolution, it requires a support that is more invested in the person who develops than any given organization of self which the personality has evolved. If one partner enters and constructs a marriage from the interpersonal balance, for example, and then begins to emerge from this embeddedness, the marriage itself becomes, or needs to become, something new. What may have been a context for exercising and celebrating a way of making meaning oriented to affiliation, nurturance, and identification might have to become something more like a context for loving which preserves, supports, and celebrates a kind of mutual distinctness, independence, or cooperation of separate interests. But if one's spouse cannot be recognized (known again) along with the rest of the world, either because of the spouse's own difficulties (our transformations can be the discrepancy which threatens meaning in those closest to us), or because of our own inability to work through the shame and anger which confuses persons with the now-repudiated construction of meaning (I see my spouse as having colluded in my dependence and subservience), then the epistemological separating of self from other may be accompanied by the actual separation from real people and places in my developing life. All of these elements are captured in a story related to me by a bewildered rabbi.

"A woman comes to see me, this is maybe thirty years ago. A woman who isn't a Jewish woman. She has fallen in love with a Jewish man. And, so that a lot of other people should be happy, she wants to make a conversion. If other people are happy she will be happy, this is what she says. She is very frank about this. Religion and politics and business—these things mean a lot to other people, she says. By her what matters is her husband and her friends, and one day, she hopes, her children. She is a good woman, a sincere person, but she has no real feeling about Judaism and I can't be much help to her.

"Seven years later, comes to see me the same woman. But it's almost a different person. Yes, she converted. Yes, she got married. Yes, she has children. But something is not right. She loves her family but she doesn't love herself, this is what she says. 'I'm thirty years old,' she says. 'I have three children and I don't even know who I am.' She thinks maybe she can figure this out by learning what is this Jewish stuff. She wants to study by me. Not to make a conversion, she says. 'I'm already converted.' But to learn who she is.

"For the next year she studies by me. What a workhorse! She learns Hebrew. She reads Talmud. She makes a Kosher house. Her husband, who I bar mitzvahed, is complaining to me, 'Stop already, you're making my wife into a rabbi.' But it wasn't me. She was taking every step on her own. She was finding out who she was.

"Then she starts to be concerned about her conversion. 'It wasn't sincere, Rabbi.' 'It wasn't kosher, Rabbi.' 'I'm not really Jewish, Rabbi.' What can I tell her? She didn't make an orthodox conversion, this is true, and, by her, this is now the only thing that counts. Do I have to tell you what happened? Almost ten years after she first comes to see me she is dipped in the ritual baths and I am signing her document, a legal convert, more orthodox than I am.

"Ah, but that isn't the end of the story. Before the next High Holidays she decides how can she live with a Jew who would marry a Gentile and so she divorces her husband."

The Growth and Loss of the Institutional Self

Michael is a man in his mid-thirties, a successful lawyer-businessman with a great deal of enthusiasm for his multiple work involvements. He brings himself to a therapist, he says, because he has begun to be concerned about what seems to him a pattern in his involvements with women, and he has started to wonder what part he himself plays in it. Never married, Michael has nonetheless "always been closely involved with women, sometimes more than one woman at once." The pattern, as Michael sees it, is that he finds a woman appealing and becomes involved with her. This part of the relationship nearly always goes well; it is filled with hope and warmth and excitement. But then as he and the woman move closer, he inevitably finds, to his regret, that there are "things about the woman which simply make her unacceptable as a long-term partner."

"She's a wonderful person and I admire her and care for her in many ways, but—(she is just too old/ she is just too young/ she really has no sense of humor and I end up feeling a whole part of myself has to be put on hold with her/ she never gets serious, everything is a joke to her/ she has too many kids/ she doesn't think she wants to have children/ she is too wealthy and I feel threatened by her independence/ I feel burdened by the poverty she calls 'the only ethical way to live'/ she only wants to make love one way/ when we make love I never have the feeling I've really satisfied her/ she's too different from me and my life/ there's not enough contrast between us/ the relationship just doesn't have enough friction or electricity, it's like a comfortable sweater/ the relationship is too much like a roller-coaster, it never settles down)." Michael's feeling about this tendency always to find something wrong—up until he started wondering about himself—was that he "just had very high standards," that some day he would meet a woman who was "just what I want," and that then he would quite naturally and without great difficulty allow himself to move closer. Until then, as he saw it, it neither felt right nor seemed fair to let a relationship get more entangled when he did not "mean it," when he already knew he and the woman were only going to have to get unentangled eventually.

Once Michael determines that the woman is "somehow just not right" or that "it just cannot work as the one big relationship," the pattern moves into its next phase. The movement toward greater depth of involvement stops. Michael continues to offer a kind of caring and connection that is neither superficial nor insincere but definitely limited. It is without commitment either to a future or to a present exploration of all that the relationship might be. Sometimes Michael begins at this point (always with the first woman's knowledge) to see another woman as well. As Michael puts it, this is the point in the pattern "where the woman decides." He finds that some women are unwilling to continue in a relationship they experience as insurmountably blocked. But many woman *do* continue, either in the hope, Michael surmises, that things will somehow change, or because they too are most comfortable in this mid-range of "mutual support without mutual dependency" as Michael describes it. A person whose work life has led him into long-term friendships and group involvements throughout this country and Canada, Michael nonetheless describes himself, and quite precisely, as "an unattached man."

Michael can be said to be having problems with "intimacy." But how much is intimacy a matter of development, even the development of subject-object relations? The "psychologic" of the institutional balance wrests the self from the context of interpersonalism and brings into being an "I" that has, rather than is, its relationships. This evolution brings into being the self as a form or system. Its strength is its capacity for self-regulation, its capacity to sustain itself, to parent itself, to name itself—its autonomy. Yet every developmental balance involves as well an illusion, a built-in falsehood or subjectivity which forms the seed of its own undoing. Given enough experience with the world, assimilative defenses which have not had to become all-powerful, holding environments which can let go of one balance and recognize another, every subject-object relation will eventually be hoisted by its own petard. This is as true of the institutional balance as it is of any other, though the requirements listed above, especially that concerning the holding environments, may, as we shall see, become a taller order with each new evolution.

The institutional balance evinces a kind of self-sufficiency which, at a whole new level of complexity, reminds us of its evolutionary cousin, the imperial balance of the school-age child. The reason they are cousins is that they are both somewhat overdifferentiated. They resolve the evolutionary tension between independence and inclusion in favor of the former. At the same time, of course, the nature of their self-determination is as different as the control of one's behavior is from the control of one's self-definition.

If the strength of the institutional balance is its autonomy, it would be as true to say that its weakness lies in its embeddedness in this autonomy. Its self-naming and self-nourishing converts the world within its reach to operatives on behalf of its personal enterprise. What is experienced from within the balance as independence and self-regulation might as accurately be seen from beyond the balance as a kind of psychological isolation or masturbation. From within the system this constraint is a matter of vulnerability to whatever threatens self-control, a vulnerability the institutional balance shares with its evolutionary cousin. For a child in the imperial balance this might involve the curtailments or goal interruptions of a superior authority, displays of behavioral incompetence, or fears of the old hegemony of the impulses. The child's rage and shame and fear of her own impulses certainly find echoes in the institutional adult's depressive self-anger, guilty self-shame, and fears about boundary loss. As we will see in this chapter, the experience of losing one's balance, when the balance is the institutional, consists in feelings of negative self-evaluation, feelings that one's personal organization is threatened or about to collapse, fears about losing one's control and one's precious sense of being distinct.

It is arguable that Michael had been for several years firmly within the institutional balance and that his relationships with women were an expression both of any system's interest in engaging the world and any system's interest in preserving itself. Does Michael's "laundry list" of discontents, which he seems always capable of generating at just those times when the relationship is getting more involved, serve to preserve his personal control over the regulation of his own psychology? But something seems to be happening with Michael; another voice, quieter, more fragile, seems to be sounding a different theme. It is possible that the psychologic of the institutional balance, like every one before it, has begun to wear itself out, that its own subjectivity or falsehood is beginning to be experienced. In this excerpt from a later therapy session with Michael we might begin to hear two perspectives on the same balance, the experience of constraining isolation commingling with that of the longer respected independence:

> I have really gotten more aware of what goes on with me in those moments when I decide, "this woman is just not for me." The whole thing probably lasts three seconds but it just stretches out in front of me and I can see it. It can be the tiniest thing. Like I'll just see the person isn't understanding what I'm saying over coffee and it happens. Or take last night: I met Andrea on a corner and we were going to walk to a restaurant and I was feeling happy to be with her and enjoying the activity on the street and I put my arm around her waist and it was just in the way she responded—or didn't respond. She wasn't kind of *with* me. We were awkward that close together. We couldn't walk in step. Her arm felt dutiful when she put it around me. I know this sounds ridiculously trivial. But it just becomes symbolic of so many ways we do not really fit together. My only sense of these moments used to be, you know, "O.K. This person isn't really for you. Carry on, it's not so awful." But now I see it isn't as simple as that. I actually go through quite a lot in those seconds. To start with, I realize now that I actually feel sort of *hurt*, like I've been abandoned, left alone. I'm feeling like I'm *needing something*, that I'm *upset*, that I'm *wanting* something I'm not getting. And this is a feeling I absolutely *hate* to have. It's the worst. When I have that feeling I can see now I just move away from the person. I never tell them or try to get what I want from the other person. I don't like to even admit to myself that I don't feel all together, let alone tell another person. I never want to *ask*. I just move away from the person and into myself. I feel, "O.K., if that's how you're going to be, it's okay. I can survive on my own. Fine. I don't need you. I can get along okay." And of course I *can* get along okay and I have *been* getting along for years. But listen to how pissed off I

sound. Of course it's *not* really fine. And I *do* need. But I hate to, and I'm mad at anyone who puts me in such a spot. I guess I feel humiliated when I need something from another person, as ridiculous as that sounds. And I guess—Why should it be so hard for me to want help, let alone to ask for it?

We can see in these words the force and intricacy of the self-regulating system, and its resistance to re-evolution. But we can also begin to hear, I think, a perspective on that system, a dawning recognition of how it works and a questioning of its costs. Most interesting to me is that we begin to hear a sense of loneliness and dissatisfaction even in its *workings* (rather than concern arising out of its failure to work), which is the experiential evidence that the system is no longer completely Michael. (If the system is all I have, I still do not have all of myself; I am missing something.) This is the sound of an evolution underway, an evolution which may be just the reason Michael has come for therapy.

In this chapter we take up the subject of evolution beyond the institutional balance, which, like every evolution, can be expected to involve a specific loss, including the loss of a home or culture and the need for a new one (see Table 11). Like every evolution, it can be expected to bring into being a whole new way of organizing inner experience and outer behavior. And often enough before doing so, it can be expected to resist mightily and mourn grievously the loss of a way of making meaning that the self has come to know as itself.

The institutional balance, which brings into being the self as a form, has its cognitive manifestation in the full development of the formal operational system which Piaget describes. What makes that system formal most of all is the new way it relates to—or gives meaning to—concrete particulars. It transcends the concrete, subordinating it to general forms, abstracted, decontextualized organizations of the particular. The same evolution which disembeds personality from context-bound interpersonalism and brings the interpersonal under the governance of an internally consistent organization (identity) is most likely reflected in the evolution of a logic which "constructs relations and movements of particulars as governed by rules or laws that have an existence without reference to the contents of the particulars" (Basseches, 1978). It may be the existence of these "abstracting rules," however unaware of them we are when we are firmly in the institu-

TABLE 11. The institutional to interindividual transformation

	Stage 4 Institutional	Stage 5 Interindividual
Underlying structure (subject-object balance)	S— Authorship, identity, psychic administration, ideology O— The interpersonal, mutuality	S— Interindividuality, interpenetrability of self systems O— Authorship, identity, psychic administration, ideology
Piaget	Full formal operational	Post-formal? Dialectical?
Kohlberg	Societal orientation	Principled orientation
Loevinger	Conscientious	Autonomous
Maslow	Esteem and self-esteem orientation	Self-actualization
McClelland/Murray	Achievement orientation	Intimacy orientation?
Erikson	Identity vs. identity diffusion	

INTERINDIVIDUAL [5]

INTERPERSONAL [3]

IMPULSIVE [1]

INSTITUTIONAL [4]

IMPERIAL [2]

INCORPORATIVE [0]

Psychologics favoring inclusion

Psychologics favoring independence

Evolutionary balance and psychological embeddedness	*Culture of embeddedness*	*Function 1: Confirmation (holding on)*	*Function 2: Contradiction (letting go)*	*Function 3: Continuity (staying put for reintegration)*	*Some common natural transitional "subject-objects" (bridges)*
(4) INSTITUTIONAL Embedded in: personal autonomy, self-system identity.	*Culture of identity or self-authorship* (in love or work). Typically: group involvement in career, admission to public arena.	Acknowledges and cultures capacity for independence; self-definition; assumption of authority; exercise of personal enhancement, ambition or achievement; "career" rather than "job," "life partner" rather than "helpmate," etc.	Recognizes and promotes adult's emergence from embeddedness in independent self-definition. Will not accept mediated, nonintimate, form-subordinated relationship.	Ideological forms permit themselves to be relativized on behalf of the play between forms. High risk: ideological supports vanish (e.g., job loss) at very time one is separating from this embeddedness. (No easily supplied age norms.)	Medium of 4-5 transition: *ideological self-surrender (religious or political); love affairs protected by unavailability of the partner.* At once a surrender of the identification with the form while preserving the form.
(5) INTER-INDIVIDUAL Embedded in: interpenetration of systems.	*Culture of intimacy* (in domain of love and work). Typically: genuinely adult love relationship.	Acknowledges and cultures capacity for interdependence, for self-surrender and intimacy, for interdependent self-definition.			

tional balance, which permits us to be self-regulating, self-sustaining, self-naming.

Suggesting that there is qualitative development beyond psychological autonomy and philosophical formalism is itself somewhat controversial, as it flies in the face of cherished notions of maturity in psychological and philosophical (including scientific and mathematical) realms. It suggests that objectivity defined in terms of abstract principles and the independence of rules of order from the phenomena they govern may not be the fullest notion of maturity in the domain of science. And it suggests that highly differentiated psychological autonomy, independence, or "full formal operations" may not be the fullest picture of maturity in the domain of the person.

But the notion of "development beyond autonomy" does not originate here. In truth, it is an idea that has begun to call notions of maturity to account in every realm. Doubts about the possibility of "scientific autonomy"—the ability of the perceiver and the perceived to exist autonomously—are central to the story of modern physics, the theory of relativity, and the Heisenberg uncertainty principle. Doubt about psychological autonomy as the hallmark of personal maturity has begun to surface in the last few years in many quarters (Kaplan, 1976; Miller, 1976; Gilligan, 1978; Low, 1978); so have conceptions of a post-formal stage of intellectual development. The work of Basseches (1980), Gilligan and Murphy (1979), and Koplowitz (1978) are three notable examples. And while these people seem to be working rather independently of each other (they do not cite each other in their publications, for example), they are joined by the work of a fourth party to whom they all *do* acknowledge an intellectual debt, William Perry. Perry's book, *Forms of Intellectual and Ethical Development in the College Years*, published in 1970, anticipated most subsequent lines of exploration in constructive-developmental psychology (this book included).

The conceptions of post-formal thought bear remarkable similarity to each other and are consistent with the notion of development—emergence from embeddedness, the whole becoming part of a new whole, the oscillating tension between inclusion and distinctness—presented here. Gilligan and Murphy find in their studies of post-college age adults that some persons begin to question the limits of their abstracted forms or principles for intellectual solution of moral problems. They do not feel any less that they alone must be the authors of their conceptions of what is true or right, but they begin to doubt whether it is possible to construct generalizable rules, which, however internally consistent they may be, seem perilously to ignore the particulars they organize. Gilligan and Murphy find these people evolving from a rather closed-system self-sufficiency to a "more open and dialectical process involving contextualization and an openness to reevaluation" (1979, p. 7). Among the central features of this new way of thinking seems to be a new orientation to contradiction and paradox. Rather than completely threatening the system, or mobilizing the need for resolution at all costs, the contradiction becomes more recognizable as contradiction; the orientation seems to shift to the relationship between poles in a paradox rather than a choice between the poles.

Koplowitz's conception is quite similar and complementary: "Formal operational thought is dualistic. It draws sharp distinctions between the knower and the known, between one object (or variable) and another, and between pairs of opposites (e.g., good and bad). In post-formal operational thought, the knower is seen as unified with the known, various objects (and variables) are seen as part of a continuum, and opposites are seen as poles of one concept" (1978, p. 32).

Basseches (1980) studied interview protocols with adults and identified twenty-four distinguishable "schemata" (ways of thinking), the logic of each of which is carefully shown to be post-formal. This logic Basseches calls "dialectical," and among its distinctive features are the following:

(a) Rather than making the form or closed system ultimate, it orients to the relationship between systems.

(b) It takes the relationship between systems as prior to, and constitutive of, the systems themselves.

(c) It regards motion, process, and change (not forms and entities) as the irreducible and primary feature of reality; this differs, too, from seeing motion as "the behavior of entities whose essential nature remains fixed and unchanging" (p. 6).

(d) Rather than orienting primarily to movement *in* a form, it orients to movement *through* forms.

(e) Beyond grasping the nature of a form or a structured system, it "views forms in a larger context which includes relationships among forms, movement from one form to another, relationships of forms to the process of form construction or organization" (p. 7).

(f) Rather than having the experience of contradiction "happen to" it, it seeks out contradiction and is not ultimately threatened by it; its organization does not exist solely for the purpose of driving out contradiction, but also recognizes its nourishment in it.

(g) Rather than exercising its dynamics in a relatively closed, self-contained dichotomous system, its dynamism is between systems, oriented not to one pole or another but to the tension between them.

In addition to these suggestions of intellectual meaning-making which transcends (and integrates) "the form," it may be good to recall the picture of post-conventional moral meaning-making drawn in Chapter 2. Here, too, we saw the possibility of emergence from an embeddedness in the system and the possibility of locating one's "ought-making" in a context prior to the construction of systems. While one did not lose one's sense of "the form," or even one's invest-ment in, or affection for, the form, it ceased to be the ultimate context by which one defined the sociomoral world. Recall, for example, the Israeli soldier-medic who, in distinction from most of his comrades, gave identical medical treatment to Arab and Israeli wounded. It did not *feel* exactly the same, the man struggled to explain. "With an Israeli I always have a desire . . . some kind of will to work and do everything, in order that he'll be saved. Regarding the Arab, I'll do the same actions, but I'll do it, not out of love, or out of—I don't know, not out of love for the man, but out of some kind of a *duty* I feel I have toward him." While there is no denying an affection for those in one's group (a part of one's "form"), one's group-identifica-tion is not, finally, the controlling context. There is some supervening affection, it seems, some higher affection, that more than *relating* groups (or relating forms) actually arises prior to them. Persons become first of all members of one human community, a community to which the Israeli medic, in a way he seems himself to find almost strange, feels finally most drawn.

It is possible that these transformations in the cognitive and moral domains—an emergence from embeddedness in "the formal" or the overarching ideology—are a reflection of yet another qualitative evolu-tion of meaning, just that evolution which we take up here.

A forty-two-year-old woman, living with her husband, is admitted because she feels "desperate." She describes herself in the past as "spontaneous, capable, self-reliant, energetic, enjoying many things, thoughtful, wise." The past year she has felt increasingly "insecure, un-happy, inadequate, not worthwhile, blocked, down, anxious, bored but unable to initiate action." Her husband concurs reporting a "complete personality change over the past year," from "creative, active, compe-tent," to "dull, flat, fearful, markedly decreased ability to function." The woman says she used to write frequent letters to members of her family and now, for the first time, "cannot write because I feel empty." She describes what is happening to her as, "I have lost my sense of self and my ability to function." Her husband says, "She complains she can't express her feelings, can't feel closeness to me, would like to talk about her feelings if she knew what they were, has lost her identity."

When the institutional balance is threatened we hear about a threat to the self, a concern about the self, the self that has been in control. This is not what we heard from the interpersonal balance under threat, where the concern for oneself is expressed in terms of the other. In the earlier balance we are hearing about a threat to the sense of inclusion; in this balance we are hearing about a threat to the sense of in-dependence, distinctness, agency.

As the emergence from the institutional balance gets underway, as with Michael, there is a frontier from which to reflect on the outworn balance. As with all transitions, there may be much that is exciting about this transformation. My attention in this book to the frame-work's understanding of distress can give the false impression that all transition is only painful; on the contrary, it can consist in extremely positive, literally "ecstatic," transcendent experience. Features of the positive experience of transition out of an ultimate orientation to one's "form" might include the relaxation of one's vigilance, a sense of flow and immediacy, a freeing up of one's internal life, an openness to and playfulness about oneself. But viewed from the old perspective, in which I have long been invested, the same loosening up may be ex-perienced as boundary loss, impulse flooding, and, as always, the experience of *not knowing*. This last can speak itself in terms of felt meaninglessness. Though every shift involves a philosophical crisis, this one may do so self-proclaimedly; while every shift involves the relativizing of what was taken as ultimate, this one raises the specter of relativism self-consciously, precisely because it is the first shift in which there is a self-conscious self to be reflected upon. It is worth considering how the knowing-in-the-world of a 4-5 subject compares to others'. Take, for example, constructions of attempted suicide:

A subject in the 2-3 transition took an overdose "not to kill myself but to go to sleep and not wake up"; the next day she became furious with her brother who had taken her to the emergency ward, and violently attacked him.

A subject in the 3-4 transition took an overdose in order "to free him" of her combined dependence upon him and upon her mother; her dependence upon her mother had led her "to being taken over by my mother's criticism of my husband, so I ended up criticizing him."

A subject in the 4-5 transition wanted to slash his wrists because he was "evil" (had "gone beyond good and evil"), but seemed equally interested in engaging those who had come to prevent him in long conversation as to the right of persons to take their own life, and the ethics of restraining them when asked not to.

All transitions involve leaving a consolidated self behind before any new self can take its place. At the 4-5 shift this means abandoning — or somehow operating without reliance upon — the form, the group, standard, or convention. For some this leads to feelings of being "beyond good and evil," which phenomenologically amounts to looking at that beyondness from the view of the old self, and thus involves strong feelings of evil. Ethical relativism — the belief that there is no (nonarbitrary) basis for considering one thing more right than another — is, on the one hand, the father of tolerance: it stands against the condemning judgment; but it must also stand against the affirming judgment, and so is vulnerable to cynicism. Every transition involves to some extent the killing off of the old self. The phenomenological side of that cold Piagetian/biological notion of differentiation is repudiation. I must for a time be not-me before I can reappropriate that old me as the new object of a new self. The first moves toward reconsolidation in stage 3 may involve the killing of *any* of my needs, the attempt to be not-me (who *is* his needs) — the early adolescent ascetic. The first moves toward reconsolidation in stage 4 may involve the ideologizing of intimacy, the killing off of all interpersonal relationships, lest I be devoured in them; an attempt, again, to be not-me (who is his interpersonal relationships) — the precipitous, temporary, and usually vacillating celibate. Similarly, in the shift to stage 5 there is often a sense of having left the moral world entirely (" 'ought' is no longer in my vocabulary"); there is no way of orienting to right and wrong worthy of my respect. This is the killing off of all standards, the attempt to be not-me (who is his standard) — the cynic, or existentially despairing.

As in the previous chapter I would like to present two cases, Kenneth and Rebecca, which might give us further understanding of this evolution. As with Alice and Diane, what may seem most striking about the two cases is how different they are, how "ill" one person is in comparison with the other. Kenneth is a hospitalized psychiatric patient who carries the label of schizophrenia, and Rebecca is a never-hospitalized, nonpsychotic therapy client managing with great accomplishment the complex responsibilities of family and career. As before, in suggesting an important similarity between the predicaments of these two people, I do not mean to ignore the differences, or pretend that persons do not differ in their capacities to cope, in their psychological resources, in the nature of their reaction to crisis, stress, and loss, or in the significance of their childhoods for their present situations. I bring them together to focus on that feature of their lives most easily lost in a pathology-oriented perspective, and in my view, the one that must *first* be understood, if one's interest is actually to engage, or in some way relate to, another person. This feature, of course, is the evolution of meaning, what I suggest is the prior ground of personality. People may live along a wide continuum of health or malaise at any evolutionary moment, but how they experience their experience is first of all a function not of where they are on that continuum but where they are in their evolution.

Kenneth came to the hospital and asked to be admitted "because I'm schizophrenic." Although he gave a history of withdrawal, few close relationships, and several years of depression, he had never been hospitalized or diagnosed as schizophrenic. He explained that he had arrived at the diagnosis on his own through reading. (Even this self-presentation, it might be noted, bespeaks a certain personal authority — and self-authored identity — which we have not seen earlier.) The situation which overwhelmed him and led him to seek help involved a relationship with a woman, but once again, it is important to see how differently this "precipitating event" *means* from the similar-sounding event that led Diane to the hospital.

Kenneth had become involved with a woman whom he knew to be involved with another man. "Every ethical sensibility said I should stay away from her, but I didn't. I suspended my ethics and went after her, and by suspending my ethics I was able to get results." But as he continued he was filled with an enormous sense of having betrayed himself. And, as he says, "I started to go out of my mind." Kenneth came to the hospital feeling that he was dangerously "beyond good and evil," that his feelings (especially sexual feelings) had taken him over and that he was losing his sense of "where I stopped and the others [the woman and her boyfriend] began." We notice again a matter of boundaries, and that the "direction" of boundary problems returns to that of Terry or Richard—a fear of losing a sense of one's distinctness ("I feel that others are being knit into me," Terry said), rather than the fear of losing a sense of inclusion which we heard from Diane or Eric in Chapter 7.

Kenneth himself experienced what was happening to him in frankly ethical and philosophical terms. Although this is not a requirement for development in or out of this balance, it makes very clear what one person's experience of emerging from an embeddedness in the self as *form* (the institutional self) can be like.

As with Terry and Diane, Kenneth's construction of the Kohlberg dilemmas was elicited in an open-ended interview. In the same Heinz dilemma which Diane discussed, Kenneth takes a very different view. Although he can see each person's point of view, and feel sympathy for one person's situation more than other, he rejects this particularistic, interpersonalist way of arriving at an ethical construction of a situation:

> I can empathize with both those guys [the husband and the drug-gist]. I see the standpoint for both. From both their standpoints I think that, at that point I see the question as being sort of amoral. I guess I tend to sympathize more with the guy whose wife is dying. He is getting pretty fucked over, while the other guy is just making a mint on this drug. This is just sympathy. That isn't a concrete ethical judgment.
> *That doesn't appeal to you as a good enough basis on which to choose—your sympathy for one or the other?*
> No. It shouldn't be.

And what should be? Kenneth is able to construct the general categories (or forms) of the right to life and the right to property, and the formal category of the law (religious and civic) regulative of particular, concrete situations. He spontaneously abstracts the particulars of the dilemma to this form—but, at the same time, because he is no longer completely shaped by the institutional truce, he is uncomfortable (in a very specific way) with this construction of the situation.

But most of him is still embedded in the institutional:

If I understand, you are distinguishing between how you would feel about a matter and what is ethical. What is the ethical?

The ethical for me is basically the Ten Commandments and the teachings of Jesus. I am not sure how well ingrained that is, but what it does mean is that I look down upon theft and I look down upon capitalism as a means of livelihood. In the case of this guy and his wife, I don't think that human life is as important as law; it shouldn't supersede the law. I think that we have laws, and if all the laws are not to be followed then people see it breaking down; it has a sort of snowball effect and then no one cares about the law. And especially laws about theft should be enforced. Stealing is a very serious transgression against another person. So for that reason I would expect first of all to find Heinz guilty because he did steal and second of all to sentence him to show everyone that people can't steal and they shouldn't. Knowing darn well that under certain circumstances people should steal.

You think you should?

That is the thing. He [the judge] cannot say that, but he would obviously realize that in giving Heinz a light sentence.

Why can't he say that Heinz should have stolen?

He can't say that because he stands for the law and the law is the structure that Heinz was going against at the time.

Kenneth's own predicament is similar to the judge he concocts. He understands, and in large part feels loyal to, his formal construction of the situation, but another part of him, a newer part, stands outside this formalism and looks at things another way:

I am pretty ambivalent toward the matter. On the one hand, I have great respect for the law, but on the other hand, it seems to me that in the circumstance there it was more important for his wife to get that drug than it was to uphold the law and the law that he was breaking was just sort of on a different scale than the death of his wife.

The institutional balance (Kohlberg's "conventionality," Piaget's "formalism") has become relativized; it is no longer ultimate; it has become unhinged. But with no new place from which to make meaning, Kenneth is left in considerable turmoil, much of the time viewing his unbalanced state from the former perspective ("It bothers me that I think very little of the law, and in this country, if everyone held my attitude about the law, there would just be anarchy").

In his interview about the dilemma Kenneth begins to speak quite consciously in two voices. One he identifies as "the ethical Kenneth," who constructs the situation within the institutional balance. The other he calls, "just Kenneth" or "the Kenneth who goes with the wind."

> I think there are times one has to forget the ethics in order to latch onto what is going on. Ethics, they can really impair you from action
> . . .
> *Your own thinking seems to be in flux on this, it's changing?*
> Yes, and I think it will continue to.
> *Can you say something about how you understand the change?*
> I understand the change in that, when I am in the middle of a situation, I will try to be very sensitive to the wind. I don't know if you have heard that metaphor, like wherever the wind carries you, follow it. At some point the wind will sort of take you away and leave your ethics behind. And hopefully one can get back on top ground and you can get your ethics back. It comes down to being whatever the situation calls for here, instinct and judgment when the situation arises. I cannot construct any hard and fast rules as to when I will ignore my moral response to something, when I will forget about it and just go wherever things go.

Although Kenneth has a sense that "going with the wind" is superior to "ethical Kenneth," he has an even stronger sense of the danger and risk of this stance, and identifies it as the cause of his hospitalization.

> *It sounds like you are saying you're not 100 percent confident about this new way?*
> I'm not. You are right. This is probably because my judgment often does not involve wisdom. In order to circumvent the law you really need wisdom because if you don't, if you just do it haphazardly, you get really shafted.
> *What would that mean to be wise?*
> It would mean you would know usually when the law could and

should be broken, and when it shouldn't, be broken. I don't know [otherwise] it is sort of like *Crime and Punishment*, it is really bad, because not only does he [Raskolnikov] separate himself from law, but he also separates himself from people, so you can go against the law, but still have your feet on the ground with things and I can't explain how I look at the law now, because I don't feel like I have my feet on the ground with it yet.

From a constructive-developmental point of view, Kenneth's predicament seems to involve the very unhinging of that most fundamental relationship which informs him both who he is and how he is to know the others with whom he lives. The state of global disequilibrium leaves him by himself—knowing himself from the balance left behind—as qualified, as heretical, as beyond good and evil. It is clear from the interview that "the ethical" is the "formal" (the Ten Commandments, the civic law, the protection against chaos) and, in company with his life circumstances, it also seems clear that "suspending my ethics" speaks to more than the relativizing of a conventional moral framework. What is cracking here is that whole construction of the self as a system, form, or institution of which "I" am the administrator who must keep the organization intact, a way of seeing now seen through. Those feelings which in the institutional balance come under the internal control of the regulative system may begin to break loose in a way which is at once, from the point of view of the old self, chaotic or psychologically anarchic, and at the same time, from the view of the emerging self, somehow rightfully honored as beyond the control of the too-constricting institutional self. At the moment (this disequilibrial moment when the old structure is being negated or rejected without yet being fully appropriated as content for the new structure), the "instinctual" is seen as antagonistic to the "judgmental." In order to give that instinctual life some play, one must "suspend" judgment and "go with the wind." But what is actually being suspended is a *form* of judgment, a form of authority bent on internal control. With the relativizing of that authority, the erotic can once again come into play. But until the new balance has evolved, the "instinctual" may be seen as in battle with the "ethical," and "victories" by the "instinctual" must be paid for by perceiving them through the lens of the not fully moved over "ethical," where they are experienced as flooding, loss of control, evil or underground activity.

The breaking of the institutional balance makes the person available to, or interested in, a kind of sharing or intimacy with others that has not been present since the interpersonal balance (at the same time, it is profoundly different from that balance in the sense that the intimacy which is possible in the new balance, 5, is the self's aim rather than its source). Yet, the very balance-breaking that signals this emerging new availability for human interpenetration leaves one temporarily unclear both as to who is the self and who are the others. This combination of heightened availability to others, the recognition that there is an important sense in which I have not been with others, the fear of losing myself in the new closeness, can leave one feeling isolated, particularly if, as Kenneth seems to be saying in comparing himself to Raskolnikov, his "suspension" does not only move him away from his old self, but moves him away from others as well.

In Kenneth's final attempt to resolve the Heinz dilemma, this time from the perspective of his emerging philosophy, he gives us a view of an evolving organism making its first efforts at a new organization:

> Can you say something about how this is going, your attempts to—your thinking about something more than the law?
>
> My thinking puts myself in a lot of different positions. It puts myself as a judge, I can put myself in a position of Heinz. I can put myself in the position of his wife. I can put myself in the position of the druggist, all of these having different outlooks on the same situation. I think whatever it is that is broader than law it takes all these people involved in a sort of entirety thing in which there is not a right or wrong, but there is a something.

If he meant he was looking for some way to empathize with each person this might be taken for the interpersonal balance, but in the context of the whole interview it seems clear he is talking about a way to make sense of their relatedness that is not reduced to (or truncated by) their subordination to a system which he sees as wrongly putting itself before them. "There is a something" being intuited which is beyond this system ("not right and wrong") that takes them all into account; and clearly, by his earlier rejection of "mere sympathy" as a basis for judging, this is not a plea for the prior balance which, unencumbered by system, might be said to engage each person. What he seems to be intuiting, this "entirety thing," is a self that travels between systems, or exists in the dynamism between them, a return to the relationship orientation of balance 3 but at a whole new level, the relationship between forms or systems. Such an organization might solve the vacillation between "judgment" or "instinct" by bringing into being a more integrative "judgment," the ultimate purpose of which is not the maintenance of the institutional self for whom feelings are often administrative "problems," but the more dynamic exercises of interindividuality, in which the self is not its duties, roles, or institutions, but the "haver" of them, which having is regulated by the recognition of one's commonality or interdependence with others, others who might even be turned to "instinctually" with no violation of one's "judgment."

Until such a new balance comes into being, Kenneth is left on the dangerous, even terrifying, side of the transformation, glimpsing a whole new way of composing himself and his world, but overrun and exhausted by its motion. This discovery and terror of the dialectical psychologic which Basseches describes is poignantly conveyed in a parable Kenneth wrote shortly before coming to the hospital:

> He left because what he wanted was not here; he came back because it was to be found only here. What he wanted was beauty, and beauty, though he did not know it at the time, is in the doorway to the room. Poor fellow. He could only be outside the room or inside the room, for it was impossible to stand in the doorway. So he kept going back and forth, in and out. He got a steady rhythm going. Each time he moved either in or out of the room he felt he was getting closer to what he was searching for, and the closer he got (or thought he got) the more enthusiastic he became about the quest. And then he made the great discovery: that beauty is in the doorway. And he knew the faster he went, the more he would see of it. He got so he could keep his eye on it as he went back and forth. But there was a problem. By now he was completely enslaved in the rhythm. He was doing nothing but forces on either side were pulling him in and out. Forces he could not see. Forces he could not fight. Because in his quest for beauty he had to have *let* them take him there. And this meant selling his soul. This meant trusting to the wind. But the wind betrayed his trust. Poor fellow kept going faster and faster and he tried so hard to keep his eye on the doorway, but he got very dizzy in this attempt and finally had to give up trying to turn his head. So here he was oscillating at an ever-increasing speed back and forth, and immediately after beauty left him, the whole thing became very strange indeed. He wondered: "I gave myself to the wind so the wind would give me beauty, but now

the wind will not let me have it. I go faster and faster wondering what I am doing in this mess if it is not for beauty's sake. What else is there for man to live for in the world? If not beauty at least good. They are the same, aren't they? Now I can't even see good." Well, you can imagine what happened. He kept going faster and faster and became more and more dizzy. Soon he could not even think, he just became more and more frightened about what was to happen to him. He left last Thursday. I am sitting here waiting for him to return. He will some day soon, I know. I hope so, 'cause he's a nice guy to be around.

Not all those who come to the limits of the institutional balance express their malaise in philosophical terms. They may as easily speak of a "loss of identity," or a sense that "the steam has just gone out of it"; or that they have let themselves down, betrayed themselves, abandoned themselves. They may speak of feeling isolated, of discovering on the other side of their psychological competence and self-sufficiency a terrible loneliness, or fear of closeness. One way or another they seem to speak of a self-conscious self that has become relativized, that they now find themselves desperately defending or standing beyond (however unsteadily). All disequilibrium is a crisis of meaning; all disequilibrium is a crisis of identity (what is the self?). But only after the institutional balance has been constructed can one speak of one's crisis in terms of "the meaninglessness of life" or an "identity crisis." For the first time a "self" known to the self *as a self* is at risk.

We first met Rebecca in Chapter 3. It may be helpful simply to listen again to her own words. They speak clearly of the personal authority and integrity of the institutional self, of its historical and evolutionary advance over interpersonalism, of the courage and fatigue of coming to its limits:

> I know I have very defined boundaries and I protect them very carefully. I won't give up the slightest control. In any relationship I decide who gets in, how far, and when.

> What am I afraid of? I used to think I was afraid people would find out who I really was and then not like me. But I don't think that's it anymore. What I feel now is—"That's me. That's mine. It's what makes me. And I'm powerful. It's my negative side, maybe, but it's also my positive stuff—and there's a lot of that. What it is is me, it's my self—and if I let people in maybe they'll take it, maybe they'll use it—and I'll be gone."

Respect above all is the most important thing to me. You don't have to like me. You don't have to care about me, even, but you do have to respect me.

This "self," if I had to represent it I think of two things: either a steel rod that runs through everything, a kind of solid fiber, or sort of like a ball at the center that is all together. What you just really can't be is weak.

I wasn't always this way. I used to have two sets of clothes—one for my husband and one for my mother who visited often. Two sets of clothes, but none for me. Now *I* dress in *my* clothes. Some of them are like what my mother would like me to wear but that's a totally different thing.

How exhausting it's becoming holding all this together. And until recently I didn't even realize I was doing it.

During the course of counseling, Rebecca reports a dream which seems to convey, with powerful precision, the risk the evolving person must take in separating from the institutional, form-bound truce:

I am in a crowded subway, rushing to get a train. I am standing. There is a woman next to me. The woman makes motions I interpret as a request for money. I open my purse but it turns out the woman is asking me to identify myself. So I begin taking out all my cards—my social security card, my license, my work identification card, my health insurance—and I show them to the woman. All the while it is on my mind that I am late and might miss the train. While I am showing my cards the subway gets into the train station. I grab up all my cards and get off the subway. I run for the train. I come to a sort of revolving door and it closes on me with my arm outside, clutching all my cards, and the rest of me looking out toward the train. I feel just completely stuck. I know that if I could just let go of all these cards, just let them drop, I could get through and catch the train. But I am completely panicked. And I am panicked both at the idea of having to give up all these cards and at the idea of missing the train.

As with every balance this one is vulnerable to evolution from the informing complexity of others who do not feel "well known" by its way of making meaning. People can come to feel manipulated by a stage 2 person's way of knowing them, devoured by a person at stage 3. By a stage 4 person they are likely to feel mediated, that they are filtered through some system rather than in direct contact with the person. But, of course, while the person lives in this balance, one *is* in direct touch. The danger in our feelings of being manipulated, devoured, or mediated is our (usually unreflected upon) assumption that the *real* person is being withheld from us, that we are being held out on, that there is someone there who could, if he or she only would, be unmanipulative, undevouring, or immediate. Only toward the end of the life of these balances, when the evolutionary truce is up for renegotiation, does there begin to be someone there to hear, however irritably, these complaints.

Thus, the hallmark of the institutional balance—its self-possessiveness—is also its limit, a limit which tends to show itself more clearly in the private regions of love and closeness than in the public light of work and career. As the imperial ten-year-old seals up her impulses and takes control over the definition and exercise of her external behaviors, the institutional adult seals up the context-embeddedness of interpersonalism and takes control over the definition and exercise of her interior self. What is a triumph at age ten is an evolutionary constraint at age sixteen, when the adolescent must struggle with the possibility of a new form of openness which neither denies the integrity of evolutionary gains (is not a return to the openness of the fantasy-filled impulsive balance) nor permits the need-embedded self-centeredness to become an overextended way of life. As always, the adolescent's success in the struggle is a function not only of a history of having to face such evolutionary risks and losses, but a willingness of the current culture of embeddedness to assist in the emergence, and of the availability of a future culture to hold and recognize the new evolutionary truce. In a similar way, the institutional adult can experience the possibility of a new openness as a seductive, regressive, and dangerous pull into what now seems the incorporation of interpersonal embeddedness. "During love-making or in sexual fantasies," Erikson says of those who would seem to be in this evolutionary predicament, "the loosening of sexual identity is found threatening. The ego is without the flexible capacity for abandoning itself to sexual and affectional sensations in a fusion with another who is both partner to the sensation *and guarantor of one's continuing identity*" (1968, pp. 167-168). The emphasis is mine; these last words indicate both how distinctly different this kind of openness (or fusion, to use Erikson's word) is from interpersonalism (there is a distinct identity), and at the same time the way in which the evolutionary gains of institutionality, while transformed, are nonetheless preserved (the love is not captive of the identity, but neither is the identity lost).

And, as in the situation of the early adolescent, the capacity of ideological adulthood to evolve to intimate adulthood is a function not only of earlier transformations from separateness to openness, but of the current psychosocial support for such development both in the culture of embeddedness to be left behind and the new one to be joined.

The culture which holds, recognizes, and remembers the institutional balance is the culture of ideology. It takes its most obvious form in the domain of work but can (and usually does) operate just as powerfully in the construction of loving relations which get organized around the exercises and preservation of one or both parties' self-contained identity. Such relations can be mutually supportive, warm, and loving; they might even be marital relations of long standing; what they cannot be is intimate. While the controversial, and possibly irritating, suggestion in Chapter 7 was that many of us who are chronologically adult are psychologically adolescent, the parallel suggestion in this chapter is that many adult relationships of closeness and affection (especially marriage) fail to be intimate. An understanding of why marriage is an increasingly perishable state (especially in an age when most of the nonpsychological reasons for remaining married have lost their potency) may depend on an understanding of intimacy that is not tied to cultural prejudice, a psychology of illness, or an arbitrary assortment of external behaviors ("stays married to same person for ten years," Vaillant, 1977; "achieves mutual orgasm," Freud, 1905), but tied instead to the meaning of intimacy to the psychological present of an adult. I will return to this understanding, but for now the question to be asked of the culture which holds institutionality, the culture of ideology—whether it holds the person in the domains of love *or* work—is how available it is to pass its charge over (or to evolve itself) into a culture which will support the post-ideological balance of interindividuality and intimacy.

While the world of work is ideally suited to the culturing of the institutional balance, work settings which can encourage, recognize, or support development beyond the institutional are quite rare. As the name of the balance suggests, in order to do so, a work setting would have to transcend an ultimate loyalty to the institution-as-it-is. It would have to have an interest in a kind of self-exploration, open-systems information seeking, and possible reconstruction of its goals, practices, and criteria, which amounts to a kind of "institutional capacity for intimacy." As many researchers and theorists of organizations suggest, work places, whether they be product- or service-oriented, tend to organize themselves in a fashion that—from the point of view of the theory in this book—amounts to a rigid defense of the institutional balance (Torbert, 1972; Argyris and Schön, 1978). Even learning-oriented or mission-oriented organizations have a tendency to suffer this kind of "displacement of value," in which the organization rather quickly moves from existing for the purpose of expressing or promoting the founding ideal, to existing for the purpose of maintaining the organization.

One of the more thoughtful students of organizations, I think, has been William Torbert, whose books speak in an uncommon blend of candid self-disclosure and scholarly rigor (1972, 1976). His understanding of bureaucratic and postbureaucratic structures for organizations speaks quite directly to the differences between those work settings which might facilitate development beyond the institutional and those which, in effect, serve to overconfirm or hold too tightly this particular evolutionary truce.

In contrast to the usual features of organizations

(a)   which focus on doing the predefined task;
(b)   in which viability of the product becomes the overriding criterion of success;
(c)   in which standards and structures are taken for granted;
(d)   which focus on quantitative results based on defined standards;
(e)   in which reality is conceived of as dichotomous and competitive (success-failure, in-group-out-group, leader-follower, legitimate-illegitimate, work-play, reasonable-emotional, etc.),

Torbert suggests features of what he considers a qualitative evolution in the development of an organization:

(a)   shared reflection about larger (wider, deeper, more long-term, more abstract) purposes of the organization;
(b)   development of an open inter-personal process, with disclosure, support, and confrontation on value-stylistic-emotional issues;

(c)   evaluation of the effects of one's own behavior on others in the organization, and formative research on the effects of the organization on the environment ("social accounting");

(d)   direct facing and resolution of paradoxes: freedom-control, expert vs. participatory decision-making, etc.;

(e)   appreciation of the particular historical moment of this particular organization as an important variable in decision-making;

(f)   creative, trans-conventional solutions to conflicts;

(g)   deliberately chosen structure with commitment to it, over time, the structure unique in the experience of the participants or among "similar" organizations;

(h)   primary emphasis on horizontal rather than vertical work role differentiation;

(i)   development of symmetrical rather than subordinate relation with "parent" organizations.

(1976, pp. 158-159)

It should be clear how such a shift echoes both that of the cognitive shift to the dialectical which Basseches et al. discuss, and the personal shift from the ideological to the intersystemic (from the institutional to the interindividual balances) which I have been discussing throughout this chapter. Although Torbert's first organization—the typical bureaucratic setting—admirably performs for the institutional balance the holding function which any culture of embeddedness must supply, it fails utterly in the equally important function of contradiction. It may salute and support those newly moving into the institutional balance, but it does nothing to contradict the oversubjectivity of the balance, and from the point of view of those who have lived in this balance a long time, it essentially serves to collude with the defensive side of personality seeking to resist the upheavals of evolution. The traditional workplace overholds ideological adulthood just as surely as a mother and father can overhold a five-year-old by failing to contradict her "subjective" confusion of her impulses with those of her parents. And just as surely as her inability to separate can manifest itself in depression or a depressive equivalent such as school phobia, an ideological adult with no supports for development beyond the institutional, who is overheld or struggling at all costs to resist a new emergence from embeddedness, is vulnerable to depression or a depressive equivalent such as workaholism.

Workaholism is the hypermasculine analogue of the institutional balance to the hyperfeminine self-abnegation of the interpersonal balance (though neither predicament is the exclusive province of men or women, respectively). The picture of the workaholic—with his or her all-consuming investment in the exercises of achievement, self-esteem, independent accomplishment, self-discipline, and control—looks like that of the evolutionary truce of institutionality in peril, working overtime lest it fall apart. I doubt very much that we would find many workaholics who have come to the interindividual or intimate evolutionary balance.

The contradiction which the institutional balance needs is similar to the interpersonal claim on the overdifferentiated preadolescent. The message a parent or potential collaborator (as opposed to cooperator) sends a typical twelve-year-old when there is an insistence that promises be kept, or that the relationship be valued, or that "my" needs be considered along with "yours," is essentially this: "It's time you came in from the cold; you have to take me into account when you put things together, and you have to take me in a way that does not make me a servant to your needs; you have to see that you are wrong when you confuse me with the operation of your self-sufficiency; I live distinct and apart from your needs; I will not be fused with the exercises of your self-sufficiency; but when you grant me my distinctness you and I can then relate to each other." This is the corrective message to overdifferentiation and it is a kind of limit setting in just the opposite direction from the type parents need to give their five-year-olds who are overincluded. Torbert's second organizational model does more than confirm the intersystemic capacities of the interindividual balance. It provides the corrective message of contradiction to the overdifferentiated institutional balance. In its attention to the larger purposes of the organization, to the receiving of information about one's way of operating, to opportunities to be confronted, to the facing of paradox, there is a continuing message that one is not to confuse a given construction of the organization with oneself, that one is not to fit the organization to the exercise of one's closed, self-reinforcing self-system. "It is time again to come in from the cold," the new culture seems to be saying. In contrast to the contradiction to the interpersonal balance, which declares, as Eric's parents do for him, "You must make your own decisions; you must satisfy yourself and meet your own expectations," the contradiction to the institutional balance recognizes the embeddedness of overdifferentiation. "You must, even in your very definition of yourself, transcend the tyranny of the form and the confusion of us with it. When you grant us [other persons and other organizations] our distinction from the exercise of your form, you can find yourself (and us, as well) in the movement which brings form into being. In this bigger context, we can seek out the experience by which we might continually alter our forms and systems which become now something we *have* rather than something we *are*." This particular shift seems at the heart of the distinction Argyris (1978) makes between what he calls "Model One," in which the person is a "single-loop learner," seeking only to maintain and confirm the system; and "Model Two," in which the person is a "double-loop learner," able to stand apart from the personal system and seek out information by which it might be modified.

What a workplace or organization actually looks like or feels like when it can culture interindividuality as well as institutionality I leave for others to elaborate. We can imagine that it creates opportunities to reflect together on "the way we are working," or "the point of our goals," or "how we went about making that decision" as well as in-suring that the work gets done, the goals get achieved, the decisions get made. The thinking of people like Argyris and Torbert and those who are interested in workplace democracy (Heckscher, 1978, 1979; Mackin, 1979) informs us not only about what such settings might look like, but what some experiments—of greater and lesser self-consciousness—actually do look like. At any rate, we can see how such an environment, as opposed to traditional bureaucratic settings, sup-ports a qualitatively different evolution of meaning. Among these differences would seem to be a shift in one's sense of responsibility. Rather than expressing itself in terms of a loyalty or fidelity to an abstracted system-preserving form (of the self or the actual public in-stitution), responsibility would seem to be more saliently a matter of taking responsibility for one's construction and transformation *of* the form. It is also possible that the kind of certainty that one has, seeks, or believes is possible and desirable in the institutional balance is replaced by a kind of tentativeness which it would take a postbureaucratic organization to respect. Where the institutional balance has a wariness about losing the stability and self-subsistence of "the form" (personal or public), the interindividual balance is more likely to be wary about losing sight of the temporary, preliminary, and self-constructed quality of any particular form. This again amounts to an unusual demand on a workplace as a culture—that it confirm, even encourage, a transcending of one's identification with the product in favor of an orientation to the process that creates the product. Where the institutional balance discovers a self who can run one's relations and sets up an organization to do so, the interindividual balance discovers a self that runs the organization. If one wants to feel how strongly a given evolutionary truce can fight to preserve itself—if one wants to see how inextricably linked epistemology is with valuing and being—one has only to look closely into efforts to inform an institution that it is actually in its interest to promote the discovery among its personnel of "the self that runs the organization." Most institutions would be mightily threatened by such a message.

Some heads and definers of organizations would probably agree that their institutions are not particularly well suited to the development of the capacity for genuine intimacy in adulthood. I imagine they would also be relatively unperturbed in this self-assessment, feeling that the workplace is not intended to serve such a function. Possibly they might even feel that intimacy flies in the very face of the smooth exercises of the organization. The usual feeling may be that sharing, closeness, surrender of oneself is a part of one's "personal life," or one's "private life." But this polarized conception of public and private, professional and personal, may itself be a very function of the ideological evolutionary balance in which some heads and definers of organizations are overembedded. If the notion that most workplaces are not well suited to the development of genuine intimacy is unperturbing to those who shape them, perhaps the notion that the workplace works against a person's growth in general might be more so. At a certain time in development, conceding the first point may amount to conceding the second. In any case, the decision any workplace must make (designedly or unselfconsciously) is identical to that which faces a community, family, a marriage, or any long-term human context which, like it or not, becomes a culture for a person's growth. The decision is simply this: to which is it more committed—the present evolutionary state of its constituents, or the bigger picture of the person as the process of evolution itself? Families which become overinvested in a child's given evolutionary truce and unwittingly dig in against the child's bigger life-project do so at great cost to the child and the family. This is well known. But the situation is really no different in the workplace. Work organizations that will not recognize the employee's growth often force the employee to choose between the job and his or her own life-project. Most workplaces are appallingly unconcerned about this choice, judging that its costs are almost entirely borne by the employee. Because the maintenance of the system is ultimate it is deemed more important to find new people who can fit in than to respond to the challenge of recognizing those who are growing in one's midst. A more progressive accommodation in the professional ranks is to grant people "leaves." Here we have the recognition that the person needs a new culture at the same time the company makes clear it is not about to try to provide it by means of its own evolution. While the company may see the loss (or leave-taking) of these employees as salutary to its continued smooth functioning, it could more convincingly be argued that what an organization is actually doing is cutting itself off from its best information and richest resource for continued growth.

If it is an enormous challenge, and relatively uncommon, for the domain of work to sponsor development beyond the ideological, we should not imagine that it must be so very different in the domain of love. After all, it is because it is difficult for individuals to reach the interindividual balance that workplaces are not more facilitative of that development, and we are the same individuals in the private domain of close and affectionate relations.

Notwithstanding the impression given by definitions of intimacy as a certain number of years married to the same person (Vaillant, 1977), it is quite possible to form long-lasting adult love relationships which are not only not genuinely intimate but actually serve to support the resistance to an evolution which permits intimacy. The framework presented in this book has as much potential for an added understanding of marital phenomena as it does for new understandings of organizational development. I will consider here only a few of the many marital alliances the theory suggests. There are two which, however rich their experience and diverse their functions, also serve to maintain one or both partners' institutional balance. These descriptions, rendered in this fashion, will have all the objectionable features of "types." They capture no one's particularity, but if they are in some way true they may suggest a kind of order or meaning for those particulars.

The first of these is a marriage between persons in the institutional and interpersonal balances. Although the marriage has quite a different

meaning to each party, the meanings can be compatible or complementary and the partnership a stable one. Speaking over-generally,
the interpersonal partner may seek a mate through whom he or she
can arrive at a self-definition; the interpersonal partner might be expected to locate himself or herself within the marriage, and probably
experience a kind of immediacy about the relationship, the other, and
whatever about the marriage travels beyond their one-to-one relationship (work, friends, the house, children). The institutional partner, on
the other hand, may be seeking a relationship which confirms, protects, even celebrates his or her self-possessedness. The institutional
partner would be more likely to locate the *marriage* within the exercises of his or her self-authored system, and this self-system would
mediate the experience of the relationship, the other, and marriage-
related involvements. Although the interpersonal partner is
"overincluded" and may seem to be bound for disappointment with
his or her "overautonomous" partner, this source of tension is not immediately or always fatal to the alliance. That it is not may be due to
the fact that what the interpersonal partner wants most of all is an
arena in which he or she can safely experience the intensity and
closeness that is longed for. The partner may be experienced as more
distanced but also as "in control" in a way which may be very comforting, especially if the partner is willing to support or even enjoys
the other's intensity or immediacy despite his or her somewhat
distanced participation in it. At the same time, the interpersonal partner's longing for closeness is not necessarily fatal to the institutional
partner's overautonomous balance, because, in the same way, the latter's greatest longing may be to experience safely his or her independence and distinctness. The dangerous and less easily faced side
of these yearnings—for the institutional partner, that one can be so
distinct as to be completely and irremediably alone; for the interpersonal partner, that one can be so close as to lose oneself
unrecoverably—are held at bay by the assurance of the continued
countervailing influence from the partner. Such an alliance between
two partners can be filled with warmth, love, support, and mutual
respect, but it also amounts to a mutual protection against one side of
oneself, a side which the other becomes. The risks here are clear: (1) at
some level one confuses one's partner with a side of oneself one has
difficulty accepting; (2) the possibilities for one's own evolution are
diminished because growth depends upon finding again that quieter

side of oneself and each is protecting the other from that discovery; and (3) the marriage has changed from a context for growth to the support of specific evolutionary truces, and the costs of growth might then become as high as the loss of the marriage itself.

What the interpersonal partner must not do if the balance is to be preserved is either demand, in the exercises of his or her closeness, a surrender of the other's distance (a request that the other become more like the interpersonal partner), or, in the process of emerging from interpersonal embeddedness, demand some more equal share in the definition and operation of the marriage (a request that the other recognize the interpersonal partner as more like himself or herself). For the interpersonal partner, there must be some sense of an appropriateness to the other's remoteness, and for the institutional partner a sense of impermissible, even life-threatening, absorption in surrendering the distance. This is a pattern, of course, that has received strong cultural support in those instances where the interpersonal partner is the woman and the institutional partner is the man. His distancing is neither perceived by the woman, nor experienced by him, as a matter of lesser involvement in the marriage; it is a matter rather of the *quality* of his involvement. He must be captain of the ship, the protector and supporter of his family. He is remote as an internal companion, but he is there as an external support. That the role may serve his own psychological needs as well as respond to traditional cultural expectations is discovered in his reaction to those situations where the wife, moving from the interpersonal to the institutional, begins in effect to offer some relief to the burdens of sole command.

What the institutional partner must not do is either require that the other take on a measure of psychological independence in the relationship, or—should he or she be in the midst of emerging from this balance—require that the other see him or her from the "inside" rather than only relating to the consequences of how the inside works. To use the same stereotypical example of the hyperfeminine wife and the hypermasculine husband, the wife may experience an ultimate risk to her meaning if he stops confirming her identification with him, insists on the distinctness between them, and insists that her feelings are first of all hers, not necessarily his or even the marriage's. Alternatively, if he invites her to see his world from the inside, as he experiences it, complete with all the doubts and deficits from the more ideal presentation of executive command, he threatens a kind of safety she may not have known she needed, and he may become undesirably weak and needy in her eyes.

The interpersonal-institutional marriage may be a common one among relatively mature and accomplished adults, although even at its most loving and supportive it bears a strong resemblance to the relationship of parent and child, especially father and daughter, a perpetuation of the apparently more comfortable roles of warm-but-distant-protector-and-world-definer, on the one hand, and loving-admiring-undemanding-affiliator, on the other. In an age that more widely supports the development in adulthood beyond interpersonalism, such an alliance may be less and less long lived. But it is important to consider here how such an alliance is as inhibiting for development *beyond* institutionality as it is for development *into* it.

I have undertaken this little excursus into a meaning-evolutionary analysis of marital dynamics in part to suggest that the domain of *Liebe* is not automatically a better culture for the development and practice of adult intimacy than the domain of *Arbeit.* We could take this a bit further by considering another marital alliance which can also serve to defend against the development of intimacy — that between two institutional partners. In contrast to the prior alliance, the partners might be expected to share a common meaning for the marriage. Each partner's personal psychological autonomy and distinctness is confirmed, supported, celebrated; and at the same time each party protects the other against the overrunning of these boundaries. Functioning smoothly, such marriages can be characterized by a close, mutually supportive, admiring, respectful, appreciative cooperation, and an implicit guarantee to stay out of each other's act in some fundamental way — psychologically and publicly. At its best the relationship furthers each party's need for a sense of self-respect, respect from others, and personal accomplishment, at the same time protecting — by means of close personal alliance — against institutionality's less easily faced fear of being so differentiated that one is utterly alone. Fundamental to the successful working of the relationship is the assurance both that each party is an appreciative member of the other's audience and that the partner will not intrude on the other's stage.

Whether a shift from the one marital alliance to the other (or any of the shifts the theory suggests) describes an evolution in the history of an ongoing marital relationship, or whether such a shift comes closer to describing the reasons why a given marriage comes to an end, is a function of how difficult a person finds it to rediscover the currently quieter yearning in himself or herself. This must certainly be a matter of how such discoveries have gone in the past, but just as surely, it must be a matter of the kinds of supports which exist in the present to help persons recognize that the upheavals they experience in their marriages may be a consequence of their own and/or their partner's natural evolution.

Among those supports least studied and of which we are most in need of increased understanding are those supports which assist individuals and couples to evolve not only to that place where each can guarantee to the other his or her distinct identity, but which allow persons to share their identities as well. The transcendence from the tyranny of the form—the theme with which this chapter began—may evidence itself *cognitively* in terms of dialectical thought, or *sociomorally* in terms of a postideological construction, but what it seems to come down to most centrally in the wider arena of the psychological self is the capacity for genuine intimacy. The choices for adulthood need not be between a form of intimacy at the expense of identity, or an identity at the expense of intimacy. Although the classic Freudian identification of intimacy with mutuality of orgasm has a depressingly humorless ring to it, there is something at least symbolically powerful about the image of at once satisfying oneself (not subordinating one's pleasure to the other's) while at the same time transcending, in resplendent play, the isolation of our separateness, our polarity, our time-embeddedness. In Erikson's words it "provides a supreme example of the mutual regulation of complicated patterns and in some way appeases the potential rages caused by the daily evidence of the oppositeness of male and female, of fact and fancy, of love and hate, of work and play" (1963, pp. 96-97).

The image of an adult relationship that is genuinely intimate—sexually, but in every other respect as well—brings to light again the theme of *reciprocity* first seen in the interpersonal balance. Traveling once more over familiar psychological terrain, the evolution of meaning, in the interindividual balance, encounters a similar theme at a whole new level of complexity. Reciprocity now becomes a matter of at once mutually preserving the other's distinctness while interdependently fashioning a bigger context in which these separate identities interpenetrate, by which the separate identities are co-regulated, and to which persons invest an affection supervening their separate identities. Reciprocity now becomes a matter of both holding and being held, a mutual protection of each partner's opportunity to experience and exercise *both* sides of life's fundamental tension. Rather than each partner speaking for the other the quieter and more frightening of life's enduring longings, each calls out the expression of that longing in the other. And rather than forming an alliance which, in investing itself in the present evolutionary position of the partner, becomes a kind of mutual protection *against* growth, the relationship is wedded most of all to that life motion which the partners do not share so much as it shares them.

NINE

Natural Therapy

In an age when psychology has become the secular religion and the practice of psychotherapy the new priestly rite, the impression is often conveyed that the solution to life's ills could be found in universal psychotherapy, if it were only practical. The natural supports of family, peer groups, work roles, and love relationships come to be seen as merely amateur approximations of professional wisdom. From a developmental perspective this view of things is quite backward. Developmental theory has a long-standing appreciation of nature as the source of wisdom. For example, the single most important contribution developmental theory makes to schooling is its exposure of the child's "natural curriculum," an active process of meaning-making which informs and constrains the child's purposes. Rather than seeing the child as a passive receptacle to whom appealing curricula must be brought in order to initiate the learning experience, the developmentalist urges curriculum designers and teachers first to recognize the agenda upon which the child is *already* embarked, and which the teacher can only facilitate or thwart, but not himself invent.

Developmental theory would seem to have a similar kind of advice for the effort to be of help to people psychologically. Rather than make the practice of psychotherapy the touchstone for all considerations of help, look first into the meaning and makeup of those instances of unselfconscious "therapy" as these occur again and again in nature. This single piece of advice has a meaning for persons and for training programs; for the intimate intricacies of working with a single person and for wide-gauge social policy-making; for those primarily concerned with helping people who seek relief from the pain or difficulty in which they already find themselves, and for those who seek primarily to prevent those extremes of psychological suffering which might be prevented; for those concerned with the improvement of those roles for professional help which currently exist, and for those looking for an intellectual foundation on which to base the development of new roles. However important and valuable the careful practice of "unnatural" (self-conscious) therapy, developmental theory would seem to suggest that, rather than being the panacea for modern maladies, it is actually a second-best means of support, and arguably a sign that the *natural* facilitation of development has somehow and for some reason broken down. Not only does an understanding of "natural therapy"—those relations and human contexts which spontaneously support people through the sometimes difficult process of growth and change—offer "preventive psychology" a sophisticated way to consider a person's supports, it offers a new guide to therapeutic practice by exposing some of the details of those interactions which it is quite possible successful therapy is replicating, whether it knows it or not. From research on the outcomes of psychotherapy we have good reason for believing the success of therapy is not a function of the particular personality theory or identifiable therapeutic approach favored by the therapist (Smith and Glass, 1977). The usual conclusion drawn from such research is that "it's the therapist not the theory," and that successful therapy is largely an ineffable matter. It may be. But it may also be that since therapeutic processes are rooted not in theory but in nature, it was a mistake to use theories (and the approaches theories give rise to) as the hoped-for determiner of outcomes in the first place. Would it not have made more sense to try to understand how a therapeutic process works—all on its own, without the presence of professionals—and then evaluate which professionals were able in some way to foster or replicate these processes?

The theory outlined in this book suggests a life history of what Winnicott, referring to the infant, called the "holding environment." I have proposed that we are "held" throughout our lives in qualitatively different ways as we evolve. The circumstance of being held, I have suggested, reflects not the vulnerable state of infancy but the evolutionary state of embeddedness. However much we evolve, we are always still embedded. Development at any period in the life history, involving an emergence from a psychobiological evolutionary state, must also involve an emergence from embeddedness in a particular human context. This is analogous to transcending my culture and creating a distinction between what now appears as the culture's definition of me and what is "really me." (That what is "really me" will one day be discovered as yet another "cultural" definition is not at the moment available to us.) The cultures of embeddedness—their sequence, their shape, their function—(summarized in Table 7) may provide additional understanding of what Erikson calls "psychosocial development." The framework outlined in this book gives us a rigorous sense of the "psychosocial" as that which is both a part of the individual ("psyche") and, from another perspective (including the individual's own, at some time in the future), a part of the "social." The theory makes clear why these psychosocial contexts are more than just social or psychological supports which do or do not aid a separate person; from the point of view of the person, they *are* him or her.

While a richly textured understanding of the cultures of embeddedness awaits careful research, the outline sketched in Table 7 is at least rich in its implications. It suggests a framework for the evaluation of psychological *support* which has the same intellectual and psychological consistency whether one considers the supports of a five-year-old or a forty-five-year-old, or whether one considers the supporting system to be a single individual (like a mother) or a complex organization (like a school). If the intrauterine environment is a model for the provision of a medium in which the growing organism can thrive, the framework suggests a basis for a kind of lifelong "psychological amniocentesis," by which the quality of holding environments, their capacity to nourish and keep buoyant the life project of their "evolutionary guests," might be assessed. A history of naturally therapeutic contexts emerges: the mothering one; the family; role-recognizing institutions of family, school, or peer groups; mutually reciprocal one-to-one relationships; identity-confirming contexts for publicly recognized, self-regulating performance (typically in work contexts; conceivably in "love" relations, too); intimate adult relations (typically in love relations; conceivably in work relations, too). How well—it can be asked at any moment in a life's development—is the individual's culture of embeddedness performing its functions of *confirmation, contradiction,* and *continuity*?

Does the *mothering culture* attend to the newborn; does it provide a warm, close, comforting physical presence; does it accept the infant's utter dependence upon and merger with it? And does the mothering context, at the appropriate time, recognize and promote the toddler's emergence from this embeddedness; does it resist trying to meet the child's every need; does it stop nursing and reduce carrying; does it acknowledge the child's displays of independence and willful refusal; can it tolerate becoming "other" to the child? And does it remain in some way that permits the child to recover it as other; does it avoid prolonged separation or psychological abandonment during the period of transition?

Does the *parenting culture* acknowledge and nurture the child's capacity for fantasy; does it accept the child's intense attachments and rivalries within the family; can it accept the child's psychological dependence on, and merger with, the interior workings of the parents? Does the parenting context, at the appropriate time, recognize and promote the child's emergence from this embeddedness; does it begin to hold the child responsible for her behaviors; locate and designate the source of the child's thoughts and feelings in the child; does it exclude the child from the inner workings of the marriage, from the marriage bed, from the home during school hours; does it acknowledge the child's displays of self-sufficiency and self-possessedness; can it tolerate becoming "other" to the child? And does it remain in some way that permits the child to recover it as other; does it avoid falling apart (stormy, uncertain marriage; divorce; separation; especially divorce or separation in which the child loses contact with one of the parents) at just that time the child is differentiating from it?

Does the *role-recognizing culture* support and acknowledge the child's tests and exercises of self-sufficiency, competence, and role differentiation; does the family or school give the child an opportunity to speak and be listened to in the public life of that institution, especially its decisions; is there an opportunity for personal responsibility, definition, control (for example, do the parents buy the child a wristwatch, or confer an allowance; is the child permitted to choose her own clothes, to wake himself up in the morning)? Does the family or school seek to discover and support at least one involvement—athletic, artistic, academic, entrepreneurial—in which the child might have a continuing opportunity for successful self-display? Can it tolerate the child's confusion of it with the maintenance of the child's competence, the prosecution of the child's own needs? And does the culture, at the appropriate time, recognize and promote the adolescent's emergence from his embeddedness; does it contradict the validity or acceptability of a self-sufficiency that will not take others into account; does it insist that the adolescent hold up his end of trusts and agreements; does it look for reports of interior states rather than exterior dispositions; can it accept becoming relativized on behalf of a new identity and a new identification? And does the role-recognizing culture remain in some way that permits the growing person not only to repudiate it, but to recover it—for example, if the young adolescent has to change schools in the middle of this transition (the usual case with the customary—and questionable—isolation of the junior high school), does he at least maintain contact with his peer group?

Does the *culture of mutuality* acknowledge and support the person's capacity for collaborative, self-sacrificing, closely attuned, idealized interpersonal relationships? Does it share the person's internal subjective states, moods, feelings, innermost thoughts? Can it tolerate the person's confusion of it with herself? Does it recognize and promote the person's emergence from this embeddedness in interpersonalism; does it resist being fused with, insist on recognizing the person as distinct while still acknowledging the possibility and value of closeness; does it require the person to assume responsibility for her own initiatives and preferences, for her own psychological self-definition; and can it permit itself to be relativized on behalf of this emerging personal authority? Are there at least some important interpersonal partners who remain during the process of transition to take some role in the new psychological landscape?

Does the *culture of self-authorship* acknowledge and support the person's exercises of psychological self-definition; does it confirm the person's gathering sense of himself as the origin of his meanings and purposes; does it recognize her as a player in a public arena in which she can exercise her personal powers, need for achievement and self-enhancement; does it give him work that allows him to exercise influence, wield power, assume responsibility; does it offer the opportunity for loyalty to and investment in, some system of belief; can it accept the person's identification of its shared meaning with himself or herself? Does it recognize and promote the person's emergence from embeddedness in independent self-definition; does it insist on some relationship to the person who is *running* the psychic administration, refusing to accept mediated, nonintimate, form-subordinated relationships? Does the culture of ideology allow itself to be relativized on behalf of the bigger context which roots and co-regulates forms, systems, organizations? And do the ideological supports remain at the very time the person is separating from this identification with them; the job is not lost, the body does not fail, the spouse does not leave?

And does the *culture of intimacy* acknowledge and support the exercises of interdependence (even interdependent self-definition), the surrender of (and play with) the form-bound autonomous self, the counterpointing of identities?

The constructive-developmental approach offers a way to think about assessing the nature of a person's psychological supports that moves beyond the *quantity* of caring others, even beyond the *intensity* of their care, to consider, in a fairly discriminating way, the structural quality of those supports. Are there others who "know" the person, who can see, recognize, understand who the person is, and who he or she is becoming? Support is not alone an affective matter, but a matter of "knowing"; a matter of shape, as well as intensity.

But beyond the questions about support to given eras and moments of individual development, the scheme also speaks to the nature of community as a whole. It would be misleading to see each culture of embeddedness as distinct and separate from the next. More even than conterminous, they tend to evolve out of each other, each one including, or potentially including, the last. The mothering culture becomes a part of the parenting culture; the parenting culture becomes a part of the role-recognizing culture, as the family is one (but again *only* one) of the important domains in which the new truce of self-possession exercises itself. But the mother, the couple, the school, the chum, and so on, are really all part of a single community, and serve as the vehicles by which that community communicates. Among its most important communications is its recognition of a person's growth and change. Each time a particular culture of embeddedness "holds securely" it insures the integrity of the wider community of which the individual is a part; each time it assists in "letting go" it attests to the community's greater loyalty to the person-who-develops than to the self-the-person-has-composed. Both functions, well-performed, assure the person that he or she can survive in the community and assure the community of the person's continued participation. We live on a turning world and are turning ourselves. We have always needed to get at the depths of these relations of private to public season. When we cannot, time itself is profaned; closed off from the dance of our own development, we live less. In a community worthy of the name there are symbols and celebrations, ritual, even gesture, by which I am known in the process of my development, by which I am helped to recognize myself. Intact, sustaining communities have always found ways to recognize that persons grow and change, that this fate can be costly, and that if it is not to cost the community the very loss of its member, then the community must itself be capable of "re-cognition." It must operate richly at many evolutionary levels, dedicating itself less to any evolutionary level than to the process itself.

I am suggesting that support is more than a given culture of embeddedness performing its three functions over a given period of development, that the human coherence of our lives is enhanced by life in a community of considerable duration, a community which gathers and subtends its era-specific expressions of support. Much of present-day stress and psychological disruption is developmental, in the sense that it is related to the processes of growth, change, and transition we have considered in this book. Left to ourselves, these processes are often negotiated by separating ourselves not only from our old meanings but from the actual people who (and commitments which) have come to stand for those meanings. This is an extremely costly life course. Its amelioration requires supports which have a longitudinal basis—that is, they know and hold persons before, during, and after their transitions; they acknowledge and grieve the losses, acknowledge and celebrate the gains, and help the person (or family) to acknowledge them himself (itself).

Psychologists in the next few decades must find better ways to support individuals, families, and communities, which are put under enormous stress by the complexities of modern institutional life. Stress, placed on every domain of life, shows up most visibly in the cultures of love and work—the family and the place of employment. The psychological and psychiatric system has *reacted* (in a well-intentioned but overwhelmed way) to the costs and casualties of our present social arrangements, rather than paying any real attention to the arrangements themselves. Schools of clinical psychology and "professional psychology" seek to train persons for positions of leadership in the practice of psychology. Should they do this by training people to take their places in the psychological services system as it now exists? Does that system represent the best use of the men and women being trained? The question of how a professional psychologist should be educated is inseparable from the question of what professional psychologists should *do*. If it is felt that the system should be reconstructed, or its range of activities qualitatively re-elaborated, then schools of clinical and professional psychology should have a hand in articulating these new roles and preparing people for them. To do so, theories are needed which are as powerful in their understanding of normal processes of development as they are in their understanding of disturbance. Among the kinds of understandings we lack (and which the theory proposed here offers the promise of rigorously pursuing) are the ways that cultural and social arrangements do or do not provide unselfconsciously therapeutic supports in times of crisis, painful change and costly growth. Increasing demand for, and need of, self-consciously therapeutic services is arguably an index of the disappearance or failure of these kinds of supports.

When "self-consciously therapeutic services" *are* needed, these can derive considerable guidance from their unselfconscious counterpart in nature. Indeed, the framework presented in this book suggests a kind of metatheory of therapy which, simply stated, amounts to viewing the therapeutic context as a culture of embeddedness in the facilitation of a troubled person's evolution. I want to elaborate here what this would mean both for an overarching perspective on therapy with persons at any age or stage, and with respect to the distinctions between different evolutionary circumstances.

We might begin by remembering the case of Violet, discussed in Chapter 4. Inadequately "held" by her mother, Violet at age two and a half had still not successfully moved out of the incorporative world of the infant. While she could not retard the life project so completely as to remain comfortably in the state of undifferentiation, she was marshaling all her forces to hold out any "information" from the world ("she was mute, she had an absolutely blank and unanimated facial expression, and she focused on nothing and nobody"—Mahler, 1968, p. 152). Like perhaps all persons in a psychotic state, for the sake of what Violet deems as her own survival, she has turned against her own life project, the movement of her own evolution.

I found the treatment which Mahler described, and which seemed helpful both to Violet and her mother, fascinating and moving. What fascinated me most of all was how it seemed to replicate the more wholesome culture of embeddedness most infants are provided. While I had begun to formulate what therapy-as-evolutionary-culture might be like when the "evolutionary guest" (the client, the patient) used *language* as the central medium of self-expression (most people beyond the age of ten or so), I was not at all sure how the same themes might apply at earlier moments of evolution. But Mahler's treatment seemed to me to reflect an attention—with a not yet speaking client—to exactly the functions of a culture of embeddedness which I had been attending to with speaking clients.

Violet's therapy seemed to move through distinct phases. In the first phase the therapist saw herself as trying to follow the child's lead, to be unintrusive but attentive, to do nothing which required Violet to acknowledge the existence of a distinct presence. The hope was that the child might gradually come to accept the therapeutic presence as a soothing phenomenon, something more comfortable to have than to be without. In just the way I spoke of the infant as physically playing out themes which would metaphorically be played out for the rest of her life (losing and finding, being in and out of balance, recognizing and being recognized), so the therapist here seems to make a choice about the beginning of therapy which is a physical, palpable version of an address which I will suggest makes the same sense at any evolutionary moment. She joins Violet from behind (or alongside) rather than face to face. And as Violet comes to accept her, not as a separate other but as an enveloping presence, the therapist seems to become literally Violet's "holding environment." The therapist is used as a chair, her chest as a backrest; she is leaned on, fallen into; her arms are used as an extension of Violet's arms to obtain things otherwise out of reach. The therapist is certainly not seen as a separate other, because any face-to-face interaction is avoided. (Even indirect and accidental visual confrontation, when Violet saw the therapist's reflection in a mirror, sent Violet into a panic.) But the therapist is being accepted in some other way, a way I would call the culture of embeddedness. She has been accepted as a psychologically amniotic environment in which Violet can float, her life project given a degree of buoyancy it has never had. This acceptance of the culture of embeddedness marks in my mind the completion of the first stage of therapy, and shortly we will consider its dynamics and various expressions at different stages of development.

Only after securely and consistently providing for some time this first function of a culture of embeddedness does another phase of therapy begin. Now the therapist gradually offers contact as a separate party. She engages in parallel play; they take turns drumming on a table; they hum a song together; they blow soap bubbles to each other. Relying on the gentle contact of sound, the therapist begins to vocalize more while still avoiding stark face-to-face interactions. She spoke very little during the earlier phase of therapy; she now begins to verbalize the child's sensations ("Oh, it hurts"). From my point of view the success of this shift in the therapeutic address is a function of (and probably cued by) a shift in Violet's own evolution. More securely held, she may be more able to rejoin her own life project; she may feel that she can emerge from embeddedness without losing her life. In beginning to present herself as a separate other, the therapist may be recognizing Violet's own growing edge, a differentiation Violet herself can begin to recognize. In giving voice to Violet's sensations, the therapist may be joining Violet in her own move from being her sensations to having sensations. The therapist is fulfilling the second function of a culture of embeddedness; she is joining Violet in Violet's own emerging contradiction of the "truth" of her embeddedness.

The heart of the constructive-developmental framework—and the source of its own potential for growth—does not lie so much in its account of stages or sequences of meaning organizations, but in its capacity to illuminate a universal on-going process (call it "meaning-making," "adaptation," "equilibration," or "evolution") which may very well be the fundamental context of personality development. Accordingly, it is to this process and its experience, rather than to stages, that I would direct the invested attention of the constructive-developmental counselor. When I meet Terry or Diane or Rebecca in counseling, my most fundamental sense of her should derive not from my convictions about "stages" or "patients" or "sick persons" or even "persons with problems," but from my convictions about "persons evolving."

Thus my most fundamental orientation toward the person I address derives from my convictions about an activity or process which I share with the client right at this moment — not a process alien to me, like "psychosis," not an activity I "once" underwent, back at a time when I was in pain, but one I share right at this moment. That activity is not presumed to be suspended for a category of people, or for periods in our life of great confusion or radical change in the way others know us. We neither escape from our own fate as lifelong meaning-makers nor escape from our lifelong community with those who may be finding that fate a greater burden. In the end, I believe, we are bound by a single fate, and we do not share it so much as it shares us.

When that fate is testing us most severely it often speaks itself in the form of "problems" or "crises"; but what are these? What is taken for crisis — divorce, death of a loved one, economic catastrophe, leaving a familiar community behind and entering a strange one — may not always *be* a crisis. People do meet these experiences, and they suffer because of them; but they do not always suffer so protractedly; they do not always suffer in a way that throws every other aspect of their lives into doubt ("it's as if everything is on the line"; "for the first time, it's like I'm just totally unsure"; "a period when everything has collapsed at once"). Is this just a matter of the intensity with which different people feel things, are affected by things, or is this a structural matter, a matter of how things mean? Is the crisis the loss of a loved one or the way that loss catches how I make things mean? Is my whole world thrown out of balance because of my grief, or am I grieving so totally because my whole world has been thrown out of balance? Is experience what happens to me, or what I do (or, in this case, am unable to do) with what happens to me? Is crisis an opportunity for growth, or is growth an opportunity for crisis? In these crises and problems we may also hear another language: "I'm just not myself"; "I can't believe I'm like this"; "if my friends saw me like this they wouldn't believe it." It is a voice that says, "I cannot recognize myself" — and, I am going to suggest, this names very precisely what is happening. One is unable to re-cognize, or re-know, oneself and one's world; one experiences, even literally, being beside oneself.

Pain — psychological pain, surely, but perhaps even physical pain as well — is about the resistance to the motion of life. Our attempt to deny what has happened and is happening causes us pain. Our refusal to accept deviation from our plans or anticipation causes us pain.

When the body tenses and defends against its reorganization, this causes greater pain than the reorganization itself; if we relax immediately after stubbing our toe the pain subsides. Our digging in and defending against the movements which make what-is what-was causes us pain. Any movement which sets us against the movement of life of which we are a part, in which we are ultimately implicated, to which we are finally obligated, will cause us pain. In defense against the losses which have already occurred, in defense against the experience of grief and mourning, we inflict on ourselves a pain which is greater than the loss itself. Grieving and mourning are not really painful; they are our reunion with life itself and our recognition of its motion. Anxiety and melancholia, which set us against life, are a greater source of pain than change itself, however much change must always have to do with loss.

In crises and problems we may hear danger and death—but danger to whom? the death of what? I have said the Chinese draw "crisis" with two characters: one means "danger," the other "opportunity." This, literally, is the character of crisis; for the crisis *is* in the transformation of meaning, the costs of evolution, and the death we hear may be, as much as anything, the death of the old self that is about to be left behind. The separation and individuation which others speak of in the course of psychotherapy (notably Mahler, 1968, 1975, in infancy and early childhood; Peter Blos, 1962, in adolescence) is always, as well, the separation from the old balance.

We may hear grief, mourning, and loss, but it is the dying of a way to know the world which no longer works, a loss of an old coherence with no new coherence immediately present to take its place. And yet a new balance again and again does emerge. This is the incredible wonder that makes clinical work worship before great mysteries. Still, it is a *new* life, not a return or a recovery. It is common, when experiencing the kind of pain we feel when we take ourselves to strangers, to think in terms of "getting back" to normal; nor is such a polar phenomenology greatly different from categories of health and illness in relation to psychological pain. When disequilibrium is weathered it can begin to lead to a new, more articulated, better organized construction of the world which differentiates and reintegrates the understanding of the prior balance. Recall Niebuhr's words: "We understand what we remember, remember what we forgot, and make familiar what before seemed alien." We will never restore the balance—but there is a *new* balance that can be achieved. We are not going back, but we are coming through—to a new integration, a new direction. The constructive-developmental perspective may support the professional helper's capacity to listen to the pain that is brought to him, or may suggest a new place from which to listen. It might also inform people generally that such crises are not sufficiently understood merely as "illness," but better understood as a move toward growth. We might learn to expect them in the course of a lifetime and teach others to. We might come to understand, and with more substance than he himself was able to muster, what R. D. Laing (1960) meant when he said, "All breakdown is not pathological; some breakdown is breakthrough." Or, as I have put it: "You're not crazy, but you may be going out of your mind."

My colleagues and I interviewed thirty-nine persons during their stay on a psychiatric ward. We used Kohlberg dilemmas and analyzed them for level of self-other differentiation. We also had the patients' permission to acquaint ourselves with their intake interviews, the reports of what life had been like prior to admission, and the events of their hospital stay. From the files we thought we detected three very heterogeneous but nevertheless qualitatively different kinds of depression:

Type A. The fundamental concern seemed to be the loss of my own needs, or an unhappiness at the increasing personal cost of trying to satisfy my own needs. When the orientation is outward I may feel constrained, deprived, curtailed, controlled, or interfered with in the effort to satisfy my needs, wishes, desires. When the orientation is self-directed there is a tension between feeling unavoidably irresponsible, a slave to my own interests, insensitive, on the one hand, and feeling compromised away, or that I have lost my own distinct personality, on the other. The overall foreboding feeling seems to be that, with the possible loss of the satisfaction of my wants, I may no longer be. At stake, directly or lurkingly, seems to be the very meaningfulness of an ultimate orientation to "my needs" in the first place.

Type B. The fundamental concern seemed to be the loss of, or damage to, an interpersonal relationship. When the orientation is outward I may feel unbearably lonely, deserted, betrayed, abandoned, stained. When the orientation is self-directed there is a tension between feeling vulnerable to incorporation, fusing, the loss of myself as my own person, on the one hand, and feeling selfish, heartless, cold, prideful, uncaring as a result of beginning to put myself first. The overall foreboding feeling seems to be that, with the rupture of my interpersonal context, I may no longer be. At stake, directly or lurkingly, seems to be the very meaningfulness of an ultimate orientation to the interpersonal context in the first place.

Type C. The fundamental concern seemed to be a blow to self-concept, a failure to meet my own standard, perform or control myself as I expect to. When the orientation is outward I may feel humiliated, empty, out of control, closed in on, that the world is unfair, that life is somehow meaningless. When the orientation is self-directed there is a tension between feeling vulnerable to crippling self-attack, identifying with my performance, isolated in self-containment, on the one hand, or feeling weak, ineffective, out of control, evil, decadent, without boundaries, on the other. The overall foreboding feeling seems to be that, with the disruption to my self-conscious psychic organization or authorship, I may no longer be. At stake, directly or lurkingly, seems to be the very meaningfulness of an ultimate orientation to the maintenance of this psychic administration in the first place.

Each subject was assigned to a depression type without the experimenter's knowledge of his or her subject-object level.[1] When subject-object levels are compared with depression type an extremely strong relation emerges between persons at stage 2 or 2-3 and Type A depression, between persons at stage 3 or 3-4 and Type B depression, and between persons at stage 4 or 4-5 and Type C depression.[2] This correlation is impressive but inconclusive by itself. For one thing, it needs to be replicated on a broader scale even to confirm the phenomenon; for another, even confirmed, the phenomenon itself only suggests a relation, not a cause. My colleagues and I are presently at work not only to confirm the phenomenon, but, by longitudinal investigation, to test the hypothesis that the depression is caused by the disequilibrium or threat to the balance of a given evolutionary truce. Still, even the present study has much to tell us beyond these numbers and correlations. However in need of elaboration and confirmation it may be, a clear picture does come through of successive processes of transformation and their costs to the evolving person.[3]

1. The Kohlberg scores, grouped as stage 2 or 2-3 transitional, 3 or 3-4 transitional, 4 or 4-5 transitional, were identical between two raters in 94 percent of the cases; depression scores were identical in 84 percent of the cases.

2. Kendall's tau = .815, < .001; Chi square + 46.43, 8 d.f., < .001

3. It is interesting that other researchers of depression, while approaching the subject from

My position amounts to a conception of depression as radical doubt, that which presents the possibility of "not knowing" with respect to the ultimate proposition: How do the world and I cohere? What is subject and what is object? It should be seen how such a conception does not reject competing understandings of depression, but rather gathers them into a more integrated whole. All theorists agree that the substrate of depression is loss. Ego psychology looks to a loss to the *self;* object relations theory to a loss of the *object;* existential theory to a loss of *meaning.* When equilibrative activity is taken as the grounding phenomenon of personality, and depression is understood as a threat to the evolutionary truce, then depression must necessarily be about a threat to the self *and* the object, *and* (since it is the relationship between the two which constitutes meaning) a threat to meaning, as well.

Table 12 schematizes this conception more particularly. Each of five types of depression is characterized by a particular concern, and each concern can be oriented to in terms of either a threat to, or a questioning of, that concern. The former orientation might be said to stand inside the concern, while the latter stands both inside and outside. What is at issue in either case is the matter of *doubt.* To doubt requires us to hold simultaneously the possible validity and invalidity of a proposition. Were we to discount either we would be without doubt; holding both we cannot know.

Depression characterized by the "threat-to" orientation lodges itself in one side of the proposition. Doing so does not eliminate doubt, it only places it in the world. The world has become doubtful; what I doubt is my capacity to continue living in such a world. I doubt whether I can make it given how things are. I experience a kind of shrinking, or diminution of my self; but what remains clear — what I am most wanting to hold clear — is *who* it is that is doing the doubting, who "I" am. As it seems to "me," what "I" doubt is whether, in the face of the way the world has become, "I" can keep myself together, my self together. From the point of view of our paradigm, that which "I" say means: I doubt whether I can keep *it* together, this balance. What is being doubted, really, from our point of view, is the capacity to continue knowing, which, phenomenologically, from the view of the self, entails the capacity to continue *being.*

---

different theoretical and methodological directions, have described depressive organizations that sound a great deal like my Types B and C (Blatt, 1974; Blatt, D'Afflitti, and Quinlan, 1979; Arieti and Bemporad, 1981; Beck, 1981).

TABLE 12. Developmental organizations of depression

Type of depression	"Threat-to" the balance	"Questioning-of" the balance
(Ego 0/0-1) *Abandonment depression* [assault on the incorporative balance]	"Separation anxiety" *(depressive equivalent: failure to thrive syndrome).*[a]	*Tension between:* "No!" - counterdependent negativism, the necessity to defend and declare distinctness [self-anger]; *and* Longing for, and feeling loss of, undifferentiated oneness (the uroboric state) [self-loss].
(Ego 1/1-2) *Disillusioning depression* [assault on the impulsive balance]	Closed out, cut off, not included, sent away, feeling others have "gone into business for themselves" *(depressive equivalent: school phobia; persistence in fantasy).*	*Tension between:* Feeling unable to curb or control my impulses, to be self-reliant, to "go into business for myself" [self-anger]; *and* Feeling the loss of the power of my own wishes to determine reality, the loss of a perfect care and attunement from another [self-loss].
(Ego 2/2-3) *Self-sacrificing depression* [assault on the imperial balance]	Constrained, deprived, curtailed, controlled, interfered with *(depressive equivalent: planful delinquent behavior).*	*Tension between:* Feeling unavoidably irresponsible, a slave to my own interests, insensitive [self-anger;] *and* Feeling compromised away, loss of my own pleasures, distinct personality [self-loss].
(Ego 3/3-4) *Dependent depression* [assault on the interpersonal balance]	Unbearably lonely, deserted, betrayed, stained *(depressive equivalent: anorexia nervosa).*	*Tension between:* Feeling vulnerable to incorporation, fusing, loss of myself as own person [self-anger]; *and* Feeling selfish, heartless, cold, uncaring as result of beginning to consider me first [self-loss].
(Ego 4/4-5) *Self-evaluative depression* [assault on the institutional balance]	Humiliated, empty, out of control, compromised *(depressive equivalent: workaholism).*	*Tension between:* Feeling vulnerable to crippling self-attack, to identifying with my performance, isolated in self-containment, unable to let myself be closer to another [self-anger]; *and* Feeling weak, ineffective, out of control, swallowed up as result of not being all together; feeling evil, decadent, loss of identity, boundary loss [self-loss].

a. I owe this idea to Judy Frieworth.

Depression characterized by the "questioning-of" orientation brings radical doubt to the self itself; the world and the self, and even the distinction between them, become doubtful. It is no longer clear who "I" am, though it may be clear who "I" am not. I doubt, not whether I will continue knowing, but whether I shall know again. I may say I do not know if I shall ever come together again; what the statement means from our view is that it is doubted whether a subject-object balance shall ever come together again.

These two orientations represent only moments in an ongoing dynamic activity. We can see that between these two orientations there may be a period of attack upon the self, where one attempts to settle the doubt not by putting it "on the world" but by putting it on the self. This purifies the world, and makes it livable, at least theoretically. No stability is suggested for these "orientations" because, as I have said, they name moments in a process. What is suggested as stable throughout any given depression is the concern which organizes the type. This, of course, is because I am suggesting that depression reflects disequilibrium and the processes of re-equilibration. Those who experience their depression generally in terms of a threatening, confusing, or problematic environment are seen as defending a threatened balance; while those who experience it self-critically have begun the separation from the old self and are thus in a position to critique it. (That is, their separation is their critique; I am not referring here to any self-consciously deliberative activity.) For example, persons over-defending stage 2 appear more likely to identify the source of their problems in others who are persecuting and curtailing the "self"; whereas persons in the 2-3 shift appear more likely to speak in terms of their own inability to do what needs to be done to get along. Persons over-defending stage 3 appear more likely to view others as pushing them to grow up, or to give up their relationships with nothing to take their place; whereas 3-4 transitionals appear more likely to understand that it is not the relationships that need to be given up, but their own dependence upon them. Persons over-defending stage 4 appear more likely to view the world as failing to hold up its end of the bargain, as betraying in its revelation that it is not what it appeared to be; whereas 4-5 transitionals appear more likely to speak in terms of their own inferiority, emptiness, and meaninglessness, or of their own need to transcend the bargain somehow. In sum, it appears that those who feel they "just don't work" are also those who are transitional; and those who feel they work okay, if others would just shape up, are those who are defending a particular shape.[4]

This summarizes what is *common* to depressions—they are the self's experiencing of assault, either assault from the outside ("threat-to"), in which the self anticipates its defeat; or from within ("questioning-of"), in which the person, dislodged from self, is caught in the imbalance between the old self's repudiation (as subject) and its recovery (as new object). In Table 12 the *distinctions* in these experiencings, by equilibrial level, are summarized. Five kinds of depression correspond with the threat-to, or questioning-of, five evolutionary positions. As can be seen, the questioning-of position amounts to a tension between a feeling of self-anger (critiquing or reflecting upon the old self) and self-loss (the old self not yet recovered as object, the new self not yet reconstructed). This self-loss experience names the stage-particular construction of that "specialness" which is always invested in the defenses of the old self; it provides an articulating glimpse into the "fear of growth" as it is experienced at each critical period in development. In the 4-5 shift the feeling of an impending loss of specialness may be connected with the sense of oneself as all together or at least honored in the attempt (to be perfect, for example). In the 3-4 shift it is more likely to be a loss of that idealized sense of oneself as all-considerate, selfless, completely charitable, or at least honored in the attempt. While in the 2-3 shift growth amounts to a reconsideration of the ideal of oneself as uncompromisingly independent. It is possible that this self-loss, in returning to the other side of the helix, is also experienced as a frightening echo of the prior balance; that is, something

4. This same distinction suggests a way of viewing depressive sleep disturbance, which, like all of the above, future research could validate or disconfirm. Depressives are commonly sleep-disturbed, and generally in a stable fashion: they are either regularly hypersomniac, sleeping many hours longer per day than usual, or they are hyperwakeful, in which case they may get their usual allotment but it might not begin until four in the morning. Both hypersomnia and hyperwakefulness are logical responses to the sense of an ultimate threat to my way of making meaning. The first seeks to shut off the irresolvably discrepant, impinging environment; the second is ever-vigilant to a suddenly inimical world. But why should some people respond fairly consistently (at least for a good stretch of time) one way and others another? We might consider the appropriateness of these defenses to the stage-defender, on the one hand, and the transitional, on the other. If I feel the *world* has become threatening I must be hypervigilant; wakefulness is action *outward*, a protection against the other. But once I have critiqued the present stage I have become my own enemy (I am me and not-me, the essence of transition) and outward vigilance will no longer do the trick. Hypersomnia is action *inward*, a protection against the self.

of the agony that looms over a system in collapse may be the memory of the former balance and a mistaken sense of the similarity of that time with the present. When, for example, the balance of ego stage 3 is giving way and personality is considering claiming the right to its own purposes independent of the shared context, might it not feel selfish in a manner reminiscent to *it* of the stage 2 world it has left behind? Might it not see its repudiation of the interpersonal balance as a repudiation of that recognition which reconstructed stage 2? Or when the institutional balance as about to give out and personality is considering allowing the affiliative or erotic impulses a freer rein, might it not feel the impending chaos or boundary loss as a return to that stage 3 balance which is now most distinguished by its lack of a self (that is, a self-conscious or systematic self)?

If the eyes are the windows of the soul, then what Terry, Diane, and Rebecca present as problems are better understood as their eyes. They are that through which each woman sees when she comes for help, and they are that through which we might get a glimpse into the workings of her soul. It is "the problem" in its particularity that opens client and counselor both into the lifetime activity of meaning-evolution, which, when the state is balanced, is rarely attended to by the client and rarely seen by another person. As the goal of psychotherapy is the development of this equilibrative activity, it is here that the constructive-developmental counselor understands the work will be done. If "the problem" is the way into this work for both of them, it should be acknowledged that "this work" at the start is more the counselor's agenda than the client's. The fact is, client and counselor do not yet have the same relationship to (for instance) Diane's problem when she presents it. No matter how sophisticated Diane may be, no matter how clearly she understands that the psychotherapeutic relationship will not consist of the counselor's curing or solving her problem, she still, like almost any other person, wants the problem to go away, and that is one reason she has come for help. She is paralyzed by her way of living, frightened, shocked at her own inability to mobilize herself, feeling she is missing a part, that "drive" which used to rally to the cause. We both know that she has come not for a "valuable learning experience" but to get herself out of this mess.

But the counselor—let us be honest—is not quite in the same rush.

Recovery, after all, means that something is covered over again, and we know what. (T. S. Eliot, "Burnt Norton": "The enchainment of past and future/ woven in the weakness of the changing body/ protects mankind from heaven and damnation/ which flesh cannot endure. Time past and future/ allow but a little consciousness. To be conscious is not to be in time.") The weakness of the changing body does not permit much consciousness but it does permit some. The constructive-developmental clinician has one primary function: to protect those opportunities for consciousness — for meaning-evolution — which the client brings to him or her as "problems." He does not seek to, and cannot, "get" the client to do anything; the choice is always the client's. The counselor only seeks to protect the choice that presents itself in the disguise of these problems. They are those particularities in time through which time is conquered. These "things" which are carried so painfully, so shamefully, represent a resource to client and counselor alike. They are chances for growth as portals to growth-work. Accordingly, the counselor is trying to hold the door open to them in his choice to resonate *to the experience* that having such a problem may entail, rather than to help solve the problem, or try to make the experience less painful. He chooses the phenomenological perspective because his loyalty is to *the person in her meaning-making,* rather than to her stage or balance. He is seeking to join the *process* of meaning-evolution, rather than solve the problems which are reflective of that process. He prizes the person-as-meaning-making, even at its most painful (what "unconditional positive regard" means constructive-developmentally), and seeks, first of all, not to relieve that pain but to join her in the fundamental context of who she is. But this can seem like just the opposite direction from the one the client wants to go. Indeed, the client may keep returning to a focus on the problem if she experiences the counselor's invitations as a *spreading out* of the problem itself; she, after all, may want to contain it, precisely to keep it from spreading into her whole life. What is the gift and grace that permits a person to move off the problem and begin the evolutionary activity of recognition? What is it that permits a person to begin "hearing" her problem rather than looking at it? I would not like anyone to imagine I believe it to be any less mysterious for having some idea of what is involved in this move.

To "hear" the problem one has to somehow leave off shoring oneself up against it. Something of what accounts for this move may be the person's sense that she can momentarily "leave" the problem without its destroying her when she turns her back on it. No matter what the content of "the problem," there is something similar about all clinical problems: they are all about the threat of the constructed self's collapse. What permits a person faced with *this* sort of problem to move beyond or under the problem is a sense that the self will still hold together, will keep defending itself against the threat even if "I" start attending elsewhere. How does one get such a sense? This is where our counselor comes in, for the process of recognition is a social one.

The defending Diane appears, and in order to keep her balance she has had to alter her gait tremendously: she has to keep her left elbow tucked at her side while her left palm is outstretched to hold whatever she feels must be held there. At the same time she is bending over at the waist to support a weight on her back, and her right hand is extended behind her, supporting something. This makes it nearly impossible to walk, of course; but at the moment, just standing is balancing enough. But what happens when Diane feels some support under that left hand? It is the counselor's hand, and it is positioned, not precisely, but almost, under the weight she has been holding all these weeks. She loosens her elbow from her side, and sure enough the weight is still suspended; gingerly, she removes her left hand entirely and allows the counselor to hold the weight. It doesn't cave in on her; the arm is safely free—for a moment, anyway. "This is just a break," she tells herself; but in the meantime it is good to have this arm free again. And while it is free who knows what it will happen upon in its explorations? Meantime a support has slipped in under her back as well, and she can straighten up. It may be many months in the process, but at some point Diane may realize she is not on a vacation from holding those weights but has actually escaped them. What they are of course is the old balance itself, that old Diane which she was trying to keep together at all costs, but which she has gradually come to separate from. Jessie Taft (1933) says the therapist is "the repository of the outworn self." But he is more like the receiver of a bank deposit than a dumping ground for a shed skin: his real role is as a kind of "bridge" in the moving over from subject to object, a facilitator of rebalancing. He is the repository of the outworn self, but the new self will, in the end, re-collect it—and with interest.

The constructive-developmental counselor is thus "phenomenological," "existential," and in a sense, client-centered—but why? He or she is seeking to become a party to the client's equilibrative activity, but in a most unusual way. Any person with whom I have a relationship is part of my equilibrative activity in the sense that they become other; I know them, hold them, according to the strictures of my current balance. When the counselor responds to the problem not in terms of assurance, or its resolution, or its interpretation, but in terms of the experience of having, or being in, the problem, the counselor is offering the client a most intimate and usually unexpected companionship—not as another object in the world, but as a fellow hanger-in-the-balance, a companion to my very experience of knowing (meaning-making) and a party to the re-cognition whose time has come. The counselor is offering the client a culture to grow in.

This suggests that developmental interventions of any kind—educational (Kohlberg and Blatt, 1975; Mosher and Sprinthall, 1971), rehabilitative (Kohlberg, Scharf, and Hickey, 1972), or clinical—require a broader conception of whom they are addressing. The original and continuing model for deliberative developmental education has been to provide experiences which might inform a person of the limits or contradictions of his or her way of constructing the world. This is good Dewey progressivism (1938), the teacher seeking thus to foster over a shorter period of time that development which would be natural over the course of an individual's lifetime, or several lifetimes if he or she had them to live. The model is consistent with the framework, but it is inadequate because its picture of the person is incomplete. An intervention which is only provocative, seeking to provide the kind of creative discrepancies which might induce disequilibrium, is essentially an address to the person in equilibrium, a presumption that the person rests in the pride of balance, in need of the ennobling Socratic itch. This conception places the intervener in the role of the environment as it faces a given meaning-balance; it is a conception of the teacher as "intentional environment." I like this conception of an aspect of the teacher's developmental role, but it can never be the whole story. We live much of our lives *out* of balance, when the world all by itself is sufficiently creative to command our irritable attention. At such a time, which party to the evolutionary conversation—the environment or the meaning-maker—is most in need of deliberate support? Developmentalists know something now about how to join the environment to stimulate development; but have we learned how to join or accompany the meaning-maker when he or she faces a world that is already heated up, already stimulating, even to the point of being meaning-threatening?

The greatest limit to the present model of developmental intervention is that it ends up being an address to a *stage* rather than a person, an address to made meanings rather than meaning-making. Terry and Diane and Rebecca are not their stages. At their best, the imperial and interpersonal and institutional balances describe something of the meaning systems the three women are departing, the biologics in which they have lived. These systems are their creations—but who are Terry, Diane, and Rebecca? They are the creators, the meaning-makers, not the made-meaning. The existing model of developmental intervention too easily translates into the goal of "getting people to advance stages," an extraordinarily reduced (not to mention presumptuous) relationship to the evolution of meaning-making. The stages, even at their very best, are only indicators of development. To orient around the indicators of development is to risk losing the *person developing,* a risk at no time more unacceptable than when we are accompanying persons in transition, persons who may themselves feel they are losing the person developing.

Let me be a bit more specific about what it means to join a person in their experience of making meaning, rather than to join, in one way or another, their made meaning. In some sense, the attempt on the therapist's part to make the therapeutic context a culture of embeddedness is an *empathic* address, an address which has long been associated with the thinking of Carl Rogers and, more recently, from a different theoretical tradition, the thinking of Heinz Kohut (1971, 1977). I think both perspectives have something to gain from a consideration of empathy in these terms. I believe Rogers' "client-centered response" is among the most misunderstood of techniques, and that the fault lies somewhat with Rogers himself, whose inability to tie it clearly to his theory of personality leaves it even more vulnerable than it would be otherwise to being appropriated as just that—a technique. Though it would be hard to tell from the way many therapists and counselors make use of it, the client-centered response is something quite different than "saying back to the client what the client said to you," "pulling for affect," or "offering support." Like any technique, it can only stop being a technique when it is embodied by a person with a specific set of ideas and hopes which he is himself trying to bring to life through the medium of the "technique." Therapy from a constructive-developmental point of view is an extremely delicate but not impossible affair. Its delicacy lies in the fact that the therapist is actually trying to join another person in an extraordinarily intimate way; he or she is trying to become a helpful part of the person's very *evolution*. Whatever else a therapist might do once he or she has established this context, establishing such a context is the first order of business. Where language is the central medium of communication I do not know a more effective way of establishing that context than by the client-centered response. Properly understood, it is an extremely powerful instrument.

Consider three crude examples which may distinguish between a therapeutic response to the situation (the meaning that is made), the interpretation of the situation (the interpretation of made meaning), and the experience of the situation (the experience of meaning-making).[5] Let us imagine we are early in the hour of a session with Lorraine. She has been talking about the changes in her relationships to her mother and boyfriend: she is especially struck by behavior which seems to her odd (her refusal to wear clothes she likes which her mother has bought her; her lack of desire for sex even though she knows she gets great pleasure out of lovemaking with Richard). Consider the following exchange (Lorraine and the counselor are represented by L and C, respectively):

L-1:   It's gotten to the point where almost anything makes me angry.
C-1:   What do you make of that?
L-2:   I dunno . . .
C-2:   You think maybe that's why you won't wear the slacks she bought you?
L-3:   I don't know . . . I'm not really so angry with *her*. I was thinking more about Richard, how even the slightest opinion of his I find it just grates me.
C-3:   I could be all wrong but it kinda seems to me like you're kind of angry with both of them, at the influence they've had over you.
L-4:   Well, maybe. But a lot of people influence me. Why aren't I angry with Betsy [best friend and roommate] or Ken [project adviser]?

5. The merits of this approach are due entirely to William Perry who taught it to me.

Any therapist's responses reveal his "where" — his sense of where he "is" or wants to be in relation to the material the client presents him. The excerpt begins with Lorraine's statement of her feeling angry, and the therapist's response is to carry it up *through* the level of *situation* (not wearing the clothes) *to* the level of *interpretation* (why she doesn't), thus lodging it finally at double-remove from its origin. This is apparently where the therapist is at home, and, further, it is apparently his assumption that it is in his home that this meeting should go on. Accordingly, good host, he takes charge of their mutual experience and gives the client/guest her options within a host-controlled context. His questions in C-1 and C-2 suggest that he is enlisting the client in a mutual process of interpretation, but it amounts to asking her to join him in taking a perspective on her experience. In L-3, the client/guest accepts the invitation (it's always easier to eat out than to have to prepare your own meal) and begins to take her place as co-interpreter, but in C-3 the therapist makes clear that Lorraine is most of all the guest, that the menu is already planned; perhaps the therapist has had his mind made up for a while now. By L-4, the client has settled into the comfortable role of the guest and now turns to the commander/therapist/host for a full tour of the house, thus completing an almost complete *reverse* of the clinical route implied by any phenomenological premise: from the excerpt's beginning when we move *from* experience *to* situation and *beyond* to interpretation; to the segment's middle where "home" is proposed to be the therapist's and the lead is taken by him; right up to the segment's conclusion where the *client* begins smoothly checking and clearing with the *therapist* about the insides of the house.

Consider now a second exchange:

L-1: I'm at a point now where I can't even make decisions, and this isn't like me at all. I'm used to myself knowing what I want to do, but now I feel like I'm going to lose something no matter which way I turn. All those purposes that directed me, I guess I've kinda lost them.

C-1: What were they, those purposes that helped you be decisive?

L-2: I don't know, it's not something I could say, like "I'm going to be a doctor," but I had a feeling that things just fit, that I fit, or could make them fit. Now nothing fits, and I feel like something's going to burst, maybe me.

C-2:   You probably have some thoughts about why this is happening.
L-2:   Yes . . . Well, nothing that really makes too much sense [ten-second pause]. I guess that's why I'm here. How does it seem to you?

Here, in her first statement, Lorraine conveys both a situation and something of her internal experience. The situation is that she is paralyzed; faced with choices, she can no longer consult herself reliably. At the level of internal experience she may be saying something like: "I feel like the ground is giving way under me; I've no solid place to stand. Whatever I do is going to hurt me or someone and doing nothing also hurts. I'm very different than I was, and I don't like it. I feel like I have to choose between losses and in not being able to choose I am already losing something I prize—my directedness, my purpose."

The therapist's response (C-1) identifies his "where" to be not in the internal experience of the client, but in her situation; not her experience of making meaning, but her made meaning. He may see his task as that of solving Lorraine's problem or helping her to solve it herself. He may feel that problems are not solved by wallowing in one's bad feelings, but by finding the inner strength and resources to whip the despondency. Accordingly, he may locate that resource in Lorraine's previous purposefulness, and so seeks to steer the conversation there in hopes of helping her recover what she has lost. In her reply (L-2), Lorraine answers, but she adds something more: now *nothing* fits; whatever glide she did have with the world has ended. Her internal experience—that she is anxious, constricted, possibly panicky, alone, different from how she used to be—has not been heard, has not been seen in their shared space, and it calls out again for recognition.

But the therapist is as tenacious that *he* be heard (C-2). He is down a level closer to the bone than the interpreting therapist of the prior excerpt, but he is lodged in the situation. Possibly he even has an interpretation but does not believe it will be heard, or that Lorraine can work on it, until the situation is solved. He may even intend for Lorraine to be unable to answer the question and may see himself as a good "teacher" who is withholding his answer until the questions "come from" (that is, are caused to be generated by) the "student."

In her last response, Lorraine says she cannot solve the problem, but she has discovered that this, anyway, is what the session will be about—solving her problem. That part of her which is asking, even without her knowing it, to be heard, has been denied, and so, at the last, the ball, which heretofore at least held out promise of being put into play, has been passed to the therapist. The likely consequences are that the therapist will run with the ball (if he wanted it all along and was working toward an attentive client-in-the-stands), or that the game will be called on account of darkness.

Consider a third exchange:

L-1: It's gotten to the point where the slightest thing he says can make me angry.

C-1: You've—ah—just kinda had it up to here?

L-2: Yeah . . . Well, not really, I . . . I don't know, I s'pose . . . [silence, ten seconds].

C-2: Or maybe, kinda, more like the tiniest thing can just mushroom into—

L-3: That's it, it just takes me over, it grows inside me. Like, he'll say something—it can be trivial, like whether we should have Chinese or seafood—and I'll pick up this feeling of his and feel it spreading in me, and I just hate that.

C-3: So you almost feel now kinda like you can't get too near to him . . . ?

L-4: Exactly. It's like he's a threat, but then—and here's another thing, it's not really his fault, I mean [and so on].

Again we can consider Lorraine's first statement in terms of a situation or problem she describes and in terms of an experience. In his response, the therapist chooses the latter as the locus for his address, and apparently has it in mind that this is where his "where" ought to be. But this is not *his* home, and now *he* is the guest. He is unfamiliar and might see dimly. Accordingly, his first attempt to let Lorraine know there is another human being in the room is not entirely successful. She is not really companioned by his way of putting her experience; it is not a space she wants to move on to. It's not that she has this large residue of rage that is waiting to go off. The therapist's words have the effect of stopping Lorraine, stuck now in this little side alley the therapist has presented. But what he can see more clearly is that he has not seen clearly. He knows the silence is "his." He has a little more time. He tries a different way, and before he can finish, Lorraine is off. This third therapist is as tenacious in the exercise of his hypothesis (as to where should be his "where") as the other two therapists. The only difference is this: as his hypothesis relies on Lorraine, he is the only one of the three who can find out from someone in the session that he is not completely fulfilling his own goals—that someone being, of course, Lorraine herself.

What it may mean for the client, when the counselor offers company to the side of knowing rather than the side of the known, is, initially, an experience of loss. I lose this person which my defended balance is hoping to hold, by whom I hope to hold that balance together. But if the counselor can establish this unusual alliance, his own holding of subject rather than object—joining self rather than other—may eventually facilitate the person's emergence from embeddedness ("someone else is there to hold [the old] me"), and the counselor may come to be found again, now as the new other of a new way of being in the world.

This amounts to a constructive-developmental way of thinking about transference. The client-counselor relationship recreates the present way of constructing meaning, and if counseling is to be about the evolution in that meaning-making, the client-counselor relationship, too, will be reconstructed. The particulars of this alliance are different at each stage, of course, and the counselor is helped in the process by knowing with which emerging balance he is seeking an alliance, and with which defensive balance he is seeking to avoid becoming a co-conspirator. The sequence of evolutionary ego balances illuminates a history of traps which a client's disequilibration can set for the unsuspecting counselor (not to mention the suspecting one), traps which amount to seductions, the counselor's perpetual nemesis, for in the counseling activity, anyway, seduction *is* abandonment.

In one's address to Terry, for example, whose "problems" invite the opportunity for development beyond the imperial balance, the question would be whether she and the counselor will have, to use Sullivan's terms, a "cooperation"—two operators, presumably spending time together in order for each to get what they want "off" the other—or a "collaboration," in which part of what is being fostered, or looked after, is the experience of the other and the enhancing of the relationship itself. At any developmental precipice the counselor must discern the way in which he or she is present for the client and the way in which he or she is not. At this particular precipice (the 2-3 shift) I might hope my words and actions are informed by an internal dialogue something like this: I will not abandon her, run out of the room, or reject her for any of the things she says to me or requests of me; nor will I condemn her in any way for the manner in which she is trying to save her life; I will try to recognize her yearnings to be safe and in control, even as that means a yearning to control me; but in my staying I will try also not to abandon her by permitting myself to be manipulated, or made use of in the exercises of her old integrity.

I will not lie to Terry's probation officer; I will not put up endlessly with Terry's late or missed appointments; I will not loan Terry five dollars. Why? The refusals have nothing to do with the fact that I mind being taken advantage of (although I do). So why? Loaning five dollars to Terry might be considered a developmentally appropriate gesture, a way of demonstrating trust in her and offering her an opportunity to hold up her end of a relationship. If we explore such a view it may help us to distinguish the developmental clinician from the developmental educator. First of all, the loan would convert the counselor from the *protector* of opportunities for growth to the *creator* of opportunities for growth. Early in a counseling relationship, especially, it would not be possible to take the latter role without risking the first, for it can permeate the relationship with a "test" quality and burden the client by her sense of the counselor's having something riding on the client's behaviors and choices. This radically alters their relationship. Second, the idea of the loan misunderstands the goal of facilitating development to mean "move from one stage to the next." This is like saying the way to earn more money is to have a higher salary. Moving from stage 2 to stage 3 will be a *consequence* of Terry's development, but the counselor's involvement is with the very processes of that development. To involve himself in this way he must resist involving himself in other ways—however well-intentioned such involvements might be. Whatever trust in her that loaning her money might show, the loan really amounts to meeting an expectation that I suggest the counselor must be brave enough not to meet—the expectation on Terry's part that, with the counselor, she will continue to know as she has known, only more so; that she will make of him the object of the old integrity.

But the counselor is there to be *of* help, not to give help; and he can only be of help by recognizing what is literally an emergency. Due to his refusal to be known in the terms of the old truce, Terry may experience a loss. She may be angry and disappointed. And these experiences, too, the counselor must acknowledge and prize. Doing so, in fact, may be the beginning of the very alliance with her meaning-making (rather than her made meaning) which he seeks. Terry may be angry and disappointed. But, if there is some beginning already made in her emergence from embeddedness, some part of the person no longer completely in balance (and this may be a requirement for therapy; but if there were no disequilibrium the person would not have come in for therapy), then the counselor's refusal to be coopted as an object in the old balance will not be entirely unwelcome. It will not be unwelcome to that fragile, emerging side of me which hopes for something new, which does not know exactly what, which will finally leave disappointed if the counselor gives in to that side of me which more conspicuously demands attention and is wily in its efforts to wrangle it. It will not be unwelcome to that side which may even experience "relief" in the counselor's refusal to be drawn into the old integrity; for in doing so, the counselor has recognized an emergency, and the emergency is me.

I am speaking here, really, of a life span developmental approach to limit-setting. The limits are set not to establish authority, curtail, or control, not even to protect the counselor (though they do so, and the counselor must be protected), but above all in order to recognize a growing person in his or her deepest ambivalence, and to assist in the expression of that voice which is weakest and newest, thereby to protect the opportunity to resolve this "projected ambivalence" in the move from subject to object.

If I were seeing Diane, my early choices might be informed by this internal dialogue: I will not leave her, she has my attention, my concern, my effort to try to understand her experience as she experiences it, including her yearning to be held and taken care of, even completed, by the caring other, even me; but in my staying I will try not to allow myself to be fused with; I will try not to become the other half which a part of her may feel she needs to survive; I will try not to let our time together be devoted to us, or what we are doing, so much as it is *her* time, *her* place, and an opportunity for *her* work.

When the shape of the old integrity, the old truce, has to do with the emergence of a self from the interpersonal, the difficulties a person may experience with a phenomenological, or experiential, counseling approach are more than just the temporary adjustment to the unfamiliarity of a consultative relationship; for the very fact of having one's *own* work about which one would consult speaks to the person's growing edge. It can be difficult for me as the client to experience this other person's attention, this stranger, of whom I have great hopes, and whom, perhaps even despite myself, I only know how to "hold" in the ways that I have been holding. Is there not something strange in this relationship that feels so close, so intimate, yet so absent of cues as to how I maintain it, preserve it, enhance it; so absent of cues as to how I reciprocate, as to what he wants in return? How do I hold this? And always I am thrown back on myself. The first few hours when I did most of the talking I guess I felt he was sort of getting to know me and would eventually tell me what was wrong with me, what I should do. I thought that he would take it in his hands somehow, but he never does.

The client might experience the difficulty of this predicament most sharply at the boundaries of the hour—the intensity of the greeting, the difficulty in separating, the feeling of having been so close and not quite understanding what it means. All of this may have something to do with trying to figure out how it can be that one both has one's own space and is not alone.

I don't know a time in the evolution of meaning-making when it is *more* important that the counselor resist speaking from a frame of reference separate from the client's. The defensive side of the client would be eager to locate the self there in the space between these two frames of reference, and in allowing this to happen the counselor would have abandoned a precious opportunity. For while the counselor's resistance to being drawn into the old integrity can initially be felt as rejection, it also creates a safe environment in which the client can separate from the old integrity. Nothing is as confirming to the counselor in this difficult refusal as the relief he sees in the client who has come to experience that refusal as the invitation—perhaps for the first time in her life—to be safe from her own self-betrayal.

The evolution their relationship assists is one Rogers describes as the most basic in psychotherapy, the movement "from living only to satisfy the expectations of others, and living only in their eyes and in their opinions, toward being a person in his own right, with feelings, aims, ideas of his own; from being driven and compelled, he moves toward the making of responsible choices" (1959, p. 310). But perhaps it can be seen that there is something not quite right about the description. While it seems an accurate account of how the transformation might feel or come to be understood once a person has come through the transition, it seems to miss the experience as it is experienced. "Compelled" by others? "A person in his own right"? No longer "living only in their eyes"? "Ideas of his own"? But in the past the other who was compelling me was not other but me! Those eyes which have *become* other were not then other but my own. My ideas *were* my own, and I *was* a person in my own right. The impression we get from Rogers' description is that the self is separating itself from an other it had been carrying around as *an other*. This may seem a fair description from the point of view of the new self, but if we are speaking of the transition process it seems most important to understand it as it is experienced at that time, and not only retrospectively. At the time of the transition the self is not in relation to some other which it sees as other and somehow permits to define or direct the self. Transition, phenomenologically, involves not so much a freeing of myself from the influence of the other, as the *creation*—the discovery or invention—of the other, which all along I had been taking as self.

Were I to see Rebecca I might inform myself with an inner reminder of this sort: I will not leave her; she has my concern, my attention, my efforts to understand her experience as she experiences it, including her yearnings to maintain her dignity, her self-respect, and her internal intactness, her allegiance to private and possibly public organizations. But in my staying I will try not to be recruited to a joint project, or taken on as a consultant to an administration, or become the apparent fellow-ascriber to some set of beliefs, hidden understandings, or private coda through which our relationship is mediated.

Meaning-making at the boundary of stage 2 threatens to coopt the counselor in terms of what can be "gotten off" him or her, with the underlying issue for the client of whether one can have a relationship of trust; and meaning-making at the boundary of stage 3 threatens to coopt the counselor in terms of his or her partnership in fusion with the underlying issue for the client of whether one can claim one's own ground and still be in a relationship. The threat at stage 4 is the counselor's being coopted as a partner in the operation of the psychic administration which the self has become, with the underlying issue for the client being whether one can have a relationship (with oneself or another) as the person who is running this organization.

Where that "administration" has taken external expression in the form of public ideology, this invitation by the old truce amounts to the effort to establish the counseling environment as a community of like-minded believers. This depends, of course, on who exactly the counselor is, but persons who construct their world this way are making these kinds of considerations in their choice of a counselor in the first place. Accordingly, "we like-minded believers" might mean we women, we men, we blacks, we Jews, we Southerners, we intellectuals, we homosexuals, we psychologists, we people in therapy — always with the assumed reference to shared membership and shared understandings that travel beyond and come to define the therapeutic relationship.

Where there is no external ideology, the effort is still to hold or enlist the counselor's allegiance to the mission of that internal administration which for so long has been the self. The person's yearnings and heartaches, fears and joys often get reported at what seems like a distance; their mediation by the self-system is what makes them even reportable. The counselor can come to experience the relationship as if he or she were in supervision with another therapist concerning the plight of a third party. So invested does the person seem in maintaining the integrity of what amounts to an internally subscribed "role" — that is, the person has become a public to herself, expecting of herself the set of behaviors that fit the given role — that the counselor can experience it as frightening or dangerous to try to make contact with someone who can acknowledge the experience of this self's decay.

And yet to fail to do so is, again, to abandon the emergency the person has become. Like all these traps we fall into them out of our own yearning to connect, to make an alliance, to bring help where it may first seem most needed. But there may be nothing more therapeutic for the person at this time than a relationship with someone who may even *be* a part of my group, value system, or ideology, but who refuses to base our relationship upon it; someone who steadfastly insists on addressing the me who I am coming to see stands behind this whole operation and runs it; someone who looks me straight in the face and says things like: "So you get to feeling like a complete failure?" "Kinda like you say to yourself, 'I just can't function anymore' . . . ?" "You feel almost ashamed of yourself . . . ?" — things which you would think would be awful for me to hear, and yet they are not.

And if they are not, might that not be because they are a way of demonstrating that the person the counselor prizes is the person in her meaning-making, not the person in her "performance" (which is the made meaning of stage 4); might that not be because such statements bear witness to someone behind the performance who can be afraid, can be ashamed, can be all in pieces and who is not thereby any less worthy of our regard?

I have been considering here the implications of the constructive-developmental theory for practice. My central point is that "practice" is not alone the activity of self-conscious practitioners and that the careful study of "natural therapy" might itself be a guide to the applications of psychological knowledge. I have discussed the way the naturally therapeutic environments (cultures of embeddedness) suggest a highly articulated context for the consideration of psychological support and "preventive" practice. I have suggested that counseling or psychotherapy, whatever else it is about, might necessarily also be about the creating of the therapeutic environment as a culture of embeddedness. Throughout this book I have been suggesting that among the promising features of this framework is its ability to establish a common ground on which badly stranded issues can be rejoined. At a theoretical level this has involved building bridges between developmental, existential, and object relations theories. At a conceptual level this has involved a new way of understanding the relationships between cognition and affect, and between the individual and the social. At the level of practice, we have seen in this chapter that it involves the relation between preventive-supportive psychology and ameliorative-clinical psychology. I would like now to suggest a last pair of issues, issues which again, it seems to me, are badly in need of reintroduction to each other, and which seem to get this reintroduction through the framework in this book. I am referring to the need to think about the *processes* of therapy in company with thinking about the *goals* of therapy.

Any framework which would be of adequate service to clinical psychology must be able to address what should be considered its two most important questions: What are the processes on which the therapist attends? Why is that attention justified? This second question, about the goals of therapy—as important as it is customarily neglected—is not, strictly speaking, a psychological question but a philosophical one. No framework that is strictly psychological can hope to address it. Any framework that *is* strictly psychological leaves its adherents to import an extratheoretical source from which to justify the use of its understandings. This means the continual challenging and refining of one's own theory does not necessarily have any relation to an ongoing examination of the goals to which it is applied; it means the framework itself cannot generate an authority to enter the conversation about what uses are made of it; it means the question of goals and uses is outside the discipline. This is a situation fraught with danger.

Behavior therapy, for example, offers a framework for the shaping or reshaping of behavior. But it is absolutely mute on the question as to what ends these practices should be put to. Such questions are guided by whatever *other* value frameworks particular behavior therapists happen to hold. Behavioral theory is of no use whatever, so far as I can see, in protecting either the client from the arbitrary preferences of the practitioner, or the practitioner from the arbitrary preferences of the client.

Let me propose three different approaches to the question of goals. The first I will call "the norms of health"; the second, "humanistic normlessness"; and the third, "the norms of growth." The first two rest, respectively, on the authorities of psychiatry and ethical relativism; they are the order of the day, and both I believe are arbitrary and dangerous. The third is suggested by the constructive-developmental framework; it rests on the authority of natural philosophy, and while it deserves, like everything else in this book, to be viewed with suspicion, it does, I believe, deserve to be viewed.

Psychotherapeutic goals based on "health" can be found in frameworks as apparently diverse as traditional hospital psychiatry and antipsychiatric humanistic psychology. In the first instance, the orientation is really toward illness and its removal, the doctor standing in relation to a depressed person, say, in a manner similar to the way a doctor stands in relation to a person with a broken bone or a virus. In the second instance, the orientation is actually toward health, not as the mere absence of symptoms, but as the move toward "full functioning" or "self-actualization." As different as these two perspectives may be, they both come down to espousing goals which are based on what some group of people value as good. Maslow (1954), has suggested that the move toward self-actualization involves a move toward becoming:

1. more perceptive of reality and more comfortable with it;
2. more accepting of self, others, nature;
3. more spontaneous, simple, natural;
4. more problem centering;
5. more comfortable with detachment, more interested in privacy and solitude;
6. more autonomous, independent of culture and environment; more self-willed; more active as an agent;
7. better able to appreciate freshly what one has experienced before;
8. more open more frequently to peak experiences;
9. more possesed of "gemeinschaftgefuhl" (a feeling for the familyhood of man);
10. more deeply and profoundly experiencing of interpersonal relationships;
11. more democratic;
12. more discriminating of the differences between means and ends, good and evil;
13. more philosophical;
14. more creative;
15. more resistant to enculturation, transcendent of particular culture;
16. more resolving of dichotomies.

These are what Kohlberg (1972) has called a "bag of virtues" — a set of traits characterizing an ideal healthy or fully functioning personality. As Kohlberg says, "The observable meaning of a virtue-word is relative to a conventional standard which is both psychologically vague and ethically relative" (p. 478). Nor does the wide concurrence of psychological experts make the goals justifiable. As Basseches writes: "Psychiatrists who feel they could agree on an instance of mental health must make clear how the observations they would make are both specific and non-arbitrary . . . their status as psychiatric experts, in and of itself, bestows no special validity on the values they espouse if those values are unsupported by philosophical justification" (1976, p. 6).

It is easy for us to delude ourselves into thinking that our notions of the healthy person are unbiased by our particular circumstances or partialities. It is comforting for us to think that, in totalitarian societies, where troublesome people are often psychiatrically hospitalized, the indigenous mental health professionals are themselves aware that their behavior is nakedly political and actually aimed at social control rather than the health of the person. But what is the possibility that American mental health workers are themselves vulnerable to what amounts to the *goals of adjustment* couched in notions of health, and which lead to equal—and probably equally unwitting—exercises of social control? How many women in the hands of male therapists have found their anger at their husbands, their cultures, and themselves, for colluding to keep them children, diagnosed as their illness, their "problems with authority," their inappropriate wishes to be included (in the parental bed, or the circle of those with penises, or whatever)? Goals oriented to health—and it does not matter whether the orientation is negative or positive—lead to people "treating" other people, acting upon them on bases that are finally quite arbitrary and vulnerable to the partialities of a given class, sex, sexual preference, age, culture, and so on. Despite all the trappings of science, on the one hand, or the humanities, on the other, "illness" can very easily become "behavior we don't like" (it makes us uncomfortable, angry, or it is not what we want from our children), and "full functioning," behavior we do like. The work of Szasz (1961) has been extremely important in its suggestion that mental illness is a kind of myth, but we remain in need of some new way to think of what Szasz calls these "problems in living" which adequately understands and addresses their very real pain, disruption, hope—their meaning—for our lives; an understanding that takes account of what Szasz recognizes is their intrinsically moral nature, and an address which protects the client from the therapist's partialities.

In actual practice many therapists and counselors become themselves goalless, and regard the exercises of respect for the client as including the temporary "living in" the client's goals. "I am not here to judge the client," they might say; "whatever his goals, beliefs or values might be, they possess a wisdom that is right for him." The therapist's regard for the integrity and individuality of each person's made meaning in the world leads to the conviction that one way of making meaning is no better than another, and that there is no justification for imposing on another one's own conception of the direction toward which personal change should tend. I want to suggest that while there is much to admire in this position, and that its refusal to impose values on another is a great discovery which must never be lost sight of, it remains a position with very grave problems. First, it confuses the judgment the therapist is or is not willing to make *on the process she and the client share* with the judgment she is or is not willing to make *of the client;* while the latter may be considered tolerance and respect for persons, the first may be considered as irresponsible. But second, and more important, it confuses integrity with validity. This distinction is a crucial one and is especially illuminated by our process conception of development.

The conviction that there are no nonarbitrary bases upon which to consider one state of meaning-making as better than another is, in a therapist, at once a philosophical confusion and a psychological confusion. Philosophically, it confuses the inevitability of subjectivity (that there is no absolute truth; that each of us is making our own truth) with what I believe is the false notion of the impossibility of thereby nonarbitrarily comparing these subjectivities. The second does not follow from the first. Psychologically, the conviction confuses the need for the clinician's unconditional positive regard for the integrity of another's meaning-making activity with what I believe is the false sense that the clinician must regard all made meanings as equally valid. Again, the second does not follow from the first. I do not judge a person's meaning-making activity, but I must admit that in an indirect way I do judge a person's made meanings. Persons cannot be more or less good than each other; the *person* has an unqualified integrity. But stages or evolutionary balances (the structure of made meanings) can be more or less good than each other; stages have a qualified validity. It is, in fact, the unequal validity of the various evolutionary truces that actually provides the basis for my sense that counseling is proceeding. In trying to avoid the traps discussed earlier, for example, I am making a judgment on behalf of one stage over another. I never voice my judgment, but not because I believe the judgment is itself unjustified; I never voice it because I do not think that doing so will be of any use. But I *exercise* my judgment in my address to the experience of the new voice emerging, and I judge our mutual process according to whether or not the person is being presented the opportunity to move from a less evolved to a more evolved state. (The judgment is made as to whether the opportunities are *presented,* not as to whether the person is so moving; the latter is not in the hands of the therapist.)

Notice, too, how this distinction between *integrity* and *validity* has a bearing on that problem which many therapists experience when they are first exploring for themselves the client-centered approach. "How do I confirm the client's experience but not be taken as necessarily agreeing with or buying into his framework?" The question is itself the question, "How do I confirm the integrity of the person's attempts to make the world cohere, without appearing to be confirming or disconfirming the validity of the way he makes the world cohere?" The answer lies in our holding ourselves to the rigors of addressing the person in the experience of meaning-making, rather than the meaning the person has made. How many times is it the case that our experience of being taken incorrectly is due to our having addressed the *stage* rather than the *process?*

As compared to approaches that emphasize norms of health and humanistic normlessness, the constructive-developmental perspective provides a basis for *norms of growth.* Among Kohlberg's most important, long-argued, and carefully exposed points is the instruction that goals for intervention cannot derive their justification from science or social science alone. Psychology can study and demonstrate the changes of personality, but the determination that a change is preferable—a matter of betterness—is intrinsically a philosophical question. At the same time our norms cannot be derived from philosophy alone; they must take account of reality, what exists in nature; with respect to questions of norms of development they must take account of biological reality.

Notions of health are one kind of address to biology, but they do not lend themselves to philosophical analysis; there is no way to assess their truth value. Notions of growth or development, as I have defined it here, do. A framework which itself is generative of justifiable goals must be more than psychological; it must, as well, be philosophical and biological. This, as suggested by Figure 6, is the nature of the constructive-developmental framework. It is biological, psychological, and philosophical; it studies the relationship of the organism to the environment (what biologists call "adaptation"), the relationship of the self to the other (what psychologists call the "ego"), and the relationship of the subject to the object (what philosophers call "truth"). The constructive-developmental framework studies one context (meaning-constitutive evolutionary activity) which it considers to be about ego, adaptation, and truth. It is a framework at once psychological, biological, and philosophical. While this may not guarantee its wisdom, it makes it an extremely promising framework for consideration of these kinds of jointly philosophical and natural-scientific questions.

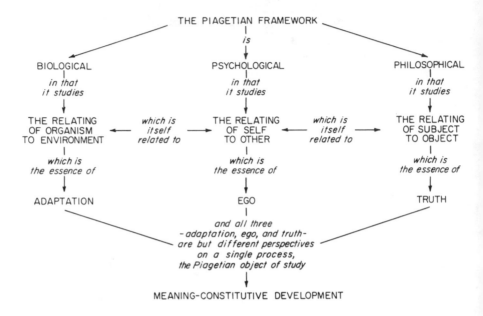

Figure 6   Complementarity of adaptation, ego, and truth

The framework suggests a demonstrable conception of development as the process of "natural philosophy," later stages being "better," not on the grounds that they come later, but on the philosophical grounds of their having a greater truth value. The popular psychological notions of greater differentiation and greater integration as goals are here given a substantive and justifiable meaning. Each new evolutionary truce further differentiates the self from its embeddedness in the world, guaranteeing, in a qualitatively new way, the world's distinct integrity, and thereby creating a more integrated relationship to the world. Each new truce accomplishes this by the evolution of a reduced subject and a greater object for the subject to take, an evolution of lesser subjectivity and greater objectivity, an evolution that is more "truthful."

Talk about truth can raise hackles because someone may seem to be claiming to know The Truth. I do not claim to know The Truth; I am not even sure what it would mean to say one did. What I do have a conviction about is what the truth is *about*. It is an activity, an activity of relation or balance. And, from a psychological point of view, it is the same activity as personality.

An orientation to growth in relation to truth does not make the therapist's address either judgmental or oracular; the truth is made, not heard. The constructive-developmental clinician locates himself or herself in the processes of growth. She regards the client's disorder not as his sickness, nor his undoing, but as the throes of his own becoming. The clinician is a phenomenologist; she takes the interior perspective; but at the same time, and without contradiction, she considers meaning-making to be more than merely subjective. That development she seeks to facilitate is itself the growth of the truth. The career of the truth is not a person's only vocation, but it may be the only one upon which the intervention into that person's life can be justified. Can any other basis—even if all parties agree to it—free itself of the partialities of convention?

If it is fair to turn the developmental framework upon this very discussion of goals, then it appears that a choice between the goals of health and humanistic normlessness is essentially a choice between the ideological categories of the institutional balance and the relativization of those categories in the transition between the institutional and the interindividual balances. Given the widespread questioning within the psychiatric community of the meaning of its categories and the efforts to construct new manuals of diagnosis which orient, at least in part, to the experience of the troubled person, it might be fairer to say that the mental health community at large is evolving beyond the institutional balance. It seems caught in this transition. It may even be in the midst of a "self-evaluative depression."

The way out of this malaise may lie in considering that the *prior* ground in personality (that context in which any further considerations—of ego strength, defenses, character, or whatever—should go on) is an activity which is naturally related to truth. So long as our goals are tied to this process alone—a process shared by all persons regardless of sex, age, class, or culture—the clients of psychological practice have some hope of being protected from the arbitrary biases of the practitioners. The benefit of a theory, so long as it remains open to its own development, is that it keeps us honest in a way an uncritical eclecticism never can. Living with a theory such as this involves imposing upon oneself a discipline, and actually allows one to "bracket" (as phenomenologists might say) particular prejudices which cannot be justified. (Is homosexuality an "illness" or an "alternative sexual lifestyle"? The very question is offensive and, essentially, unintelligible from a constructive-developmental perspective which immediately defeats the fiction of a monolithic category, "homosexuality" (Henderson, 1979).)

Among the many things from which a practitioner's clients need protection is the practitioner's hopes for the client's future, however benign and sympathetic these hopes may be. The constructive-developmental perspective leads us to bracket every hope, save the growth of the truth. But what a harsh-sounding thing to say! What about the hope that a person might become more loving, more gentle, a better parent, more spontaneous and playful, more open to the experience of awe, of beauty, or irony? Shouldn't we care about that? These sound like good hopes to me. In fact, I do care about them — and to be honest, if I never saw such developments in therapy I might quit being a therapist. But it is equally true that they are *my* hopes. As much as I care about them, I care even more that people be protected from arbitrary influences upon them to shape up to someone else's favorite value. And this supervening "care" is *not* merely another of "my values" but itself rooted in the psychological and philosophical development of the truth. It arises out of a recognition of the other's distinctness.

Perhaps people *do* become more loving and more gentle, and so on, as they develop; but perhaps they do not, and if they do not, while we can continue to hope that they might (should those be our values), the client all the same must be protected from our hopes. The "career of the truth" may turn out to include a far greater degree of personal functioning than we might at first imagine, but the fact remains that in a world where people increasingly will put themselves in the hands of "mental health professionals" it is the professionals above all who must understand that much of human personality is none of their business.

REFERENCES

INDEX

References

Angyal, A. 1965. *Neurosis and treatment: a holistic theory.* New York: Wiley.

Argyris, C. and Schon, D. 1978. *Theory in practice.* Reading, Mass.: Addison-Wesley.

Arieti, S., and Bemporad, J. R. 1980. The psychological organization of depression. *Journal of Psychiatry* 137: 11.

Bakan, D. 1966. *The duality of human experience.* Chicago: Rand McNally.

Baldwin, J. M. 1906. *Social and ethical interpretations in mental development.* New York: Macmillan.

Bandura, A. 1969. Social-learning theory of identificatory processes. In *Handbook of socialization theory and research,* ed. D. A. Goslin. Chicago: Rand McNally.

Basseches, M. 1976. Development as the aim of higher education. Unpublished manuscript, Harvard University.

———— 1978. Dialectical operations. Ph.D. dissertation, Harvard University.

———— 1980. Dialectical schemata: a framework for the empirical study of the development of dialectical thinking. *Human Development* 23: 400-421.

Beck, A. 1981. Cognitive theory of depression. Paper presented at APPA.

Bellow, S. 1965. *The adventures of Augie March.* New York: Crest.

Binswanger, L. 1963. *Being-in-the-world.* New York: Basic Books.

Blakeney, R., and Blakeney, C. 1977. Knowing better: delinquent girls and the 2-3 transition. Unpublished paper, Harvard University.

Blatt, S. M. 1974. Levels of object representation in anaclitic and introjective depression. In *The psychoanalytic study of the child,* vol.

29, pp. 107-157. New Haven, Conn.: Yale University Press.

Blatt, S. M., D'Afflitti, D., and Quinlan, D. 1979. Experiences of depression in normal young adults. *Journal of Abnormal Psychology* 85 (4): 383-389.

Blos, P. 1962. *On adolescence.* New York: Free Press.

Boring, E. G. 1930. A new ambiguous figure. *American Journal of Psychology* 42: 444.

Bowlby, J. 1969. *Attachment.* New York: Basic Books.

———— 1973. *Separation: anxiety and anger.* New York: Basic Books.

Broughton, J. M. 1975. The development of natural epistemology in adolescence and early adulthood. Ph.D. dissertation, Harvard University.

———— 1978. The development of concepts of self, mind, reality, and knowledge. In *Social Cognition,* ed. W. Damon. San Francisco: Jossey-Bass.

Buber, M. 1960. *The origin and meaning of Hasidism.* New York: Horizon Press.

Burlingham, D., and Freud, A. 1942. *Young children in war-time.* London: Allen & Unwin.

Byler, R., Lewis, G., and Totman, R. 1969. *Teach us what we want to know.* New York: Mental Health Materials Center.

Colby, A., Kohlberg, L., Gibbs, J., Candee, D., Speicher-Dubin, B., Power, C., and Hewer, R. In press. *Moral judgment interview scoring manual.* New York: Cambridge University Press.

Damon, W. 1977. *The social world of the child.* San Francisco: Jossey-Bass.

Darwin, C. 1962. *On the origin of species.* New York: Macmillan.

Originally published in 1889.

Dewey, J. 1963. *Experience and education.* New York: Collier. Originally published in 1938.

Eliot, T. S. 1948. *Four quartets.* New York: Harcourt, Brace and World.

Elkind, D. 1968. Editor's introduction. In J. Piaget, *Six psychological studies.* New York: Vintage.

———— 1974. Egocentrism in children and adolescents. In *Children and adolescents.* New York: Oxford University Press.

———— 1979. Cognitive development and psychopathology: observations on egocentrism and ego defense. In *The child and society.* New York: Oxford University Press.

Erikson, E. H. 1963. *Childhood and society.* New York: Norton.

———— 1968. *Identity: youth and crisis.* New York: Norton.

Fairbairn, W. R. D. 1952. *Psychoanalytic studies of the personality.* London: Tavistock Publications.

———— 1962. *An object relations theory of personality.* New York: Basic Books.

Feuerbach, L. 1846. *Sammtliche Werke.* Leipzig: Otto Wigand.

Fingarette, H. 1963. *The self in transformation.* New York: Harper and Row.

Fogelson, R. 1981. The anthropology of the self: some retrospects and prospects. In *The self: psychology, psychoanalysis and anthropology,* ed. B. Lee and G. Noam. New York: Plenum Press.

Fowler, J. W. 1974. Toward a developmental perspective on faith. *Religious Education* 69: 207-219.

———— 1981. *Stages in faith.* New York: Harper and Row.

Freud, A. 1936. *The ego and the mechanisms of defense.* New York: International Universities Press.

Freud, S. 1917. Mourning and melancholia. *The standard edition,* volume 14, pp. 243-258. London: Hogarth Press.

———— 1905. Three essays on the theory of sexuality. *The standard edition,* vol. 7, pp. 125-245. London: Hogarth Press.

———— 1911. Formulations regarding the two principles in mental functioning. *The standard edition,* vol. 11, pp. 409-417. London: Hogarth Press.

———— 1926. *Inhibitions, symptoms and anxiety.* In *The Standard Edition.* Vol. 20. London: Hogarth Press.

Freud. S., and Jung, C. G. 1974. *The Freud/Jung letters: the correspondence between Sigmund Freud and Carl Jung,* ed. W. McGuire, trans. R. Manheim and R. F. C. Hull. Princeton, N.J.: Princeton University Press.

Frost, D. 1978. *I gave them a sword: behind the scenes of the Nixon interviews.* New York: Ballantine.

Gardner, H. 1978. *Developmental psychology.* Boston: Little, Brown.

Gibbs, J., Erickson, L., and Berkowitz, M. 1978. Sex differences in moral judgment during adolescence and young adulthood. Unpublished manuscript, Harvard University.

Gilligan, C., Kohlberg, L., Lerner, J., and Belenky, M. 1971. Moral reasoning about sexual dilemmas: the development of an interview and scoring system. In *Technical report of the U.S. Commission on Obscenity and Pornography,* vol. 1.

Gilligan, C. 1978. In a different voice: women's conception of the self and of morality. *Harvard Educational Review* 47 (4): 481-517.

Gilligan, C., and Murphy, J. M. 1979. Development from adolescence to adulthood: the philosopher and the dilemma of the fact. In *Intellectual development beyond childhood,* ed. D. Kuhn. San Francisco: Jossey-Bass.

Glasson v. City of Louisville. 1975. 518 F.No.2.d, 899.

Goethals, George. 1978. The first three weeks. In *Conference record: dean's conferences on the freshman experience.* Cambridge, Mass.: Harvard University Records.

Guntrip, H. 1968. *Schizoid phenomena, object relations and the self.* New York: International Universities Press.

———— 1971. *Psychoanalytic theory, therapy and the self.* New York: Basic Books.

Haan, N. 1977. *Coping and defending.* New York: Academic Press.

Haan, N., Block, J., and Smith, M. B. 1968. Moral reasoning of young adults: political-social behavior, family background, and personality correlates. *Journal of Personality and Social Psychology* 10: 184-201.

Hartmann, H. 1958. *Ego psychology and the problem of adaptation.* New York: International Universities Press. Originally published in 1939.

Heckscher, Charles. 1978. Directions in the democratization of work: management's interest in worker participation. Unpublished paper, Group for Work Democracy, Somerville, Mass.

———— 1979. Directions in the democratization of work: the interest of unions in worker participation. Unpublished paper, Group for Work Democracy, Somerville, Mass.

Hegel, G. W. F. 1892. *The science of logic.* Oxford: Clarendon Press.

———— 1967. *The phenomenology of mind,* trans. J. B. Baillie. New

York: Harper & Row.

Hemingway, E. 1953. *The short stories of Ernest Hemingway.* New York: Scribners.

Henderson, A. F. 1979. College age lesbianism as a developmental phenomenon. *Journal of the American College Health Association* 28: 176-178.

Heyert, M. 1978. The new kid. In *Projection in Literature,* ed. E. Daniel. New York: Scott Foresman.

Hickey, J. E., and Scharf, P. 1980 *Toward a just correctional system.* San Francisco: Jossey-Bass.

Holmes, L. 1974. The nature of hope. Unpublished senior thesis, Harvard College.

Holstein, C. 1969. The relation of children's moral judgment to that of their parents and to communication patterns in the family. Ph.D. dissertation, University of California, Berkeley.

———— 1976. Irreversible, stepwise sequence in the development of moral judgment: a longitudinal study of males and females. *Child Development* 47: 51-61.

Homer. 1950. *The Iliad,* trans. A. H. Chase and W. G. Perry. New York: Bantam Books. Originally published in the 8th century B.C.

Hudgins, W., and Prentice, N. 1973. Moral judgment in delinquent and nondelinquent adolescents and their mothers. *Journal of Abnormal Psychology* 82: 145-152.

Huxley, A. 1972. Visionary experience. In *The highest state of consciousness,* ed. John White. New York: Archer.

Inhelder, R., and Piaget, J. 1958. *The growth of logical thinking from childhood to adolescence.* New York: Basic Books.

Jacobsen, E. 1964. *The self and the ob-*

ject world. New York: International Universities Press.

Joyce, J. 1965. *Portrait of the artist as a young man.* New York: Viking Press.

Kagan, J. 1971. *Change and continuity in infancy.* New York: Wiley.

———— 1972. A conception of early adolescence. In *Twelve to sixteen: early adolescence,* ed. J. Kagan and R. Coles. New York: Norton.

Kant, I. 1969. *Critique of pure reason.* New York: St. Martin.

Kaplan, A. 1976. Androgeny as a model of mental health for women. *Beyond sex-role stereotypes,* ed. A. G. Kaplan and J. P. Bean. Boston: Little, Brown.

Kaplan, A., and Sedney, M. A. 1980. *Psychology and sex roles.* Boston: Little, Brown.

Kegan, R. 1976. Ego and truth: personality and the Piagetian paradigm. Ph.D. dissertation, Harvard University.

———— 1977. *The sweeter welcome: Martin Buber, Bernard Malamud and Saul Bellow.* Needham Heights, Mass.: Wexford.

———— 1978. Child development and health education. *Principal* 57 (3): 91-95.

———— 1979. The evolving self: a process conception for ego psychology. *Counseling Psychologist* 8 (2): 5-34.

———— 1980. There the dance is: religious dimensions of developmental theory. In *Toward moral and religious maturity,* ed. J. W. Fowler and A. Vergote. Morristown, N.J.: Silver Burdette.

———— 1981. A neo-Piagetian approach to object relations. In *The self: psychology, psychoanalysis and anthropology,* ed. B. Lee and G. Noam.

New York: Plenum Press.

Kernberg, O. 1966. Structural derivatives of object relationships. *International Journal of Psychoanalysis* 47: 236-253.

_____ 1976. *Object relations theory and clinical psychoanalysis.* New York: Jason Aronson.

Kohlberg, L. 1966. A cognitive-developmental analysis of children's sex-role concepts and attitudes. In *The development of sex-differences,* ed. E. Maccoby. Stanford, Calif.: Stanford University Press.

_____ 1969. Stage and sequence: the cognitive developmental approach to socialization. In *Handbook of socialization: theory and research,* ed. D. Goslin. New York: Rand McNally.

_____ 1971. From is to ought: how to commit the naturalistic fallacy and get away with it in the study of moral development. In *Cognitive development and epistemology,* ed. T. Mischel. New York: Academic Press.

_____ 1976. *Collected papers on moral development and moral education.* Cambridge, Mass.: Center for Moral Education.

Kohlberg, L., and Blatt, M. 1975. The effect of classroom moral discussion upon children's level of moral judgment. *Journal of Moral Education* 4: 129-161.

Kohlberg, L., and Gilligan, C. 1972. The adolescent as a philosopher. In *Twelve to sixteen: early adolescence,* ed. J. Kagan and R. Coles. New York: Norton.

Kohlberg, L., and Kramer, R. 1969. Continuities and discontinuities in childhood and adult moral development. *Human Development 12:* pp. 93-120.

Kohlberg, L., and Mayer, R. 1972.

Development as the aim of education. *Harvard Educational Review* 42: 449-496.

Kohlberg, L., Scharf, P., and Hickey, J. 1972. The justice structure of the prison: a theory and an intervention. *Prison Journal* 51: 3-14.

Kohut, H. 1971. *The analysis of the self.* New York: International Universities Press.

_____ 1977. *The restoration of the self.* New York: International Universities Press.

Koplowitz, H. 1978. Unitary operations. Unpublished manuscript.

Kramer, R. 1968. Changes in moral judgment response pattern during late adolescence and young adulthood: retrogressions in a developmental sequence. Ph.D. dissertation, University of Chicago.

Krebs, D., and Rosenwald, A. 1977. Moral reasoning and moral behavior in conventional adults. *Merrill-Palmer Quarterly* 23: 79-84.

Kris, E. 1975. *Selected papers of Ernst Kris.* New Haven, Conn.: Yale University Press.

Kuhn, T. S. 1970. *The structure of scientific revolutions,* 2nd ed. Chicago: University of Chicago Press.

Laing, R. D. 1960. *The divided self.* New York: Pantheon.

Lang, D. M. 1973. Love of country. *New Yorker,* July 30, pp. 35-48.

Langer, Jonas. 1969. Disequilibrium as a source of development. In *Trends and issues in developmental psychology,* ed. P. Mussen, J. Langer, and M. Covington. New York: Holt, Rinehart and Winston.

LaPlace, Pierre. [1832.] 1969. *Celestial mechanics.* London: Chelsea.

Lecky, P. 1945. *Self-consistency.* New York: Island Press.

Lévi-Strauss, C. 1963. *Structural anthropology.* New York: Basic Books.

LeVine, R. 1981. Psychoanalysis and other cultures: an African perspective. In *The self: psychology, psychoanalysis and anthropology,* ed. B. Lee and G. Noam. New York: Plenum Press.

Lickona, Thomas, ed. 1976. *Moral development and behavior.* New York: Holt, Rinehart and Winston.

Loevinger, J. 1976. *Ego development.* San Francisco: Jossey-Bass.

Low, N. S. 1978. The mother-daughter relationship in adulthood. Paper presented to the Massachusetts Psychological Association. May.

Lyell, Charles. [1833.] 1970. *Principles in geology.* Monticello, N.Y.: Lubrecht & Cramer.

Maccoby, E. 1966. *The development of sex differences.* Stanford, Calif.: Stanford University Press.

Mackin, C. 1978. Workplace democracy: problems and prospects. Unpublished paper, Group for Work Democracy, Somerville, Mass.

Mahler, M. S. 1968. *On human symbiosis and the vicissitudes of individuation,* vol. I: *Infantile Psychosis.* New York: International Universities Press.

Mahler, M. S., Pine, F., and Bergman, A. 1975. *The psychological birth of the human infant.* New York: Basic Books.

Marx, K. 1931. *Capital.* New York: Charles H. Kerr & Company.

Maslow, A. H. 1954. *Motivation and personality.* New York: Harper and Row.

Masterson, J. F. 1976. *Psychotherapy of the borderline adult.* New York: Brunner-Mazel.

May, R., Angel, E., and Ellenberger, H. F., eds. 1958. *Existence: a new dimension in psychiatry and psychology.* New York: Simon & Schuster.

McKim, Marriott. 1981. The open Hindu person and the human sciences. In *The self: psychology, psychoanalysis and anthropology,* ed. B. Lee and G. Noam. New York: Plenum Press.

Mead, G. H. 1934. *Mind, self and society.* Chicago: University of Chicago Press.

Milgram, S. 1974. *Obedience to authority.* New York: Harper & Row.

Miller, J. B. 1976. *Toward a new psychology of women.* Boston: Beacon Press.

Miller, N. E., and Dollard, J. 1941. *Learning and imitation.* New Haven: Yale University Press.

Mischel, W. 1970. Sex-typing and socialization. In *Carmichael's manual of child development,* ed. P. H. Mussen. New York: Wiley.

Mosher, R., and Sprinthall, N. 1971. Psychological education: a means to promote personal development during adolescence. *Counseling Psychologist 2:* 3-81

Niebuhr, H. R. 1941. *The meaning of revelation.* New York: Macmillan.

Offerd, D., J. J. Lawton, and S. Z. Gross. 1969. Presenting symptomatology of adopted children. *Archives of General Psychiatry* 11: 635-643.

Ovid, 1963. *Metamorphoses,* translated by Rolfe Humphries. Bloomington: Indiana University Press. Originally published in the first century A.D.

Parsons, M. In press. Baldwin and aesthetic development. In *The foundations of cognitive developmental psychology,* eds. J. M. Broughton and D. J. Freeman-Moir. Norwood, N.J.: Ablex Press.

Perry, W. G., Jr. 1970. *Forms of intellectual and ethical development in the college years.* New York: Holt, Rinehart and Winston.

Piaget, J. 1948. *The moral judgment of*

the child. Glencoe: Free Press.

――――― 1952. The origins of intelligence in children. New York: International Universities Press. Originally published in 1936.

――――― 1954. The construction of reality in the child. New York: Basic Books. Originally published in 1937.

――――― 1962. Plays, dreams and imitation. New York: Norton.

――――― 1964. Relations between affectivity and intelligence in the mental development of the child. In Sorbonne courses. Paris: University Documentation Center.

――――― 1965. Psychology and philosophy. In Scientific psychology, ed. B. Wolman. New York: Basic Books.

――――― 1968. Le structuralisme. Paris: P.U.F.

――――― 1969. The psychology of the child. New York: Harper Torchbooks.

――――― 1970. Piaget's theory. In Carmichael's manual of child psychology, ed. P. Mussen. New York: Wiley.

――――― 1973. An autobiography. In Jean Piaget: the man and his ideas, ed. Richard Evans. New York: E. P. Dutton.

Richardson, N. J. 1981. Developmental shifts in constructions of success. Ph.D. dissertation, Harvard University.

Rieff, Phillip. 1966. The triumph of the therapeutic. New York: Harper and Row.

Robertson, J. 1958. Young children in hospital. London: Tavistock.

Rogers, C. 1951. Client centered therapy. Boston: Houghton Mifflin.

――――― 1959. A theory of therapy, personality, and interpersonal relationships as developed in the client centered framework. In Psychology: a study of a science, vol. 3: Formulations of the person and the social context, ed. S. Koch. New York: McGraw-Hill.

Sandler, J., and Sandler, A.-M. On the development of object relations and affects. International Journal of Psychoanalysis 59: 285-293.

Schachtel, E. 1959. Metamorphosis. New York: Basic Books.

Schaefer, E. S., and Emerson, P. 1964. The development of social attachments in infancy. Monographs of the Society for Research in Child Development.

Schleiermacher, F. 1956. The Christian faith. Edinburgh: T. and T. Clark.

Sears, R. R., Rau, L. and Alpert, P. 1965. Identification and child rearing. Stanford: Stanford University Press.

Selman, R. L. 1969. Role-taking ability and the development of moral judgment. Ph.D. dissertation, Boston University.

――――― 1974. The development of conceptions of interpersonal reasoning based on levels of social perspective taking. Unpublished scoring manual, Harvard-Judge Baker Social Reasoning Project.

――――― 1976a. The development of social-cognitive understanding: a guide to educational and clinical practice. In Moral development and behavior, ed. T. Lickona. New York: Holt, Rinehart & Winston.

――――― 1976b. A developmental approach to interpersonal and moral awareness in young children: some educational implications of levels of social perspective taking. In Values and human development, ed. T. C. Hennessy. New York: Paulist Press.

――――― 1980. The growth of interpersonal understanding: developmental and clinical analyses. New York: Academic Press.

Selman, R., and Jaquette, D. 1978. Stability and oscillation in interpersonal awareness: a clinical/developmental analysis. In *XXV Nebraska symposium on motivation,* ed. C. B. Keasy. Lincoln, Nebraska: University of Nebraska Press.

Smith, M., and Glass, G. V. 1977. Meta-analysis of psychotherapy outcome studies. *American Psychologist* (September): 752-761.

Spitz, R. A. 1946. Anaclitic depression. *Psychoanalytic Study of the Child* 2: 313-342.

———— 1950. Anxiety in infancy: a study of its manifestations in the first year of life. *International Journal of Psychoanalysis* 31: 138-143.

Steinberg, R. and Kegan, R. 1978. Israeli soldiers' attitudes toward Arab enemies: moral judgment and moral action. Unpublished manuscript, Harvard University.

Straus, T. 1981. The structure of the self in northern Cheyenne culture. In *The self: psychology, psychoanalysis, and anthropology,* ed. B. Lee and G. Noam. New York: Plenum Press.

Sullivan, H. S. 1953. *The interpersonal theory of psychiatry.* New York: Norton.

Szasz, R. 1961. *The myth of mental illness.* New York: Harper.

Taft, J. 1933. *The dynamics of therapy in a controlled relationship.* New York: Macmillan.

Torbert, W. 1972. *Learning from experience: toward consciousness.* New York: Columbia University Press.

———— 1976. *Creating a community of inquiry: conflict, collaboration, transformation.* New York: Wiley.

Turiel, Elliot. 1969. Developmental processes in the child's moral thinking. In *Trends and issues in developmental psychology,* ed. P. Mussen,

J. Langer, and M. Covington. New York: Holt, Rinehart and Winston.

Turiel, Elliot. 1972a. Stage transition in moral development. In *Second handbook of research on teaching,* ed. R. M. Travers. Chicago: Rand McNally.

———— 1972b. A comparative analysis of moral knowledge and moral judgment in males and females. Unpublished manuscript, Harvard University.

Uzguris, I., and Hunt, J. 1968. Object permanence. From *Ordinal scales of infant psychological development—a film series.* 40 min. Champaign: University of Illinois Visual Aids Service.

Vaillant, G. E. 1977. *Adaptation to life.* Boston: Little, Brown.

Waldfogel, S., Coolidge, J., and Hahn, P. 1957. The development, meaning, and management of school phobia. *American Journal of Orthopsychiatry* 27: 754-780.

Watts, A. 1936. *The spirit of Zen.* London: J. Murray.

Wells, H. K. 1972. Alienation and dialectical logic. *Kansas Journal of Sociology* 3 (1).

White, R. W. 1959. Motivation reconsidered: the concept of competence. *Psychological Review* 66: 297-333.

White, S. 1970. Some general outlines of the matrix of developmental changes between five and seven years. *Bulletin of the Orton Society* 20: 41-57.

Whitehead, A. N. 1929. *Process and reality.* New York: Macmillan.

Whorf, B. L. 1956. *Language, thought, and reality.* New York: Technology Press and Wiley.

Winnicott, D. W. 1965. *The maturational processes and the facilitating en-*

vironment. New York: International
Universities Press.

Yankelovich, D. 1969. *Generations*
apart. New York: Columbia Broad-
casting System.

Index

Accommodation, 43–45, 78, 170
Acting out, 75
Adaptation, evolutionary, 43–45, 107–108, 113–121, 293–294; treatment of, in various theories, 6, 85, 108–110
Adolescence, 19–20, 38, 178–179, 242; and identity formation, 96, 187–194; and limit setting, 168–169, 188–189; questions of, 35–36, 205–206; and psychoanalytic theory, 142–143, 187. *See also* Formal operational thought; Interpersonal balance; Interpersonal concordance moral orientation
Adulthood: evolutionary supports in, 207–215, 217–228, 242–253; and sex-role identification, 142–144, 153–155. *See also* Formal operational thought; Institutional balance; Interindividual balance; Principled moral orientation; Societal moral orientation
Affect. *See* Emotion
Allen, W., 1
Ambivalence, 88, 96, 138; across self-other balances, 105–106; between separation and attachment, 107–108, 207–208; projected, 99–101, 145

Anger, 82–83, 97
Angyal, A., 3, 4–5
Anxiety, 5–6, 102, 266; experience of, 124–127; and loss of organization, 11, 81–82, 139–140; and separation, 85, 186–189. *See also* Case material; Separation
Argyris, C., 244, 247
Arieti, S., and Bemporad, J. R., 268n
Assimilation, 41–45, 78; and defense, 170
Attachment, 81–83, 133, 168; to primary caretaker, 17, 78, 121–124. *See also* Infancy; Integrating
Attention: to another's meaning evolution, 15–20, 27–29, 32–33, 54–55, 122, 162; failure of, 148–158, 177–178
Authority: constructions of, 201–203
Autism, 122–123
Autonomy, 5–6, 154–156; development beyond, 228; Erikson's concept of, 117–121, 127. *See also* Impulsive balance; Institutional balance; Interindividual balance

Bakan, D., 176
Balance. *See* Equilibrium; Evolutionary

truces, 149–150, 173–176, 182–183, 186; at incorporative balance, 129, 132; at impulsive balance, 156, 158–160; at imperial balance, 176; at interpersonal balance, 185, 189, 217–220; at institutional balance, 243–253. *See also* Cultures of embeddedness, functions of

Contradiction: of meaning, 123, 140–145, 158, 168–169, 188–189, 245–246; at incorporative balance, 126–128; at impulsive balance, 141–142, 144–149, 151–153; at imperial balance, 168–169; at interpersonal balance, 188–189, 212–215; at institutional balance, 245–252. *See also* Cultures of embeddedness, functions of

Control. *See* Defense

Coping. *See* Meaning-making

Crisis, 41, 59, 240; and opportunity for growth, 61–62, 264–267, 273–275, 283. *See also* Emergency; specific cognitive and moral stages, limits of

Cultures of embeddedness, evolutionary, 115–132, 173–174, 118–120, 242; functions of and dysfunction within, 121–132, 140–141, 162, 168, 173–179, 257–260; and particular holding environments, 115–116, 140–142, 162–163, 186, 257; and sociopolitical cultures, 210–215, 380; and therapy, 124–132, 256–288. *See also* Psychopathology; specific self-other balances

Darwin, C., 13

Defense: defending, 5, 6, 14, 102, 272–275; and assimilation, 169–170; and control, 75, 91, 100–102, 108–110; defined, 41; and evolution, 81–82, 245; and integrity, 170; and pain, 265–266

Dependency, 5–6, 107, 179. *See also* specific self-other balances

Depression, 73, 131, 184–185, 267–273; and anger, 82–83; and loss, 82, 130, 185–186, 193–194, 196–197; and mourning, 130, 266; and pain, 265–266. *See also* Loss; Separation

Determinism, 42–43, 187–188

Development, 8–10, 12–18, 26, 41–42, 66–67, 108–109, 182, 257; vs. adjustment, 290–291, 293–296; cognitive and

affective, 83; and constructive-developmental tradition, 4, 79, 81–85, 293–296; as internalization sequence, 30–31; and sex differences, 209–215; theories of, 5, 186–187. *See also* Cognitive development; Moral development

Developmental transition. *See* Transformation

Dewey, J., 4, 276

Dialectic: between entities and processes, 7–8; between limit and possibility, 44–45; between structure and content, 103–104; dialectical reasoning, 86–87, 225–230; and dichotomy, 8, 154–155. *See also* Evolutionary tension

Differentiating, 28–31, 39, 44, 50–51, 65; and adaptive development, 66–67, 75–76, 85, 107–108, 142–144, 294; and loss, 81, 139; overemphasized in psychology of normality, 108–110, 207–215; and separation, 5–6, 18, 75–81, 106–107, 117, 161, 217–219

Disembedding. *See* Emergence; Transformation

Disequilibrium. *See* Equilibrium

Ego, 3, 6–7, 83–84, 96, 293–294; and equilibrium, 103–104; and identity, 96; strength, 14, 96. *See also* Self-other balancing

Ego psychology, 3, 6; and depression, 269

Egocentric perspective. *See* Preoperational thought

Einstein, A., 13, 28

Eliot, T. S., 23, 62, 111, 274

Elkind, D., 85

Embeddedness, 31, 32–33, 79; emergence from (*see* Emergence); limits of, 40–41, 170; as prior to internalization, 31, 91, 94–95. *See also* Cultures of embeddedness; Structure; Subjectivity; specific self-other balances

Emergence, from embeddedness, 29–31, 78, 126–132, 242, 266; as differentiation, 39, 50–51; as re-cognition, 42, 82–83, 129, 182. *See also* Transformation

Emergency, natural, 29–30, 39, 71–72, 110, 129, 147–152, 283–285

Emotion, 15, 81–83; lability of, 88; in Piaget's work, 4, 169; source of, 44–45, 81–82, 169

Reciprocity, 37–38, 48, 51–57, 167–168; in mature intimacy, 253–254. *See also* Reversibility

Recognizing. *See* Continuity; Transformation

Reflecting: and integration, 82–83; and internalization, 30–31

Reflexes, 30–31, 40, 79, 85–88. *See also* Incorporative balance; Sensorimotor intelligence

Regression: as development detention, 123–124, 155–156; vs. recurring phenomena of development, 187–189, 203–204

Relativism: socio-ethical, 65–67, 232–233; as transitional disequilibrium, 103–104, 231

Reversibility: cognitive operation of, 32–33, 36–39, 40, 54; and reciprocity, 37–38, 54–57, 167–168

Richardson, N., 87

Rieff, P., 13

Robertson, J., 130

Rogers, C., 3, 4–6, 209, 274, 277–278, 285

Role-recognizing culture, 118–120, 161–166

Role-taking, 48–54, 157–158; and compromise, 163; and impulse control, 89, 137–139; and reciprocity, 54–57, 94, 167–168

Sandler, J., and Sandler, A. M., 83

Saxon, C., 152

Schachtel, E., 31, 78, 85

Schizophrenia, 233–240

Schliermacher, F., 107

School, 161–163, 255; and school phobia, 148–158

Secondary process. *See* Psychoanalytic theory

Self, 3, 5, 12, 17–18, 43–44, 71–72, 74; coherence of, 96, 100–101; defined, 110, 169; and other, 6–7, 11, 82, 113–116, 293–294; separation from, 82–83 (*see also* Differentiating); and subjectivity, 96–97 (*see also* Subjectivity). *See also* Self-other balancing, construction of self and other

Self-concept, 89, 101, 138–139, 161, 163

Self-consciousness, 18, 240. *See also* Reflecting

Self-esteem, 96

Self-other balances: compared with cognitive stage, 40, 54, 86–87; compared with moral stage, 54, 71, 86–87; compared with various developmental systems, 86–87; specific (*see* Incorporative balance; Impulsive balance; Imperial balance; Interpersonal balance; Institutional balance; Interindividual balance). *See also* Evolutionary truce

Self-other balancing, 6–7, 12, 43–45, 28–29, 30–32, 35–39, 103–106, 113–116; and construction of self and other, 75–84, 169; and equilibration, 81–82; and knowing, 81–82, 156–157, 169 (*see also* Cognition; Emotion); sequence in and theories of development, 39, 50–51, 74, 84–87; vulnerability in, 27–28, 90–91, 99–101, 108–109. *See also* Meaning making; Subjectivity; specific self-other balances

Self-sufficiency, 138–139, 155–156, 158–160; of over-differentiated balances, 228. *See also* Imperial balance; Institutional balance; Latency

Selman, R., 50, 54, 55, 58, 210

Sensations, 30–31, 40. *See also* Sensorimotor intelligence

Sensorimotor intelligence, 17–18, 30–32, 34, 39–40; and incorporative balance, 86–87. *See also* Incorporative balance

Separation, 5, 67–68, 85, 106–107, 133, 186–187; in infancy (*see* Infancy); ease and timing of, 81–82, 129–131, 158–159, 168, 185–186; and holding on, 125–126, 149–161; physical and psychological, 149–151, 217–220

Sex differences, 208–215; and sex-role identification, 143–144, 151–154

Sexuality, 204; and impulse management in interpersonal balance, 205–207; in mature relations of intimacy, 242–243, 253–254

Skinner, B. F., 13, 174. *See also* Behavioral theory

Smith, M., and Glass, G. V., 256

Societal moral orientation (stage 4), 52–53, 58, 61–66, 70; and institutional balance, 86–87, 100, 234–235; limits of, 63–64; object in, 58, 71; structure of, 52–53, 58, 63–65, 71; and transitional "4½" relativism, 62–63, 85–87, 235–237